Backyard Living

Time-Life Books is a division of Time Life Inc.

TIME LIFE INC.
President and CEO   Jim Nelson

TIME-LIFE TRADE PUBLISHING
Vice President and Publisher   Neil Levin
Senior Director of Acquisitions and Editorial Resources   Jennifer Pearce
Director of New Product Development   Carolyn Clark
Director of Trade Sales   Dana Coleman
Director of Marketing   Inger Forland
Director of New Product Development   Teresa Graham
Director of Custom Publishing   John Lalor
Director of Special Markets   Robert Lombardi
Director of Design   Kate McConnell

BACKYARD LIVING
Director of Creative Services   Laura McNeill
Senior Editor   Linda Bellamy
Technical Specialist   Monika Lynde
Production Manager   Carolyn Bounds
Quality Assurance   Jim King, Stacy L. Eddy

Cover Design by Kathleen Mallow

Produced by Lark Books, Asheville, North Carolina.
Project Management   Chris Rich
Design and Production   Thom Gaines
Production Assistance   Theresa Gwynn and Megan Kirby
Editorial Assistance   Amy Elizabeth Cook and Jan Menon
Project Acquisition   Kim English
Primary Photography   Evan Bracken
Secondary Photography   Richard Hasselberg
Photo Styling   Skip Wade
Illustrations   Orrin Lundgren
Watercolors   Lorraine Plaxico

Pre-Press Services, Time-Life Imaging Center
Printed in China.
10 9 8 7 6 5 4 3 2 1

TIME-LIFE is a trademark of Time Warner Inc., and affiliated companies.

ISBN 0-7370-0612-9

CIP data available upon application:
Librarian, Time-Life Books
2000 Duke Street
Alexandria, VA 22314

Books produced by Time-Life Trade Publishing are available at a special bulk discount for promotional and premium use. Custom adaptations can also be created to meet your specific marketing goals. Call 1-800-323-5255.

Backyard Living

FROM Gardening & Grilling TO Stone Walls & Stargazing

TIME LIFE BOOKS

Alexandria, Virginia

Contents

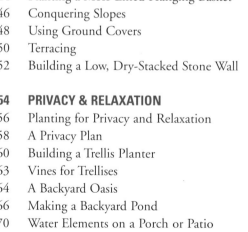

Introduction

Take a minute to stand at your back door and look outside. . .

What do you see?

Chances are the space behind your house doesn't bear much resemblance to the backyard of your dreams. But with the help of this book, it can! You don't have to be a master gardener or a landscape architect to transform your yard into a place that you love and enjoy. *Backyard Living: From Gardening and Grilling to Stone Walls and Stargazing* will walk you through every step.

Start by browsing through the first chapter for a great introduction to gardening basics. Then pick a few simple projects: Plant a small flower bed, build and set up a birdhouse or two, or make painted glass lanterns for your deck. Invite a few friends over to share an outdoor meal using some of the delicious recipes provided. Before long, you'll be adding a small fountain to your garden design, a shade screen to your patio, or even a miniature orchard to a sunny corner of your property.

Whether your goal is to win your local garden club award, barbecue a perfect rack of ribs, throw a successful soiree, or spend summer weekends tending container plants on your patio, you'll find all the information you need within these pages: hundreds of inspirational design ideas, a wealth of useful gardening tips, menus and recipes for delicious backyard meals, practical backyard projects, and beautiful garden plans.

The Backyard Gardening Workshop

No matter how you picture your ideal backyard—as an open, sunny gathering place for friends and family; as a shaded and serene oasis for moments of solitude; as a neatly clipped lawn or a terraced slope bright with blossoms and foliage—that yard will be shaped by two powerful forces. The first is Mother Nature, who provides such a wealth of materials that even master gardeners are awed by her generosity. The second, believe it or not, is you.

Once you've learned what to bring to this partnership—a few simple skills, a few sturdy tools, and an adventurous spirit—you'll soon be on your way to the backyard of your dreams. If you've never gardened before, this chapter will introduce you to all the basics. In it, you'll discover how to select tools, test and enrich your soil, prepare garden beds and set out plants, and protect your garden from pests. Once you've completed this simple "workshop," you'll be ready to walk hand-in-hand with nature toward the many joys of backyard living.

Garden Tools and Storage

Find a garden that you love—one that leaves you almost breathless with delight. Then ask the gardener who created it to let you take a look at his or her gardening tools. Chances are that you won't be shown a collection of designer gadgets from glossy, mail-order catalogs. Instead, you may very well find a simple assortment of well-used tools, much like the ones your grandparents used: a sturdy spade and metal rake, humble trowels and hoes, pruning shears and clippers, a good hose, and perhaps a long-handled garden fork for turning the compost pile. No matter how well worn these tools are, however, they will share a few common characteristics: They'll be exceptionally well made, lovingly maintained, and carefully stored when they're not in use.

TOOL SELECTION TIPS

If you're new to gardening, don't rush out to purchase a complete tool collection. Buy your tools one at a time, and buy the highest-quality tools you can afford. If your budget is tight, by all means shop at yard sales and flea markets, but don't make compromises in your search for quality. Inexpensive secondhand tools aren't a bargain if they're flawed. And as you shop for tools, keep the following rules in mind:

Select tools made with forged or tempered high-carbon or stainless steel blades, and with handles made from straight-grained ash or hickory, or from high-strength fiberglass. Avoid buying tools with painted wooden handles, as the paint may very well cover knots or flaws in the wood. The blade extension of any tool (where the blade and handle meet) must be strong and should surround the handle completely.

Also be sure to choose tools that are the right size and weight for you. A good tool is an extension of your own hands; it shouldn't feel cumbersome or awkward when put to use. A shiny new spade that's too heavy to lift or a trowel that's too large to grip will end up spending its working life in your garden shed.

CUTTING TOOLS

Your completed collection of gardening tools should include gardening scissors, grass shears, pruning shears, and an asparagus fork. A sturdy pair of garden-

ing scissors, with reinforced handles, is the ideal tool for cutting flowers and may also be used for trimming hedges. Grass shears come in handy for shearing annuals and trimming grass along garden walks. (The best models have long, sharp, scissorlike blades, reinforcing springs, and metal squeeze handles.) Pruning shears are best for cutting thicker stems, up to ¾ inch in diameter. And an asparagus fork is the tool you'll turn to when battling or pruning roots. Its 12- to 18-inch metal shank has a sharp, V-notched head at the tip, which works to prune the roots of plants you love and to sever the long taproots of those you don't.

Don't forget to purchase a high-quality pair of gardening gloves, too.

Using hand tools without wearing gloves is begging for blisters. Also make sure that your gloves are thick enough to protect your hands from thorns.

DIGGING AND CULTIVATING TOOLS

The trusty hand trowel, with its scoop-shaped pointed blade, is the garden tool that you're likely to use most frequently. Look for a trowel with a handle that's comfortable to grip and with a forged, heavy-gauge metal blade. A three- or four-clawed hand cultivator makes hand weeding a simple task, and will also prove useful while cultivating soil and breaking up soil lumps.

A garden spade with a rounded blade is indispensable. You'll use it for

digging garden beds and holes for large plants. Shovels with rectangular blades are best for moving gravel and large quantities of soil. As you select your shovels, keep in mind that although the larger, heavier models may penetrate the soil more deeply and hold more soil, unless you have the strength to wield them, they'll wear you out in a matter of minutes. Don't be embarrassed to "try on" a new spade just as you would a new pair of shoes. Go through the motions of digging some imaginary soil for a minute or two; the salespeople may giggle, but you won't make the mistake of purchasing a spade that's too heavy to use.

No backyard garden—or its owner —should be without a metal garden rake. Unlike the long, flexible tines of its lighter cousin the leaf rake, the short, heavy-gauge metal tines of a garden rake are ideal for combing through and leveling the soil in garden beds. For turning the compost pile, breaking up or aerating soil, and lifting and dividing perennials, a garden fork with thin, lightweight tines, is the tool of choice.

TOOL MAINTENANCE

Every minute you spend protecting your tools from moisture, cleaning and sharpening their blades, and caring for their wooden handles will lengthen

their working lives and simplify your gardening tasks.

Tool maintenance is easier than it sounds. Just set aside five minutes at the end of each gardening day, and perform a few simple tasks. Rust is the greatest foe of garden gear. When metal heads and shanks take regular nose dives into moist soil or cut through plants, battling rust becomes inevitable, so cleaning and oiling blades is the first tool-maintenance step. (Though fiberglass tools have recently become a viable option, steel garden tools remain the most popular.)

If the tool blades are coated with compacted soil, hose them down and dry them off thoroughly. Then wipe them with an oily rag in order to prevent rust. If oily rags sound too messy to you, fill a container with a mixture of sand and motor oil, and plunge the clean blades into the sand a few times. This coarse mixture will scour any remnants of soil from the blade and will leave a light coat of oil on the metal. To remove light rust spots from a metal tool, use steel wool and elbow grease. If the rust is heavy, you'll find that it's easier and more effective to use an electric drill with a rotating wire-brush attachment.

Next, check the wooden handles of any tools you've used that day, and sand away any splinters that may have formed on them. A coating of linseed oil, applied once or twice a year, will help preserve them. Alternatively, you may want to paint the handles with exterior-grade paint. (A bright-colored handle has the added advantage of being easy to spot when you've accidentally left a tool out in the yard.)

Finally, you'll want to keep all tool blades sharp; dull blades will double your labor. Either sharpen the blades yourself, or take them to a professional sharpening service.

TOOL STORAGE

If you're the kind of gardener who thinks of "tool storage" as propping your rakes and shovels against the exterior wall of your garage and tossing the trowel into an empty basket under its eaves, you might want to read this section carefully. You don't need to hang every gardening gadget on a pristine, wall-length tool rack, but you do need to learn a few simple habits that will

help you preserve the tools you own and prevent serious accidents.

First, no matter what kind of storage system you develop, put away all garden tools as soon as you've finished using them. There's nothing quite as frustrating as spending an hour trying to remember where you left the rake last time you used it—or quite as dangerous as stepping on its grass-disguised tines as you amble across your lawn.

Second, store all tools in a dry, well-ventilated area. You'll not only lengthen their lives, but will also save yourself from the tedious task of rust removal.

Third, make sure that your tools—and all garden chemicals—stay well out of reach of children and pets. The ideal tool-storage site will have a door with a lock.

Organizing your tools isn't critical, but it will make them easier to find and, if your storage space is limited, will also help you make wise use of available space. Traditional tool racks and cupboards, in many shapes, sizes, and materials, are widely available at home-improvement and garden centers. Pegboards also make useful tool organizers. After arranging the tools on a pegboard, use a marker to outline the shape of each one so that you'll know right where to place it next time you put it away.

Have you ever started an afternoon of gardening by grabbing an armful of garden tools, only to find at day's end that they're hidden all over the yard? Portable storage, in the form of garden baskets, or wooden or canvas tool totes, will help keep your tools from playing hookey as you move from one garden task to another.

Creative tool-storage solutions can also bring a bit of humor to the end of a gardening day. Fasten the head of an old metal rake to a shed wall, with the metal tines pointing outward. Then use the tines as hooks for hanging smaller tools and gloves. Salvage the frame of an old umbrella, hang it upside down, and drape your oily tool-wiping rags over the spokes. Or suspend a bicycle wheel horizontally, hang S-hooks from the spokes, and use these hooks to hold your lightweight hand tools.

Building a Garden Tool Shelf

Remember the last time you found a rusted trowel half-buried in a garden bed? Or discovered your favorite clippers hiding beneath a pile of mulch? This project—the perfect home for wayward gardening tools and supplies—was designed for you. Just set aside a free afternoon, gather some inexpensive materials and a few basic tools, and follow the simple instructions.

MATERIALS & TOOLS

- Handsaw or circular saw
- Pencil
- Tape measure
- Straightedge
- Electric drill with ⅛" bit and 1" spade bit
- Wood glue
- No. 2 Phillips-head screwdriver
- No. 6 decking screws: 1¼" and 1⅝"
- Sandpaper
- Paint or finish (optional)

TIPS

- When you purchase the front trim stock, ask for ¾" "S4S" (surface four square) stock or any narrow molding.
- Rectangular 4' x 8' sheets of lattice are available at many home-improvement centers. Have the sheet cut to size for you there.
- Use your drill and ⅛" bit to drill pilot holes at every screw location. These holes will make inserting the screws much easier. Unless the instructions tell you otherwise, locate the holes ⅜" in from each board's edge.

Instructions

1 Cut all the parts except for the lattice (see "Tips") to the lengths specified in the "Cutting List."

2 To mark holes in each side panel (B) for the dowel rod (C), measure and mark a point 2¾" up from one end of the side panel and 2¾" in from either of its edges.

3 Using a drill and 1" spade bit, carefully bore a hole at each mark, but stop drilling as soon as the point of the bit begins to exit from the opposite face of the board. (The dowel will fit into the 1"-wide portion of the hole, and the narrow opening left by the point of the bit will serve as a pilot hole.)

4 Place the upper shelf (A) on the top ends of the side panels (B). Drill a row of three evenly-spaced pilot holes through the upper shelf and into each end of a side panel.

5 Apply wood glue to the ends of the dowel rod (C), and insert the ends of the rod into the holes in the side panels (B). Then fasten the upper

shelf (A) to the side panels with three 1⅝" screws through each joint.

6 After drilling a pilot hole, secure the dowel rod (C) by inserting a 1¼" screw through each side panel (B) and into the rod.

7 Measure 24¾" down from the top face of the upper shelf (A), and mark a line across the outer face of each side panel (B).

8 Along each of the 24¾" lines on the side panels (B), drill three evenly-spaced pilot holes. To complete the tool rack frame, fasten the lower shelf (D) to the sides by inserting 1⅝" screws through the pilot holes.

9 Check the lattice (E) for fit by placing it into the opening formed by the sides (B) and the shelves (A and D). Trim the lattice if necessary, and set it aside.

CUTTING LIST

CODE	DESCRIPTION	QTY.	MATERIAL
A	Upper shelf	1	1 x 6 x 49"
B	Side panel	2	1 x 6 x 30"
C	Dowel rod	1	1" diameter x 48¾"
D	Lower shelf	1	1 x 6 x 47½"
E	⅜" lattice	1	23⅝" x 47½"
F	Long rear trim pieces	2	1 x 2 x 49"
G	Short rear trim pieces	2	1 x 2 x 22⅛"
H	Long front trim pieces	2	¾" x ¾" x 47½"
I	Short front trim pieces	2	¾" x ¾" x 22⅛"

10 Using four evenly-spaced 1¼" screws, attach one of the two long rear trim pieces (F) to the back of the upper shelf (A), with its wide face down and its upper edge flush with the upper face of the shelf. Attach the other long rear trim piece in the same fashion, positioning its bottom edge flush with the bottom face of the lower shelf (D).

11 Position and secure the two short rear trim pieces (G) in the same fashion, using three 1¼" screws on each piece. Make sure the outer

edge of each short trim piece is flush with the outer face of a side (B).

12 Place the assembled frame, trim side down, on a flat work surface. Then position the lattice (E) in the assembly.

13 To secure the lattice (E) in place, position the long and short front trim pieces (H and I) against the lattice, as shown in the illustration. Attach the long trim pieces with four evenly-spaced 1¼" screws driven into the top face of the lower shelf (D), and the short trim pieces with three evenly-spaced 1¼" screws driven into the inner faces of the sides (B).

14 Using sandpaper, round over and smooth all the edges.

15 Paint or finish the tool rack as desired.

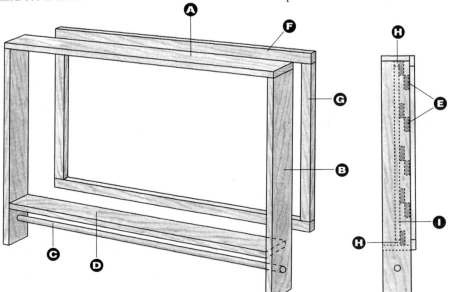

Testing and Amending the Soil

Beneath every great gardener is a foot or two of healthy soil that drains well, is rich in organic matter, has a near-neutral pH, and contains ample nutrients. Every hour you spend preparing and enriching your soil before you plant will pay off in the long run. That cheerful daisy gazing at you in the nursery will only be happy and healthy three weeks later if you provide a fertile, friable home for it.

SOIL TEXTURE

The ideal soil is made up of fine rock particles (sand, silt, or clay), organic matter, soil organisms, and open pore spaces that hold both water and air. Knowing your own soil's composition will help you to choose the plants best suited for it—and to amend the soil so you can grow a wider variety of plants.

Sandy soil, which doesn't hold water or nutrients well, feels gritty and is difficult to form into a ball. Clay soil is slippery; when you squeeze it into a ball, it holds its shape. This soil doesn't allow water to reach plant roots; it inhibits root growth and can be difficult to dig.

To test your soil texture, add one cup of soil and one teaspoon of non-sudsing dishwasher detergent to a clean, one-quart glass jar. Fill the jar two-thirds full with water, place the lid on tightly, and shake the jar hard for two minutes; then set it on a level surface. After one minute, mark the outside to indicate where the soil has settled—this will be the sand layer. After two hours, mark the new soil level—this is the silt layer. After two days, mark the final soil level—this is the clay layer. This will give you a visual "graph" of the percentage of each rock particle in your soil. Ideal soil (known as loam) is 40 percent silt, 40 percent sand, and 20 percent clay. If your soil has too much sand or clay, you can improve it by adding compost (see page 18) or other organic matter.

SOIL pH AND FERTILITY

The acidity or alkalinity of soil (its pH level) affects soil fertility. When soil is too acid or alkaline, the minerals in it bind together and become unavailable to your plants. Simple kits that test pH and fertility are available at most gardening centers. For a small fee, the Cooperative Extension Service in most states will provide a more detailed soil analysis.

Soil pH is measured on a scale of 1.0 to 14.0. Soil with a pH below 7.0 is acid (sour), while soil with a pH above 7.0 is alkaline (sweet). Most flowers prefer a pH of 6.0 to 7.0. If your soil pH is between 5.5 and 7.8, you can balance the pH level (up or down) by adding organic material. If your soil tests above or below this range, choose plants that prefer the acid or alkaline soil conditions, or add amendments to adjust the pH. Dolomitic limestone will raise pH, and sulfur will lower it.

For strong roots and healthy leaves and flowers, most plants need nitrogen, phosphorus, and potassium, as well as trace elements. Compost, well-rotted cow manure, and leaf mold will provide most of the nutrition your plants require, while also improving soil texture. If you decide to add fer-

tilizer, you'll need to choose between organic and inorganic types. Organic fertilizers tend to be environmentally safer, are less likely to burn plants, and don't pollute the environment.

CULTIVATING THE SOIL

Cultivation loosens the soil for plant roots and allows you to work in amendments. Before digging, test the soil's readiness by picking up a fistful and squeezing it. When you open your hand, the clump of soil should crumble. If it remains in a ball, the soil is too wet to dig; if it turns to dust, the soil is too dry.

Most annuals, which tend to have shallow roots, will be happy with soil that's loosened to a depth of one foot. Remove any sod (and all but its smallest roots). Then turn over spadefuls of soil to a depth of one foot. Add any

amendments to the loosened bed by working them in with a spade or gardening fork.

Perennials thrive in double-dug soil. Dig a trench across one end of the bed, one foot wide and one spade blade deep. Place the soil you remove into a wheelbarrow. Next, loosen the soil in the trench's bottom, adding amendments such as compost while you do. Dig another trench alongside the first one, but this time, toss the topsoil onto the amended soil in the first trench. Repeat these steps to double dig the entire bed. Finally, place the reserved topsoil from the first trench on top of the subsoil in the last trench.

Compost

Smart gardeners always have something rotting in their backyards. Something so valuable that it's called gardener's gold. Something made from ingredients that you may be in the habit of setting out on the curb for the trash collectors. That something, of course, is compost, and its effect on gardens is almost magical. Compost adds pore spaces to clay soil to loosen it and help it drain better. When added to sandy soil, compost helps the soil retain moisture and fertility. Compost is also chock-full of microorganisms that feed on organic matter and release nutrients to your plants.

COMPOST MATERIALS

You make compost by combining materials that are rich in nitrogen with materials that are rich in carbon. Common nitrogen sources (these tend to be moist and green) include fresh grass clippings and other green plant material, fruit and vegetable scraps, well-rotted manure, and coffee grounds. Carbon sources (typically brown and dry) include dry leaves, shredded bark or sticks, dry grass clippings, and hay or straw. The smaller you chop or shred these materials before adding them to the compost pile, the faster the microorganisms in the mixture will break them down. Do not add weeds, diseased plants, dairy products, meat or bones, or human or pet wastes to your compost pile.

MAKING COMPOST

Either the tortoise or the hare approach to composting will work. The tortoise approach is to pile mixed fresh green and dried brown yard wastes into a mound, add more yard waste as it becomes available, and toss in a shovelful of fresh soil from time to time. During dry weather, aim the garden hose at your pile now and then. When your stack is three to four feet tall, start a new one. The completed pile will become usable compost, via benign neglect, in about a year and a half.

If you want compost and you want it now, you'll need to take the hare approach by creating optimum compost-pile conditions: an internal temperature of 140°F to 160°F (60°C to 71°C), adequate moisture, and good air circulation. Rotating composters, which are spun in order to aerate their contents thoroughly, can produce finished compost in only three or four weeks.

If neither the hare nor the tortoise route appeals to you, try a middle-of-the-road approach by composting in a low-tech plastic compost bin or in a simple cylinder of hardware cloth. Chopping materials finely, keeping the pile as moist as a damp sponge, and turning the pile every two to four weeks will all speed up the process.

USING COMPOST

Finished compost is dark brown, crumbles easily, and has a rich, earthy aroma. Work compost into the soil as an amendment during cultivation, or scatter it around plants as a top dressing. Compost tea (water in which compost has been steeped for several days) makes an excellent liquid fertilizer.

Mulch

Of course you don't really *want* to mulch your garden. Napping in the dappled shade of your pergola or splashing in the sprinkler while you water the lawn would be much more pleasant ways to pass an afternoon. But mulching correctly will save you from many a day of gardening chores. A blanket of mulch helps retain moisture in your soil, while regulating soil temperatures and suppressing weeds. Mulch works to prevent soil-borne diseases from reaching your plants and prevents dirt from splashing up onto flowers and leaves. It also insulates against soil shifts from repeated freezes and thaws in winter, and eventually decomposes to add organic matter to the soil. On top of all that, mulch is to gorgeous gardens as makeup is to Hollywood starlets—it makes them look terrific.

MULCH MATERIALS

Pine needles, straw, leaf mold, dried grass clippings, compost, shredded bark, and bark nuggets are all organic mulches. Sand and gravel are sometimes used as mulch around plants that thrive in hot, dry conditions. Inorganic mulches such as black plastic and landscape fabric suppress weeds, but they also prevent perennials from spreading, and they don't add organic matter to the soil.

USING MULCH

Mulch perennials when most of the new growth has sprouted, after the soil has warmed up in spring and you've removed all weeds. When starting plants from seed, apply mulch only after you've thinned the seedlings and the remaining ones have several sets of leaves. Transplants can usually be mulched as soon as they're set out. A two- to four-inch-thick layer of mulch is generally recommended. To prevent rot, push the mulch back a couple of inches from plant stems or tree trunks.

Winter mulches are also useful. They are not meant to keep plants warm but to insulate the soil from sudden freezes and thaws, which can push plants out of the ground and kill them. Airy materials, such as straw, hay, and pine boughs, serve especially well as winter mulches. If you live in an area of heavy snows, you're in luck: Snow is nature's ideal winter mulch.

Building a Potting Bench

Although this potting bench may never win prizes in the "elegant garden furniture" category, it's perfect for the backyard gardener—sturdy, functional, inexpensive, and unpretentious. You don't need to be an expert woodworker to construct it, either. In fact, this simple bench was designed for people who care more about puttering in their backyard gardens than developing expert woodworking skills.

MATERIALS & TOOLS

- Handsaw or circular saw
- Measuring tape
- Electric drill with $\frac{1}{8}$" bit
- Hammer
- No. 2 Phillips-head screwdriver
- No. 6 decking screws: 2" and $1\frac{5}{8}$"
- 12d ($3\frac{1}{4}$") nails
- Primer and exterior paint (optional)
- Paintbrushes (optional)

TIPS

- Buying standard lumber that's the correct size can be confusing for beginning woodworkers because the numbers by which the board sizes are named (for example, 1 by 10, 1 by 12, and 2 by 4) don't represent the boards' actual sizes. A 2 by 4 (or 2 x 4) is approximately 1½" thick and 3½" wide. A 1 x 10 is about ¾" thick and 9¼" wide, and a 1 x 12 is about ¾" thick and 11¼" wide.

- The stringers (B), front piece (E), and spacers (F) in this project are all 2 x 4s that have been "ripped" (cut along their grain) to 2½" in width. The easiest way to rip these boards is with a table saw, but if you don't have one, just substitute 2 x 4s cut to the correct lengths. Your finished potting bench may not look quite as graceful, but it will work just as well.

- The top and bottom shelves shown in the photo were actually made with ⅞"-thick lumber. In the "Cutting List," however, they're replaced by ¾"-thick 1 x 10 and 1 x 12 lumber, which is sometimes easier to find.

- When the instructions call for drilling "pilot holes," use your drill and ⅛" bit.

CUTTING LIST

CODE	DESCRIPTION	QTY.	MATERIAL
A	Legs	4	2 x 4 x 35"
B	Stringers	2	1½" x 2½" x 20"
C	Side pieces	2	2 x 4 x 23"
D	Back piece	1	2 x 4 x 48"
E	Front piece	1	1½" x 2½" x 48"
F	Spacers	2	1½" x 2½" x 13"
G	Narrow bottom shelf	1	1 x 10 x 45"
H	Wide bottom shelf	1	1 x 12 x 45"
I	Top shelves	2	1 x 12 x 48"

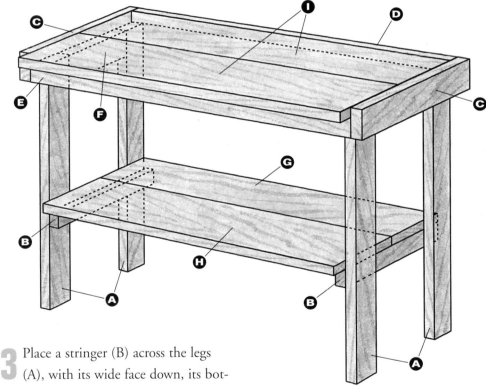

Instructions

1 Cut all the lumber to the lengths specified in the "Cutting List."

2 Place two legs (A) on a flat work surface, with their wide faces down and their outer edges 20" apart. Measure and mark a line across each leg, 12" up from its bottom end.

3 Place a stringer (B) across the legs (A), with its wide face down, its bottom edge at the 12" lines, and its ends flush with the outer edges of the legs. Fasten the stringer to the legs by drilling two pilot holes at each joint and then inserting 2" screws in the holes.

4 Repeat steps 2 through 3 to fasten the second stringer (B) to the remaining two legs (A).

5 At both ends of each side piece (C), measure and mark across the board's wide face, ¾" in from the end. Drill three evenly-spaced pilot holes along this line on one end of each side piece.

6 Position the side pieces (C) on edge, and insert the back piece (D), also on edge, between them so that the outer face of the back piece is flush with the end of each side piece. (Check to make sure that each side piece has three holes at this end.) Then secure the side pieces to the back piece by driving 12d nails through the pilot holes.

7 Position the front piece (E) so that its outer face is flush with the unsecured ends of the side pieces (C) and its lower edge is flush with the lower edges of the side pieces. (If you use a 2 x 4 for the front piece, position its upper edge ¾" below the upper edges of the side pieces. Its lower edge won't be flush with the lower edges of the side pieces.) To secure the side pieces to the front piece, first drill two evenly-spaced pilot holes through the ¾" line on each side piece. Then drive a 12d nail through each hole and into the front piece.

8 To attach a legs-and-stringer assembly (A and B) to the rectangular frame you have just made, first position the frame upright, with one side piece (C) flat on the work surface. Mark a straight line across the inner face of this side piece, ¾" down from its top edge.

9 Center a spacer (F), wide face down, on top of the side piece (C), so the spacer's top edge is flush with the ¾" line, and the lower edges of both parts are flush. (If the spacer is a 2 x 4, it won't rest flush at the bottom.)

10 Place the leg assembly (A and B) on top of the side piece (C). The ends of the legs should be flush with the top edge of the spacer (F) at the ¾" line, and the spacer should fill the space between the legs.

11 Drill three pilot holes through each leg (A) and into the side piece (C), and secure each leg to the side piece with three 2" screws.

12 Drill three evenly-spaced pilot holes through the spacer (F) and into the side piece (C), and secure the spacer with three 2" screws.

13 Repeat steps 8 through 12 to attach the other legs-and-stringer assembly (A and B) to the other end of the frame.

14 With the bench standing on its legs, position the narrow bottom shelf (G) across the back of the stringers (B); its outer edge should be flush with the ends of the stringers.

15 Drill two pilot holes through the narrow shelf (G) and into each stringer (B), about 1½" in from each edge of the shelf and ¾" in from its end. Secure the narrow shelf in place by driving 1⅝" screws through each pilot hole.

16 Position the wide bottom shelf (H) across the stringers (B) so that one edge is against the edge of the narrow bottom shelf (G), and the other edge overlaps the edges of the front legs by ½".

17 Drill two pilot holes at each end of the wide bottom shelf (H), about 1½" in from each long edge of the shelf and ¾" in from its end. Then fasten the shelf to each stringer (B) with two 1⅝" screws.

18 Repeat steps 14 through 17 to attach the top shelves (I) to the legs (A) and spacers (F). At the front of the potting bench, the top shelf will overlap the front piece (E) by 1".

19 If the bench will be exposed to the elements, be sure to apply a primer and a couple of coats of high-quality exterior paint.

Putting in Plants

You've made your soil all fertile and fluffy. You've purchased your containers of plants, and you're ready to tuck them into their new homes. Take a few extra precautions to get them off to a good start, and they'll thank you with robust foliage and abundant flowers.

GETTING STARTED

The move from container to soil is stressful for plants, so pamper them. To guard against wilting, give the plants a long drink while they're still in their pots and plant on an overcast day or in the early evening. Remove most flowers and pinch leggy growth from annuals before you plant them to encourage strong root growth and a summer's worth of blooms.

Before you start digging holes for the plants, set them in their containers on your garden bed, spaced according to label instructions. (If labels are missing or instructions aren't provided, check a plant encyclopedia for proper planting distances.) Plants look best grouped in odd numbers, so set them out in clusters of three, five, or seven.

PLANTING

Dig a hole almost twice as wide and deep as the plant's container. Refill the hole with amended soil (see page 17) until the hole is as deep as the height

of the container. Then carefully remove the plant by turning its pot upside down and tapping the bottom. (Don't tug on the plant's stem; if you can't get the plant and soil ball out easily, carefully cut the container apart.)

Gently loosen any tangled roots and adjust the hole if necessary so the roots fit without breaking or bending. Place the plant in the hole, making sure it sits at the same soil level as it did in its container.

Refill the hole around the plant with the excavated soil, press the top of the soil gently to remove any air pockets, and then water the plant thoroughly. (As always, a gentle soaking will allow the water to be absorbed down near the plant's roots.) When all your plants are in, spread a two- to four-inch layer of mulch over the bed, leaving a two-inch diameter circle around each plant's stem to prevent rot.

If your new transplants are in an especially sunny spot, you may want to rig up some temporary shade to help them through the first few days of the move. Water all plants well until they're established. The stress of transplanting makes your plants less able to tolerate lack of water, insect damage, and diseases, so check on them often for the first couple of weeks they are in their new homes.

Water-Thrifty Gardening

Daylilies and purple coneflowers

L et's face it: A garden can be demanding. Without a certain amount of tender loving care, plants will fold in the face of the elements. After a particularly ruthless day of sun, you'll probably have to unwind the hose and soak those garden beds until each drooping flower looks happy again. But garden watering should be more than a matter of damage control. To keep plants thriving and not just surviving, you'll need to devise a regular watering program— one that satiates both your backyard soil and the vegetation it supports, while conserving water and time.

XERISCAPING

As municipal water supplies decline and unpredictable weather patterns increase, it's more important than ever to work with, rather than against, your yard's ecosystem. One way to do this is by learning the art of xeriscaping. Derived from the Greek word *xeros*, which means dry, xeriscaping is actually a method of landscaping that conserves water. Plan your garden with xeriscaping in mind, and you'll save yourself hours of garden maintenance down the road.

First, as you design your backyard, group together plants with common watering needs. There's an obvious

logic to segregating roses and rhododendrons from daylilies and coneflowers: The water required to keep the former healthy would be wasted on the latter. You can grow thirsty plants such as roses, but do so in an area that you've designated as water-intensive— preferably close to your water source.

Selecting native plants and wildflowers that have naturalized in your area is another wise way to keep garden maintenance to a minimum. After all, if a plant thrives naturally in your region, without the benefit of water from a hose or sprinkler, chances are it will flourish in your backyard with very little attention. Coreopsis, Stokes' aster, and blue flax are just a few of the many drought-resistant wildflowers to consider. Native-plant societies and local arboretums can suggest many more plants for your region. You may be surprised to learn

that some species of the prickly pear cactus are not only water-thrifty, but are also natives as far north as Canada.

Another vital aspect of xeriscaping is attention to soil quality. Keeping your soil well drained and moisture retentive allows your garden to do more with the water it's given. A layer of mulch such as leaf mold will help improve soil quality as it decomposes, reduce weed growth by smothering weed seedlings, minimize competition among plants for water, and reduce evaporation by cooling the soil beneath it.

IRRIGATION

After planting your garden with an eye to water conservation, the next step is to design a watering program. The rule of thumb is that plants need an inch of water per week. This rule can be difficult to apply, however, given the countless variables involved: how much sun each plant gets, the soil composition in its bed, and the vagaries of the weather.

The real trick to keep in mind is that when you water (typically about once a week for most perennials), always water deeply. If you continually supply water only to the top few inches of soil, your plants will form shallow root systems. This is harmful since the top few inches of soil heat up and dry out more quickly than the soil farther down. Instead, soak the soil slowly until it is moist to a depth of 12 inches. This will encourage

Prickly pear cactus

roots to penetrate deep into the soil. Deeply rooted plants can tap into the soil's moisture reserves during dry spells, and they are also well anchored and able to reach soil nutrients.

The most efficient, low-maintenance tools for deep watering are soaker hoses and drip systems. A soaker hose generally consists of a single length of foam, vinyl, or rubber tubing, with holes along its length. Water seeps out to soak a two- to three-foot-wide band around the hose. To implement this type of irrigation, simply snake the hose through your garden and turn on the tap.

Drip systems, which consist of multiple hose components, are slightly more complex than soaker hoses, but are much more efficient. Why? Because you can assemble the hose components so that their drip points are right where you want them to be—over the root zones of specific plants. Unlike a soaker hose, which releases water along its entire length, a drip system can be tailored to the actual layout of your garden.

And one final water-conservation tip: No matter how thirsty your plants look at midday, resist the temptation to water them right away. Fifty to seventy-five percent of any water you provide during the hottest part of the day will evaporate. Avoid watering in the evening, too; you'll just be providing an open invitation to slugs and diseases. Wait until morning to give your plants a drink. Stems will rise, blossoms will perk up, and leaves will spread. Your plants will thank you.

Good Bugs, Bad Bugs

When a slimy slug munches its way through your prized hosta leaves, leaving lacy green doilies behind, you may be tempted to adopt the motto that the only good bug is a dead bug. The truth is, it's a bug-eat-bug world in your garden, and some of those bugs are on your side. Learning which insects nibble leaves and which insects eat the leaf nibblers will help you work with nature, rather than against it, to keep your garden healthy.

THE BAD GUYS

The thugs in your yard will usually leave clues behind. Slugs and snails like to dine while you're sleeping or on cool, cloudy days. Trailing slime to and from the scene of the crime, they consume seedlings and sometimes entire leaves or chomp ragged holes in

Praying mantis

Garden slug

the foliage of low growing plants. The more precise Japanese beetle chews round or oblong holes in flowers and leaves (unless it decides to eat the whole leaf; then it will devour all but a skeleton of leaf veins). Aphids—tiny, pear-shaped insects—leave distorted, curled, and sticky leaves in their wake. The larvae of leafminers feed between the upper and lower surfaces of leaves. Maze-like tunnels, blotches, and blisters are all evidence that they've been feasting on your foliage.

THE GOOD GUYS

It's important to remember that at the same time aphids are sucking on your tulip stems, another insect is out there, ready to sup on the aphids.

Those cute, polka-dotted ladybugs (also called lady beetles or lady birds) strike terror in the hearts of many garden pests who know there's nothing ladylike about the beetles' appetite for bad bugs. Parasitic wasps and tachinid flies lay their eggs in caterpillars and other bugs so their larvae hatch inside their first meal. A delicate spider web, bejewelled with morning dew, is actually a deadly snare set to entangle a bug that will become the arachnid's lunch. The praying mantis is not worshipping; its lethal forelimbs are poised for attack.

Encourage beneficial insects to take up residence in your yard by providing a few luxuries for them. Most require water (a one- to two-inch-deep container with a small stone to serve as a raft works well). Plants that attract beneficial insects include dill, coriander, fennel, lavender, black-eyed Susan, and Queen-Anne's-lace.

Most important, unless your garden is suffering from a downright plague of destructive insects, don't panic and reach for the poisons as soon as you see insect damage. Pesticides kill not only the bad guys but also your allies in the battle of the bugs. Most plants recover from insect attacks, and a few holes in your zinnia leaves won't matter in the long run.

THE CONVERTS

Finally, we have the bad guys who reform. Before resorting to chemical sprays, remind yourself that those caterpillars you are cursing now may metamorphize into lovely butterflies. That tomato hornworm devouring vegetables will soon be a sphinx moth pollinating night-blooming flowers. Read a good book on garden insects to learn to identify friend from foe. Then welcome beneficial insects into your yard while using more selective (and environmentally friendly) ways to give the bad guys the boot.

Tomato hornworm

REPELLING THE HORDES

Don't despair if the leaf-munching hordes in your garden outnumber the beneficial bugs. An entire arsenal of home remedies exists to help you snuff out those bad bugs—or at least send them scurrying. Following are a few examples:

- Place several grapefruit rinds upside down in your garden (melon rinds or cabbage leaves will also work); slugs will be attracted to their protection and shade. Check the rinds early in the morning and destroy the slumbering slugs and any other insects that have availed themselves of your hospitality.

- Study up on companion planting. Many believe that planting garlic near roses will repel Japanese beetles. Both marigolds and nasturtiums are said to send a variety of garden pests packing.

- Make a toad abode out of an overturned clay pot, with a hole broken out for a door. Insects make up 90 percent of a toad's diet.

- For an effective spray, steep a dozen minced garlic cloves in one pint of mineral oil for 24 hours. Strain out the garlic, and add one teaspoon of liquid dish soap. Remember when using this spray that it can also harm beneficial insects.

- Use a hand-held vacuum to suck beetles and other insects off your plants. Just remember to empty the pests from your bug-buster and destroy them.

Visual Variety

A carpet of summer grass may be deeply satisfying to mow, but you won't find yourself spending much time on that carpet if grass is all your yard has to offer. Why? Because staring at a lawn, no matter how green or lush, is just plain boring. Variety is the spice of any garden, just as it is of life.

An appealing backyard offers a wealth of visual delights, from the continuously changing colors of its blossoms and foliage to the heights of its plants and the contours of the land itself. This yard may include a swath of green grass and bright-blooming annuals in it each summer. A truly inviting backyard, however, will offer a feast for the eyes—throughout the year.

In this special yard, you'll find beds of perennials and bulbs, bursting with color from spring to autumn; leaves in hundreds of shades of green, gold, and brown; planted berms or terraced slopes; beautiful container plants arranged in groups by a gate or doorway; evergreen ground covers peeking from under a blanket of snow; and more. And lest you think that this special yard can't be yours, read on...

Annuals, Perennials, and Bulbs

In spite of their sometimes intimidating Latin names, most flowers are easy to grow. Give them the soil they need, the sun they want, and a deep drink now and then, and most blooms won't care what you call them. Becoming familiar with the three main categories of flowers, however—annuals, perennials, and bulbs—will help you decide where to place your plants and how to nurture them.

ANNUALS

Think of annuals as the gerbils of flowers. Their job is to reproduce as prolifically as possible in the short time they're with us—usually one season. Luckily, in order to create the seeds from which they reproduce, annuals must first flower—hence, their popularity.

ANNUAL: **Morning glory**

Annuals are an inexpensive, season-long source of color and sometimes of fragrance. The plants—many of which are easily started from seed—creep, climb, and cascade. Unlike most perennials and biennials, they flower within weeks of germination, and after blooming for weeks on end, many will even sow seed for the following year. For quicker color, purchase and set out bedding plants, which are often available in inexpensive six packs.

While a true annual is a plant that completes its life cycle in one season, the term "annual" is often used to describe any plant that will flower for only one season in a given climate, including biennials, which sprout from seed, produce only leaves the first year, and then flower and die during the second year. The term is also used for tender perennials that are unable to survive a particular region's harsh winters. In fact, many plants that we call annuals are perennial in milder climates.

Because they don't live long, annuals put down only shallow roots. Most aren't finicky about soil conditions and need only the correct amount of sunlight and water. Since an annual's goal in life is to produce seed, deadheading (removing faded flowers) is usually necessary to keep the plants blooming.

PERENNIALS

Although perennials die back to the ground each year, most have roots that can survive freezing temperatures to produce new shoots each spring. All perennials live at least three years, and some outlive their owners. Unlike annuals, most perennials flower for only a few weeks at a time. A perennial bed will change continuously (and with luck and planning, will bloom continuously) throughout the growing season.

Because a perennial has a short bloom time and a long life, you must consider its shape, foliage, and texture before deciding where to place one in

your garden. Also remember that if an annual is like a gerbil, a perennial is more like a puppy; leave plenty of room for growth!

Perennials, which most home gardeners start from plants rather than from seeds, are usually more expensive than annuals, but the only care they require is occasional division or pruning. Of course, pruning reaps cut flowers and division produces more plants, so in the long run perennials are also economical backyard companions.

BULBS

Bulbs might be considered the camels of flowers; they store both moisture and nutrients in their fleshy tissues. Crocuses, daffodils, and tulips are well loved as harbingers of spring, but some bulbs (lilies and allium, for example) can also brighten perennial beds in midsummer, and some (as in the case of fall-blooming crocus) add color to autumn gardens.

PERENNIAL: **Shasta daisy**

BULB: **Siberian iris**

Bulbs do offer some challenges. Gardeners in the North must overwinter dormant tender bulbs indoors or plant new ones each spring. Gardeners in the Deep South must refrigerate hardy bulbs (40°F to 50°F or 4°C to 10°C) for six to eight weeks in winter because these bulbs require a period of cold in order to bloom. What's more, a bulb's foliage must be left to wither and brown so the bulb can build up nutrients for the following spring. To disguise the withered leaves, plant bulbs in beds with perennials or annuals that will grow to hide them.

Bulbs (the term is used for corms, tubers, rhizomes, and true bulbs) provide an astonishing variety of plants, from towering six-foot-tall cannas to tiny two-inch crocuses. As an extra bonus, some bulbs—when provided with well-drained soil—will naturalize (multiply and spread), either by seed or natural division, to provide a stunning return for a small investment of money and labor.

An Annual, Perennial, and Bulb Plan

There's no need to segregate your flowers by type: This combination of annuals, perennials, and bulbs offers knock-your-socks-off color all summer long. The perennials in this garden will only get better with time, the summer-blooming bulbs require practically no care, and the annuals will flower with gusto all season. Because the low-growing annuals are at the front of the bed, they can be replaced easily each year.

A LADYBELLS
Adenophera confusa

Hardiness zones 3–8

36 inches tall

Spires of nodding, bell-shaped, deep blue flowers in summer; toothed leaves; rich, moist, well-drained soil; full sun to partial shade

B ROSE CAMPION
Lychnis coronaria

Hardiness zones 4–9

30 inches tall

Small, rounded, magenta flowers in summer; wooly, gray-green leaves; moist, well-drained soil; full sun to partial shade

C LILY
Lillium 'Mont Blanc'

Hardiness zones 3–8

30 inches tall

Large, unscented, bowl-shaped, white flowers, flecked with brown, bloom in summer; glossy, dark green leaves; moist, well-drained soil; full sun to light shade

D PETUNIA
Petunia 'Purple Wave'
and 'Lilac Wave'
Annual

up to 18 inches tall

Trumpet-shaped, 3- to 5-inch flowers all summer (*P.* 'Purple Wave' is magenta; *P.* 'Lilac Wave' is lavender); sticky, hairy green leaves; well-drained soil; full sun

E GOLDEN EYE
Bidens 'Golden Eye'
Annual

up to 12 inches tall

Small, daisy-like, golden yellow flowers all summer; finely cut, delicate leaves on wiry stems; moist, well-drained soil; full sun

F CANDYTUFT
Iberis

Hardiness zones 5–9

6 to 18 inches tall

Clusters of tiny white, pink, red, or violet flowers spring through summer; dark green leaves; well-drained soil; full sun

G TOADFLAX (BUTTER AND EGGS)
Linaria vulgaris

Hardiness zones 4–8

12 to 36 inches tall

Small, pale yellow and white flowers resembling snapdragons from late spring to autumn; pale green, linear leaves; light, well-drained (preferably sandy) soil; full sun

H SPEEDWELL
Veronica alpina 'Alba'

Hardiness zones 4–8

up to 16 inches tall

Long spikes of tiny white flowers spring to summer; soft-textured, narrow leaves; well-drained loam; full sun to light shade

I YARROW
Achillea millefolium

Hardiness zones 4–9

24 inches tall

Flat-topped clusters of white, yellow, pink, or red flowers in summer, green or gray green fernlike foliage; well-drained, poor soil; full sun

Improving Your Lawn

A lush, green lawn ties landscape elements together, provides play areas, and even increases a home's value. Beautiful lawns do take some work, but too much coddling (over-watering, mowing, and fertilizing) does more harm than good. The best lawn-care system is one that concentrates on improving the soil and root growth.

AERATING YOUR LAWN

The soil beneath many lawns suffers from compaction. The cure is *aeration* —removing plugs of turf and soil in order to allow water, oxygen, and helpful microorganisms to enter the ground.

The size of your lawn will probably determine how you aerate your soil. A spading fork will work for small areas, while a gas-powered aerator (available at tool-rental stores) will remove plugs from large lawns. If you've never aerated your lawn, do so twice a year (once in the spring and once in the fall) for the first two years. After that, aerate once every year or two.

FERTILIZING YOUR LAWN

Test your soil every few years to determine its fertilization needs. Then embark on a regular fertilizing program and add sulfur (to lower pH) or lime (to raise pH) only as needed.

Self-mulching lawn mowers help fertilize your lawn by spreading finely-cut clippings, which provide nitrogen-rich organic material as they decompose. Other natural fertilizers, such as compost and manure, contribute to soil health and help your grass tolerate drought and compaction. Although synthetic fertilizers are less expensive than organic alternatives, they often leach out of the soil easily and do not offer long-term soil improvement.

Apply fertilizers right before periods of active growth—not during midsummer. (A well-maintained lawn should need fertilizing twice a year at most.) And remember that overfertilizing will cause excessive leaf growth—increasing the need for mowing—and insufficient root growth.

WATERING YOUR LAWN

Your lawn's water needs will depend on the type of grass planted and on the weather. Light, frequent watering discourages strong root growth (when water and nutrients are always available nearby, the roots have no reason to extend farther). To promote good root growth, provide large amounts of water less frequently, watering until the soil is moist to a depth of six to twelve inches.

Keeping the blade of a gasoline-powered lawn mower sharp and allowing the grass to grow a little longer than usual will decrease your lawn's need for watering. (Reel mowers necessitate more frequent mowing; they don't function well in very tall grass.)

OVERSEEDING YOUR LAWN

Overseeding (sowing grass seed on an established lawn) can improve an unattractive lawn or provide a temporary cool-season grass to cover dormant, brown grass in mild climates. It's an easy way to take advantage of the new grasses that are bred to resist pests and diseases and to tolerate shade, drought, and traffic.

When selecting a seed mix for overseeding, consider your climate, the amount of sun or shade your lawn receives, how much time you have for mowing and other maintenance, and how you use your lawn. (Yards that double as soccer fields need grass that can take abuse.) Consult with your local Cooperative Extension Service regarding mixes suitable for your area.

Overseed lawns in the North just before active growth begins in the early spring or late summer. Lawns in areas with mild climates should be overseeded when nearly dormant in the fall.

WEEDING YOUR LAWN

The healthier the soil, the fewer weeds you'll have to battle. (Of course, developing an appreciation for dandelions can also reduce weeding tasks!) When weeding is necessary, either remove the entire root by hand or apply herbicides. (The latter are toxic, so follow the manufacturer's directions carefully.)

ODE TO THE REEL MOWER

It begins shortly after daybreak on Saturday morning in suburban neighborhoods everywhere: a distant, whining drone that slowly gathers strength until its earsplitting racket drives children indoors and dogs beneath couches.

Up and down the street, gasoline-powered, rotary lawn mowers are chewing up and spitting out grass, while belching fumes and complaining loudly.

Consider the reel mower. Its spiraled blades whirl and snip the grass with a satisfying swish and click—the sound of a dozen busy barbers. You can hear birds singing while you push a reel mower; you can smell the juicy green scent of fresh-cut grass. You can even hold a conversation over the fence with your next-door neighbor, assuming the neighbor isn't riding high in the saddle of a lawn tractor and wearing ear protection.

A reel mower does cut a narrower swath than a gasoline or electric mower, and because it works best on grass that isn't very long, you'll need to mow more frequently. But for people with relatively small yards, the reel mower offers "reel" advantages. While rotary mowers bruise and tear grass blades, reel mowers cut cleanly. And speaking of clean, one recent

study showed that lawn tools in Southern California put forth more pollution in a single day than all the aircraft in the Los Angeles area. What's the point of having manicured grass if you can't breathe when you go outside to see it?

Low-tech reel mowers are also economical. Although their blades require professional sharpening every other year, reel mowers don't require oil changes or last-minute trips to the gas station. They don't have a lot of complicated parts, so repairs are seldom costly. You can buy an old reel mower at a yard sale or purchase a newer model, which will be lighter and easier to maneuver. Either way, you'll be doing your part to make the world a little quieter and cleaner.

Planting for Color

Remember how exciting it was to open a new box of crayons when you were a child? Remember when you did things just for the joy of doing them, before you'd decided that you were good at some things and not at others? Well, you don't need a degree in landscaping or fine arts to plant a beautiful, colorful backyard.

COLOR THEORY

Children soon discover that when the green crayon is missing, they can color in a frog by blending blue and yellow. In the same way, a little knowledge about color theory will help you make each plant contribute more effectively to the color scheme of your yard. This is true whether you're the kind of gardener who sketches out every last leaf onto draft paper before heading to the nursery, or the kind who pulls into the drive with a carload of plants, wondering how on earth you'll cram them all in.

Let's imagine that your house has a patio with a small, fenced yard around it. If you know that warmer colors (yellow, orange, and red) tend to make objects appear closer, while cooler colors (blue, green, and purple) make objects recede, you might plant blue bellflowers beside the back fence in order to make your yard appear larger. If you'd like one part of your yard to stand up and shout, and another section to offer a peaceful sanctuary, knowing how color combinations affect mood will come in handy. Colors directly across from each other on the color wheel—red and green, blue and orange, yellow and violet—are called complementary colors. Placing complementary-colored flowers next to each other tends to create an exciting, vibrant effect. Colors adjacent to one another on the color wheel harmonize and produce a more tranquil, relaxing atmosphere.

FOLIAGE COLORS

Of course, you'll also need to consider foliage when you're planting for color. The leaves of different plants can vary from deep purple to silver to lime green. Certain foliage combinations can be quite dramatic and usually last longer than flower combinations. (See pages 38–39 for more on foliage.) Trees, shrubs, and ground covers that are evergreen, as well as berries and dried grasses, all lend color to the landscape in winter.

INFLUENCES ON COLOR

Consider, too, when designing with color, every element of your yard. The house, its trim and roof, and even paving materials will add their own colors to the final composition—a composition that will change continuously from hour to hour, week to week, and season to season. In mixed perennial beds, the color scheme will change almost weekly, so you must consider bloom time when planting. (No matter how perfect that pink peony might look next to a purple aster, you'll never see their flowers at the same time.) Pale evening primroses, lost in the glare of the afternoon sun, will practically glow in twilight. The light during different seasons of the year will also change the appearance of colors.

Luckily, nature helps out when it comes to coordinating seasonal colors. The bulbs and blossoms of early spring are often pastel; late summer flowers tend to be red, orange, and violet; while the fall palette is usually gold, rust, and purple.

All this information may seem like a lot to juggle, but if you trust your intuition and play around, you'll hit upon color combinations that will surprise and delight you. And if, as is almost inevitable, you also wind up with some hideous combinations, just grab your gardening spade and do what your third-grade art teacher always advised: "If at first you don't succeed . . ."

Toadflax (butter and eggs)

Glorious Green

Japanese painted fern

Are the shady sections of your yard forlorn and neglected? Does your garden look limp and exhausted in autumn and shamefully naked come winter? The antidote is to begin a love affair with leaves, and that means cultivating a passion for the various shades, hues, and tints of green.

The word *green* comes from the Old English word for "grow"; knowing this gives us a hint of green's importance to life. In fact, the green in plants comes from chlorophyll, which converts sunlight to energy through photosynthesis—a process upon which all life depends. Backyards with landscape designs that aren't working (yet!) often include too many plants selected for their flowers and too few for their foliage.

COLORS

From the reddish green leaves of a Japanese maple to the shocking chartreuse of a sweet potato vine, some shades of green can step forth from the backdrop of your yard to become outright show-stealers. Others—the silver, blue, and gray variations on green—can work to calm your color schemes and tone down hot spots. Do your fluorescent pink petunias clash with the red impatiens nearby? Tuck some silver dusty millers between them, and the effect will be magically harmonizing.

Then there are the plants that can't seem to make up their minds and put forth variegated foliage. These highly prized mutations, such as *Hosta* 'Royal Splendor,' can light up a shady corner of your yard. The huge yellow-and-green striped leaves of the *Canna* 'Bengal Tiger' add an exotic, tropical touch to any landscape.

SHAPES

Foliage shapes vary widely. Think about the delicate fronds of a maidenhair fern; the huge, bold leaves of a rhubarb plant; and the stiff, swordlike leaves of an iris. When you group plants together, you should aim for both variety and repetition of foliage shapes. A garden bed filled with leaves that are too similar in shape will be boring. A bed cluttered with too many different leaf shapes will look busy. Once you begin noticing the shapes of leaves, you'll soon discover the fun of finding pleasing combinations. Teaming the lacy leaves of peonies with the upright blades of Siberian irises is a favorite foliage combination. Another is simple, heart-shaped hosta leaves planted beside the intricate foliage of ferns.

TEXTURES

Texture is as important as color and shape when it comes to designing with foliage. The leaves of some plants seem to beg for our touch. Two good examples are the feathery foliage of fennel and the woolly leaves that give lamb's-ears its name. Some leaves warn us to keep our distance—the shiny, sharply pointed leaves of holly and the spiny shields of thistle, for example.

In any landscape design, coarse-leaved plants come forward to meet the eye, while fine-textured plants recede. Setting a tree with fine-textured foliage (such as the honey locust or willow) toward the rear of your yard will make the yard appear larger, especially if you set a plant with bold-textured leaves (hostas work well) toward the front. Remember, though: Plants with large, coarse-textured leaves may overwhelm a very small space, just as fine-textured plants can get lost in large, open areas.

SEASONAL INTEREST

The fresh green of a perennial's new growth is always welcome in spring, but if you choose your perennials carefully, you can get autumn color from their leaves as well. Plumbago, cranesbill, and cushion spurge all have foliage that colors beautifully in the fall. Evergreens, of course, offer winter color, and also provide an ideal backdrop for spring and summer flowers.

Even if a love of flowers will always be what inspires you to grab the trowel and start planting, once you begin to see the potential of foliage in your landscape designs, you'll have both beautiful blossoms and a yard rich in visual variety all year long.

'Great Expectations' hosta

10 Great Foliage Plants

- **'Blue Moon' hosta**
  Hosta 'Blue Moon'

- **Cushion spurge**
  Euphorbia polychroma

- **Dusty miller**
  Senecio cineraria

- **Gunnera**
  Gunnera

- **Japanese maple**
  Acer palmatum

- **Japanese painted fern**
  Athyrium niponicum

- **Lady's-mantle**
  Alchemilla mollis

- **Lamb's-ears**
  Stachys byzantina

- **Maidenhair fern**
  Adiantum

- **Plume poppy**
  Macleaya cordata

Lady's-mantle

Container Gardening

Who can forget the sense of childlike wonder that came from planting seeds in a coffee can and waiting—not so patiently—for the first signs of green to poke through the soil? Container gardening takes us back to childhood—to the joys of planting, nurturing, and watching things grow.

Whether you're challenged by limited space or longing to enhance your existing garden, container plants can bring color, texture, dimension, and charm to any garden sanctuary. And one of the joys of container gardening is that you're not bound by any hard and fast rules. Let your whims and dreams lead the way.

CHOOSING CONTAINERS

As you shop for containers (a vast array of pots, bowls, troughs, barrels, urns, and tubs awaits you at your local home or garden center), consider the containers most suitable for your setting. If you'd rather indulge in a treasure hunt for "found" containers, try browsing at flea markets or antique stores, cleaning out the garage, or visiting your grandmother. Old boots, rustic baskets, your grandmother's wash basin, or an antique urn all make creative containers for plants.

As a general rule, natural materials make the best homes for plants— wood, stone, terra-cotta, and copper. The subtle earthiness of terra-cotta blends naturally with most plants, and these pots come in virtually every shape and size. Ceramic and terra-cotta pots, however, are vulnerable to freezing and cracking during harsh winters. Synthetic imitations are usually less costly, offer comparable visual appeal, and can withstand seasonal variations in temperature. Reconstituted stone and fiberglass containers also make good alternatives.

Keep in mind that large pots lend themselves to lush, dramatic displays. Plants will also have more room for growth and require watering less frequently. Large containers are usually heavy, so try placing them on dollies with casters to make them easy to move.

Whatever containers you choose, good drainage is necessary to avoid soggy roots, which can lead to root rot. Ideally, you'll want to select containers that have adequate drainage holes. For outdoor pots, you won't need to purchase drainage saucers; water that becomes stagnant in these can become a breeding ground for damaging pests. And don't despair if you find just the right pot only to discover that it has no drain holes! There is a way to remedy this problem if favorite pots don't offer optimal drainage (see "Pot Luck" on pages 42–43).

CHOOSING DECORATIVE PLANTS

As you shop for plants, keep your choices simple. You can always add complexity to your garden once you've established a basic plan. Start out by determining the visual effect you hope to achieve—formal or informal, permanent or seasonal, or a combined effect. Choose colors that lift your spirit and scents that take your breath away. (Aromatic displays will soon invite butterflies, bees, and hummingbirds.)

On the practical side, consider the amount of available sunlight, as well as the rate of growth and scale of plants that will thrive in your space. You don't want "creepers and climbers" showing up as unwelcome guests in your neighbor's backyard!

While a few plants prefer solid ground to container life (roses and deciduous clematis fall into this category), almost any plant will thrive in a suitable container if it's given proper light, water, and periodic grooming. For visual variety, mix annuals with perennials or combine common plants with more exotic ones.

CHOOSING EDIBLE PLANTS

For people whose yards aren't large enough for an orchard or garden, containers provide a wonderful way to grow fresh vegetables and fruits. Fresh green lettuce, sweet young carrots, radishes, tomatoes, peppers, and strawberries all grow well in pots, and with a few extra-large containers, you can even establish your own orchard by planting dwarf fruit trees. If you'd like to try your hand at growing edibles this way, keep a few tips in mind.

Never use a container that has ever held a substance toxic to humans or plants, and if you use wooden containers, make sure the wood hasn't been treated with a preservative. (Naturally rot-resistant woods such as cedar or redwood are fine.) Make sure your pots are large enough to support the plants once they're mature, and use only containers with drainage holes in them.

Avoid the light, soil-free potting soils that are sold for houseplants; they don't contain enough organic matter for edible plants and aren't heavy enough to keep outdoor containers from blowing over on windy days. Instead, select a potting mixture that's rich in organic matter, or make your own by combining sand, peat moss, and rich garden soil in equal proportions. Commercial potting soils generally provide enough fertilizer for about eight weeks' growth, but vegetables and fruits will require periodic use of a water-soluble fertilizer after that.

No container garden is really complete without a collection of aromatic herbs: basil, oregano, parsley, chives, rosemary, and thyme. Whether they're planted in separate pots or together in a large container, herbs provide decorative appeal and delectable culinary pleasures.

CREATING YOUR DESIGN

To achieve a balanced design, select plants that suit their containers' forms and the materials from which they're made. In decorative pots or works of art, use upright plants that complement rather than overwhelm the container. Less attractive containers can be dressed with flowers cascading over their rims. Plant colorful containers with flowers of matching hues.

For optimal effect, group pots in key locations—beside a door, a garden gate, or the edge of a pond. To give structure to your design, use pedestals, posts, and stands that will vary the heights of plants. For a less structured look, scatter pots throughout surrounding beds and terraces, or along a favorite path. And when you tire of a design, just rearrange the landscape by mixing and matching containers and plants to create a new one.

"POT LUCK": RECIPES FOR SUCCESSFUL CONTAINER GARDENING

The tools for container gardening are few and simple. You'll need a small hand trowel and a fork, preferably stainless steel with wooden handles; a pair of good-quality pruning shears; and a watering can or hose with an adjustable outlet.

Before setting plants in any used container, clean the container thoroughly with dish soap and hot water. Then sterilize the container by scrubbing it with a ten-percent bleach solution (rinse it thoroughly when you're finished); or with a handful of rock salt in a mixture of two parts white vinegar and one part water. Small pots can be run through the dishwasher.

When you're ready to begin the planting process, first place a layer of drainage materials in the bottom of your container: marble chips, pebbles, pottery shards, or polystyrene "peanuts" will all work well. Spread a one-inch-deep layer in each small pot and a two-inch-deep layer in each larger one. The type of potting soil you use will also influence drainage, so be sure to

buy one that contains perlite or coarse sand. (To remedy poor drainage in pots you've already planted, carefully remove the plant and soil. Then use an electric drill and the appropriate bit for the material from which the pot is made to bore extra holes in the container's bottom.)

Fill the container with potting soil, to within two inches of its rim. Gently remove the plant from its cell pack or pot and spread its roots. Using a trowel, dig a hole in the potting soil, insert the plant, add potting soil, and press it down to firm it. Water the plant well, using either a watering can or a garden hose that has a long-handled wand with a flat rose at its end. Apply the water directly to the soil, not to the foliage.

Check the moisture levels of containers daily at the edges and near the center, and water early in the day when the air is cool. During the growing season, fertilize the plants once every seven to ten days. Feed them in the morning, after watering, using water-soluble plant food or organic fertilizers (fish emulsion, liquid kelp, or blood meal).

As part of your ongoing plant-care program, remove faded flowers daily to encourage new growth and prevent certain plants from going to seed. To deadhead properly, cut or pinch below the flower pod, just above the node, rather than pulling the flower from its pod. Using sharp, clean pruning

shears, prune all diseased, dead, or weak growth to promote health and preserve the shape of your plants. Try to prune sensitively, cutting at an angle, away from the leaf joint.

REPELLING PLANT PESTS

When pests become a problem, avoid using chemical pesticides if possible. Many pests can be kept at bay by placing unpeeled garlic cloves one inch deep in the soil, near the rim of each pot—about three cloves for a 14-inch pot. To deter "crawlers," sprinkle cayenne pepper on the soil near the rim of the pot. To keep slugs away from tender foliage, place a shallow container (a jar lid or tin tray) of beer near the bases of the pots.

As an alternative to chemical sprays, try making your own organic spray by mixing the tobacco from four cigarettes, four crushed garlic cloves, one teaspoon of white pepper, two tablespoons of liquid insecticidal soap, and two tablespoons of ammonia into two quarts of hot water. Steep the mixture for several hours; then strain it thoroughly. Spray plants three times a week until health is restored.

Planting a Moss-Lined Hanging Basket

A cheerful profusion of color contained in a moss-lined basket will be a stunning eye-catcher, enlivening your garden with variety and visual interest. Its earthy texture, with plants trailing in the breeze, lures us back to nature and is perfect for any setting. As well as their aesthetic charm, hanging baskets offer a practical and attractive way to bring visual balance or contrast to your surroundings.

MATERIALS & TOOLS

- Open-mesh wire basket or other open-weave container
- Green sheet moss (available at garden centers, craft stores, and florists)
- Plastic sheeting
- Top-grade potting soil
- Plants
- Trowel
- Scissors
- Wire hanger or wall mount
- Slow-release plant food

TIPS

- Be sure to match your plant selection with the hanging site to ensure proper growing conditions.
- Over-watering your basket can be a problem. To check for moisture, gently insert your finger into the soil. Water only when the soil feels dry.
- Replenish plants in your hanging basket by replacing them with others. When bulbs have stopped blooming, for example, replace them with spring or summer annuals. (Grocery stores and garden centers are excellent sources for blooming annuals and bulbs.)

Instructions

1 Water the plants in their packaged containers so they'll be well hydrated when you place them in the soil. To hydrate the sheet moss and make it easier to use, allow it to soak in water for 10 to 15 minutes. Then squeeze it out to eliminate excess moisture.

2 Line the basket with a layer of damp moss, placing the more attractive green side out. Adjust the thickness of the layer to eliminate any holes. To check for shallow spots, hold the pot up to the light; then add more moss if necessary.

3 Cut a layer of plastic sheeting to fit the size of the basket. Using the scissors, punch drainage holes, spacing them about 1" apart. Then place the plastic on top of the moss to form an inner lining that will conserve moisture.

4 Fill the basket half full with potting soil. For proper drainage, use a quality, name-brand soil with a combination of peat, perlite, and bark.

5 Position the basket on an upturned bucket or pot to allow sufficient clearance for trailing or cascading plants. Plant trailing plants such as English ivy first. Insert small clumps or segments from cell packs around the perimeter of the potting soil. Cover the roots with soil, and press the soil gently with your fingers or trowel to eliminate air pockets. Then give the basket a gentle shake to settle the contents.

6 Plant the largest plant next, either in the center of the basket (if you plan to hang the basket) or toward the back (if you plan to display the basket against a wall).

7 Fill in with remaining plants—tallest to shortest, in descending order—working either from the back or center to the outside edge of the basket. Remember to firm the plants, add more soil as needed, and periodically shake everything down. If you plan to hang the basket rather than display it with a wall bracket, be sure to leave room for the hanging chains.

8 When all the plants have been placed, add additional potting soil if necessary to cover the roots completely and fill in any gaps between plants. Then cover the soil with a thin layer of sheet moss.

9 Water the basket gently but thoroughly with a diluted solution of slow-release fertilizer, until you see water trickling out around the base. Allow the basket to drain completely before you hang it.

10 Attach the wire hanger to the basket, being careful not to damage surrounding plants. If you prefer a wall display, secure the basket with a wall mount or a heavy-duty nail.

11 Mist the plants for the first week or two, until they're established in their new home.

VARIATION

For a variation on your planting theme, either select a different basket material, as shown above, or create a lush, rounded look by arranging some of your trailing plants to extend through the sides of the wire basket.

Start by placing a thin layer of damp moss in the bottom of the basket. Fit a layer of plastic sheeting over it, punching drainage holes as described in step 3. Arrange a shallow layer of potting soil on top of the plastic liner and insert your small trailing plants through the lowest openings in the basket. Cover their roots with soil and press gently to eliminate air pockets. Continue this process, until you reach the top of the basket. Line the basket with moss as you progress upward, followed by additional layers of soil and plants. Avoid adding too many plants; three layers is usually adequate to create the desired look.

Conquering Slopes

First the bad news: Landscaping a steep slope can be frustrating. Even if you manage to coax grass to grow on it, mowing can be either treacherous or impossible. The soil on slopes is usually too dry for flower gardening. What's more, hard rains have a tendency to erode dry soil and leach out its nutrients.

Now the good news: Solutions for these problems exist. Some of the most beautiful gardens imaginable thrive on slopes that have been terraced or stabilized with rocks. The rise of a hillside shows many flowers to their best advantage, and rocks, which make handsome additions to almost any landscape, actually create

a more moderate microclimate, which in turn will allow you to grow plants that might not otherwise survive in your zone. Attractive ground covers can serve to hold sloped soil in place as well. In addition, artificial streams and waterfalls look most natural when cascading down naturally sloping yards.

TERRACING

Terracing (creating a level section or sections) transforms a steep bank into usable land, fights erosion and nutrient loss by slowing and rechanneling water flow, and provides flat areas in which to plant or, if these areas are large enough, to dine or play.

Landscaping timbers, stones, and cinder blocks are all common materials for the walls with which terraces are constructed.

Whether or not you can create a terraced slope on your own will depend in part on the size and difficulty of the job, but anyone with a healthy back can create a low, dry-stacked terrace wall. (See pages 52–53 for instructions.)

MAKING STEPS AND PATHS

Steps make a hillside garden more inviting and accessible, as well as easier to tend. The only firm rule to keep in mind as you build them is that they must be wide and deep enough to traverse easily. Many materials are suitable for making steps, including rocks, landscape timbers, and railroad ties. Some of the easiest steps to build—and the most convenient when you're dealing with large expanses—consist of gravel or wood chips spread within open frames constructed from landscape timbers.

Gentle slopes are often best served by meandering paths that cut back and forth across the slope rather than

steps that rise straight up the hillside. In fact, paths and steps that run across slopes are almost always your best bet for erosion control.

PLANTING GROUND COVERS

Many ground covers (see page 48) will quickly blanket a hillside and help curb erosion. Most require little maintenance, and the adverse conditions of the slope will cut down on the invasiveness of some ground covers. Evergreen ground covers, such as periwinkle, English ivy, and pachysandra, will give year-round coverage and may be interplanted with flowering bulbs. Low-growing shrubs, such as creeping juniper and cotoneaster, provide easy coverage for sloping terrain and are often able to thrive in spite of poor soil conditions.

WATERING SLOPES

Because water tends to run off sloping ground before it's absorbed, slopes should be watered at a slower rate than flat areas. Buried drip hoses positioned horizontally across a slope will allow water to weep slowly into the ground. Also keep in mind that because much of the water will run downhill, the top of a slope needs more water than the bottom.

Planting drought-tolerant flowers, shrubs, or ground covers on slopes will reduce the need to water. When you dig a hole for a plant on a slope, create a pocket by mounding the dirt just below the hole. Then, to hold the mounded dirt in place, bury a rock in its downhill side, tilting the top of the rock in toward the plant. The pocket will help hold water near the plant's roots until it is absorbed.

Using Ground Covers

Ground covers (low growing, spreading plants) can add color and texture to shady areas, help control erosion on banks that are too steep to mow, and unite separate sections of the yard. Once established, ground covers both spread and thicken to become more attractive, usually with little if any maintenance.

CHOOSING A GROUND COVER

Before choosing a ground cover, consider the growing conditions of your particular site. Note the amount of sunlight the area receives and the condition of the soil. Some ground covers will grow in deep shade, while others need full sun. Some, such as vinca and ajuga, do well in dry spots, while others, such as sweet woodruff, will thrive in moist areas.

Think, too, about how you will use that section of yard and how you would like the ground cover to function. A creeping rose will blanket a slope with delicate color in summer. Pachysandra will provide year-round color and texture for your yard. Roman chamomile or thyme planted between paving stones will spread to provide a fragrant pathway to your

Cotoneaster

front door. (See pages 148–149 for instructions on planting aromatic paths.) Low growing evergreen shrubs planted as ground covers can also add a vertical element to your landscape and will serve as visual transitions between grass or flowers and trees or tall fences.

PLANTING GROUND COVERS

Prepare the soil for ground covers as you would for any plant. If you're planting a large, flat area, rototilling

may be best. On a steep bank, you'll need to dig individual holes for each plant instead. Test the soil and amend it if necessary; then set out the plants, spacing them as directed. The most economical way to start fast growing ground covers is to put in a few plants and be patient. To ensure even coverage on a slope, start at the top and stagger rows of the individual plants down and across.

Keep plants mulched and well watered until they're established. Vigilant weeding for the first year or two will reward you with a ground cover that needs very little weeding or other maintenance thereafter.

CONTROLLING INVASIVE GROUND COVERS

Some ground covers spread very rapidly and are planted for precisely this reason. These same ground covers, however, can get out of hand. When you come across catalog descriptions such as "extremely vigorous," or "covers that problem spot," watch out. Invasive ground covers can overtake an entire bed and threaten to swallow the house! Always plant these ground covers (English ivy, crown vetch, and ribbon grass are a few examples) alone and in areas bordered by hardscapes (cement pathways and stone terraces, for instance); solid barriers will keep the plants in check. Leaving a four-inch-deep, four- to five-inch-wide border of soil around the ground cover will also help control spreading. But even barriers won't prevent the need for regular pruning of underground stems and aboveground shoots at the edge of a vigorous ground cover's bed.

Ground Covers

COMMON & BOTANICAL NAME	HARDINESS ZONES	SOIL & LIGHT CONDITIONS	DESCRIPTION
African daisy *Osteospermum*	9–10	*well-drained* FULL SUN	tender perennial; purple to lavender to white daisy-like flowers; oblong leaves; blooms heavily in late winter and early spring; spreads to create a dense mat
Bugleweed *Ajuga*	3–9	*well-drained, acid loam* FULL SUN TO PARTIAL SHADE	perennial, but often evergreen in mild winters; whorled, violet, blue, pink, or white flowers in summer; thick mats of foliage in shades of green, deep purple, bronze, or creamy mottled white
Cotoneaster *Cotoneaster dammeri* 'Coral Beauty'	6–8	*well-drained* FULL SUN	prostrate, evergreen shrub; white flowers in summer; coral-red berries in fall; rich green foliage tinged purple in fall; fast growing
Creeping juniper *Juniperus horizontalis*	2–9	*light, well-drained* FULL SUN	evergreen, creeping shrub; scalelike foliage ranging in color from dark green to emerald to silvery blue-green, usually purple-bronzed in winter
English ivy *Hedera helix*	5–10	*average to poor, moist, well-drained* PARTIAL SHADE	evergreen trailing perennial; foliage ranges from butter yellow to dark green to purple, sometimes variegated; tolerates many conditions; can also be used as a climber
Pachysandra *Pachysandra*	5–9	*moist, well-drained, acid* PARTIAL TO FULL SHADE	evergreen or semi-evergreen perennial; short spikes with white or pink flowers in spring; whorls of toothed, dark green leaves; grows well beneath trees
Thyme *Thymus*	3–9	*average to poor, dry, well-drained, alkaline* FULL SUN	evergreen perennial or shrub; aromatic with rose-purple flowers in summer; tiny oval leaves; tolerant of heat and drought

Terracing

Through the ages, people around the world have used terracing to transform steep slopes into land suitable for planting. Today, terraced gardens are built for decorative as well as practical purposes—to create nearly level areas for planting and to make slopes more attractive and accessible. Cutting a series of level plateaus into a slope also provides a perfect solution to drainage problems and adds visual variety to your overall landscape design.

VARYING YOUR PLANTING THEME

With careful planning, just about any kind of gardening is possible on a terraced slope. Trees provide pockets of shade for ferns, hostas, mosses, and hardy geraniums, while sunny spots offer perfect homes for bright perennials and annuals. Rock gardens brimming with phlox, sedum, purple sage, thyme, and other easy-care "creepers" add texture and variety to your garden theme. Terraces are also ideal settings for meandering trails and paths among seasonal flower beds and ground covers. An overall plan that is well suited to your site creates a stunning backdrop for a focal point such as a pond, bench, or stone wall.

Keep in mind that drought-tolerant plants grow well along steeper terraces, while "thirsty" plants thrive near the bottom. And remember that the most cherished garden evolves over time. Your terrace garden does not have to happen overnight. So relax and enjoy—one step at a time.

CHOOSING RETAINING WALLS

A terrace requires a retaining wall to hold back the soil in it. Desirable effects for terraced walls can be achieved with any number of creative combinations of building materials. Combining stacked stones with locust logs creates a warm, primitive look in a rustic backyard setting. Railroad ties and landscape timbers make good retaining-wall materials, as do slabs of recycled concrete walkway, and concrete blocks made to look like stone. Dry-stacked stone walls combined with dry-laid steps are not only practical but also provide decorative focal points that draw the eye.

SLOPING TERRACES TO ENHANCE DRAINAGE

Rather than making terraced levels flat, gently slope them from the center outward, allowing rainwater to run off to the sides. Avoid too much sloping, or heavy rain will wash away topsoil from beds and mulch from pathways. If your terraces include pathways, consider digging the paths six to nine inches below the level of planting beds, so that water will drain slowly along the path rather than pooling on the terraced bed.

PREPARATIONS

First you'll need to calculate the *rise* and *run* of your slope. Set a vertical stake at the top of the slope and another at the bottom. Tie a string between them, with a line level on it to make sure the string is level. Measure the longer stake from the string to the ground; this distance is the rise. The length of the string is the run. Divide the run by the desired number of terraces to determine the width of each terrace. Then divide the rise by the desired number of terraces to calculate the height of each terrace.

Also check the condition of the soil before deciding what to plant. Dig several test holes, and if you encounter many rocks, consider building a raised bed or planting a ground cover around the rocks. If you don't mind doing a little excavating, larger rocks can be dug out and used for building a dry-stacked wall.

To transform a large hillside or embankment, you'll probably need more than a shovel and your own two hands to do the job—consult a landscape professional. But for mild to moderate slopes that can be conquered "by hand," a dry-stacked stone wall can turn a sloped area into a productive and beautiful garden (see pages 52–53 for instructions).

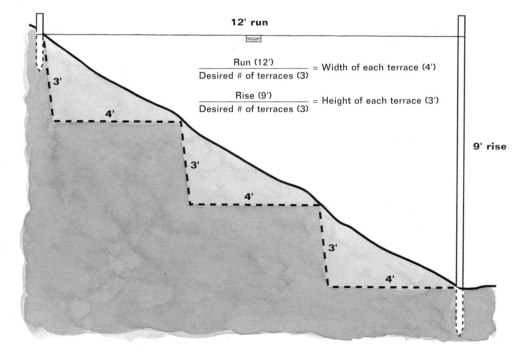

$$\frac{\text{Run (12')}}{\text{Desired \# of terraces (3)}} = \text{Width of each terrace (4')}$$

$$\frac{\text{Rise (9')}}{\text{Desired \# of terraces (3)}} = \text{Height of each terrace (3')}$$

Building a Low, Dry-Stacked Stone Wall

Dry-stacked stone walls require no mortar and are easier to create than you might think. Just be sure to complete only as much work in a day as your muscles can handle comfortably! The instructions that follow will work for any retaining wall two feet or less in height. If you like, you can adapt them to create either steps or terraced planting beds on a backyard slope. As you can see in the photo below, you may also taper a wall from one end to the other in order to match the incline of your yard.

MATERIALS & TOOLS

- Leather gloves
- Protective boots
- Shovel
- Mattock
- Stones
- ⅜" to ½" gravel
- Sturdy wheelbarrow for stones
- Sturdy 5-gallon bucket for gravel
- Steel rebar, 3' long

TIPS

- Calculate the amounts of gravel and stone you'll need by using the formulas below:

  Stone: (Wall length x wall height) + (wall length x wall width) = square feet of exposed wall. Divide square feet by 30 to calculate the number of tons of stone required.

  Gravel: (Wall height x wall length x 1 foot) ÷ 27 = cubic yards of gravel required

- Ideal stones are hard (basalt, gneiss, granite, and limestone are best) and have flat surfaces and well-defined corners. Order 35 percent more stone than required for your wall and select the best stones from the pile.

- Either order your stones from a stone yard or collect them from your property. Gravel is available from sand and gravel companies.

Instructions

1 Select some of the largest, flattest stones for the top layer of your wall and set these "capstones" aside. (Be sure to wear protective clothing, including leather gloves and boots.)

2 Using your mattock and shovel, cut away the soil bank, angling it slightly backward from bottom to top. (Save some of the soil; see step 10.)

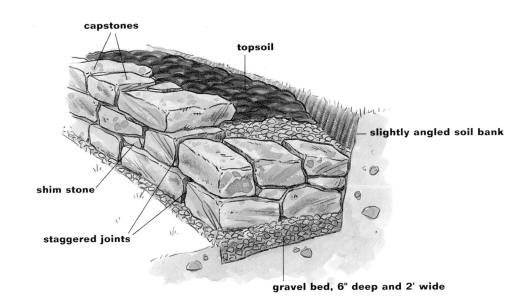

capstones

topsoil

slightly angled soil bank

shim stone

staggered joints

gravel bed, 6" deep and 2' wide

3 Dig a 6"-deep, 2'-wide trench at the base, and fill it with gravel. Then spread a 2"-thick layer of gravel from the base of the cut bank to the front of the trench.

4 Select very large stones, each with at least one wide, flat surface, for the first layer. Position their front ends as close to each other as possible, at the front of the trench, and their flattest surfaces facing up. (The distance between the soil bank and the back of each stone will vary, but should average about 1'.) Slant each stone slightly downward from front to back, and set any long, rectangular stones with their short ends positioned at the front and back of the layer.

5 To create corners at each end of your wall and to keep the gravel from filtering out, set stones to fill the gap between the soil bank and the first and last stones in this layer.

6 Add gravel behind the first layer of stones, filling the gaps between the back ends of the stones as well. To lock the stones in place and fill all the voids between them, "set" the gravel around their sides and backs by jabbing it repeatedly with one end of the rebar. (Add more gravel as necessary.) When you're finished, brush away any gravel on top of the stones. Backfilling a wall with gravel and setting the gravel can be tedious, but both steps are essential for wall strength and stability.

7 Lay out the next layer of stones. To make your wall stronger, stagger the joints between the stones in each layer by setting each stone on top of a joint in the layer beneath. Stabilize wobbling stones by using small rocks as shims. Use especially long stones as "ties" by setting them with one short end in front and the other short end right up against the soil bank in back.

8 Add gravel behind the stones in the second layer, and set the new gravel with the rebar.

9 Continue by adding layers of stone, backfilling with gravel, and setting the gravel after each layer is complete. As you work, check frequently to make sure that each layer is level from end to end and angled slightly downward from front to back. Also make sure the outer face of the wall angles slightly backward from bottom to top. The slope of the wall should match the slope of the cut soil bank.

10 Using the capstones that you set aside in step 1, lay out the last layer of your wall, and then backfill with gravel as before. Then cover the gravel with the soil you reserved in step 2.

Privacy & Relaxation

Read this chapter with your feet up. For a few minutes, set aside thoughts of stacking stones, pulling weeds, and mowing grass. Stretch out on a chaise or curl up in a swing. And think relaxation.

Imagine yourself lounging in a hammock, late one summer afternoon. The breeze is playing in the leaves above; a waterfall spills into a small pond nearby. Or envision yourself sitting on a rustic bench in your own private garden nook, watching birds play at your garden fountain. Perhaps you'd rather read while resting in the shade of trellised vines, or amble along the path that winds gently through your yard.

Every yard needs a private sanctuary— a place that offers respite from the rest of the world and promises peace of mind. And don't worry. A private place doesn't have to be ringed by high, ugly fences or gloomy hedges: Tall plantings that shelter and water features that soothe are more calming—and much more attractive. Let yourself be inspired, but don't grab that shovel yet! First, sit back and practice the fine art of relaxation.

Planting for Privacy and Relaxation

Imagine your house without any walls. How could you possibly relax and enjoy yourself, exposed to both your neighbors and the elements? Our backyards, like our homes, are places in which we need a sense of privacy and comfort. Unfortunately no one told that to the designers of many modern housing developments, where adjoining yards sometimes merge into one and are open on all sides.

Fences, trees, hedges, trellised vines, and even tall perennial plantings will define the boundaries or "walls" of your property to make you feel more secure and protected. Yards designed with careful attention to these vertical elements will put you and your guests at ease and encourage relaxation.

Tall plantings often serve more than one function at a time. As we scan seed catalogs in January, most of us crave sunlight, but on a July afternoon, lounging on an unsheltered patio may make you feel as relaxed as a hot dog on a grill. A strategically placed, vine-covered trellis can provide color and even fragrance while it casts cooling shade onto your patio.

Trees and shrubs that screen out the sights and sounds of traffic can also buffer a seaside home from strong winds. The fence that offers privacy from the neighbors can become the home for an espaliered apple tree.

Even if your property is already fenced or hedged, vertical elements within the yard itself can break the space into a series of "rooms" that will greatly enhance your enjoyment of the space. Small yards actually feel larger when divided into separate areas. They're also easier to use. A line of low shrubs may be just enough to separate the kids' play area from your prized perennial bed, and during the summer, a tall perennial planting can set off a dining area from the rest of the yard.

As with all aspects of backyard landscaping, you'll want to keep vertical elements properly scaled to their site. Make sure that vine won't turn into Jack's beanstalk, and never plant a tree impulsively. Consider carefully the mature height of the species and the specific variety of any tree you'd like to plant. Removing an established tree that has grown too large or was planted in the wrong place is difficult and often costly. The right tree in the right place, on the other hand, will do wonders for your yard and might easily be enjoyed by future generations.

RELAX!

Why toil in the backyard all season if you're not going to prop up your feet and reap the benefits? Why fuss and fret over that perfect lawn and then deny yourself the pleasure of sprawling out on its fresh, cool grasses? Pick a sprig of that mint you've grown, drop it into a tall glass of iced tea, and review some relaxing basics.

Sleeping. A nice, wide hammock wins the prize for best outdoor napping spot—hands down. Strung between two trees or spread out in its own stand, a hammock in dappled shade is the perfect place to read or sleep. Or read and then sleep. Or intend to read but fall asleep instead.

Sunbathing. Tsk-tsk, you know better than to bask unprotected. A big, floppy hat will help guard your face and shoulders, but you'll still need sunscreen with an SPF of 15 or higher to survive the sun's dangerous rays. Slather it on, and keep a big pitcher of ice water nearby to avoid dehydration.

Reading. There's no easier way to lose yourself than to slip between the pages of a good book. Settle into your favorite garden nook and check out these authors' observations of the natural world:

> *Pilgrim at Tinker Creek,* **Annie Dillard**
> *My Favorite Plant,* **Jamaica Kincaid**
> *New and Selected Poems,* **Mary Oliver**
> *Plant Dreaming Deep,* **May Sarton**
> *Walden,* **Henry David Thoreau**

Gathering with Friends. Whether you want to grill kabobs, raise the volleyball net, or just sit and talk, there's no better place to host guests than in your well-tended backyard.

Observing Wildlife. You didn't plant all of those butterfly bushes for nothing, did you? Take time to find a quiet spot where you can sit and watch with fascination as butterflies flutter by, mantises pray, and cocoons burst. Even the smallest patch of a garden is teeming with life.

A Privacy Plan

An intimate backyard nook for leisurely chats or quiet contemplation is often the most treasured spot in the yard. The tall plantings in the garden plan provided here offer privacy, shade (if you set out your tallest plants to block the late afternoon sun), and cheerful bursts of color that will continue through the end of summer and into the fall. Space perennials (and the tree mallow) at least 18 inches apart. Keep the holly hedge sheared to 18 inches in height or replace the annuals behind it with taller perennials after the first year.

A JOE-PYE WEED
Eupatorium maculatum
Hardiness zones 3–7
up to 7 feet tall
Large, flattened clusters of white to deep purple flowers from midsummer to early fall; oblong, medium-green leaves on purple-tinted stems; moist, well-drained loam; full sun to partial shade; attractive to bees and butterflies

B TREE MALLOW
Lavatera 'Barnsley'
Hardy annual
up to 6 feet tall
Funnel-shaped, white flowers with red centers in summer, flowers fade to soft pink; gray-green leaves on vigorous, shrub-like branches; well-drained soil; full sun; deadhead to promote flowering

C PHLOX
Phlox paniculata 'David'
Hardiness zones 4–8
40 inches tall
Fragrant, flat, panicle-like, white flowers from midsummer to early fall; thin, lance-shaped leaves on sturdy stems; moist, fertile loam; full sun to partial shade; deadhead to prolong flowering

D PURPLE CONEFLOWER
Echinacea purpurea
Hardiness zones 3–9
2 to 4 feet tall
Deep purple to rose to white, drooping petals, with dark brown conical centers, blooms midsummer to early fall; lance-shaped, dark green leaves; well-drained loam; full sun to light shade

E FLOWERING TOBACCO
Nicotiana alata
Nicki Series 'Nicki Red'
Hardy annual
16 to 18 inches tall
Fragrant red, tubular flowers from midsummer to fall; spoon-shaped to ovate leaves; fertile, moist, well-drained soil; full sun to partial shade; flowers are especially fragrant at night

F ZINNIA
Zinnia elegans
Ruffles Series 'Pink Ruffles'
Annual
24 inches tall
Pink, ruffled, fully double flowers in summer; lightly hairy, oval leaves; fertile, well-drained soil; full sun; deadhead to prolong flowering

G JAPANESE HOLLY
Ilex crenata 'Hoogendorn'
Hardiness zones 5–7
3 to 4 feet tall
Dwarf evergreen shrub with small, glossy, medium-green leaves; moist, well-drained loam; full sun to partial shade

H ZINNIA
Zinnia angustifolia 'Star White'
Annual
24 inches tall
White, daisy-like flowers, with golden yellow centers, bloom until frost; oblong leaves lightly covered with hairs; fertile, well-drained soil; full sun; deadhead to prolong flowering

Additional Plants

1 **Weeping willow** (*Salix babylonica*)
2 **Hollyhock** (*Alcea*)
3 **'China Doll' rose standard** (*Rosa* 'China Doll')
4 **Whirling butterflies** (*Gaura lindheimeri* 'Whirling Butterflies')
5 **Bearded iris** (*Iris*)
6 **Globe amaranth** (*Gomphrena globosa*)

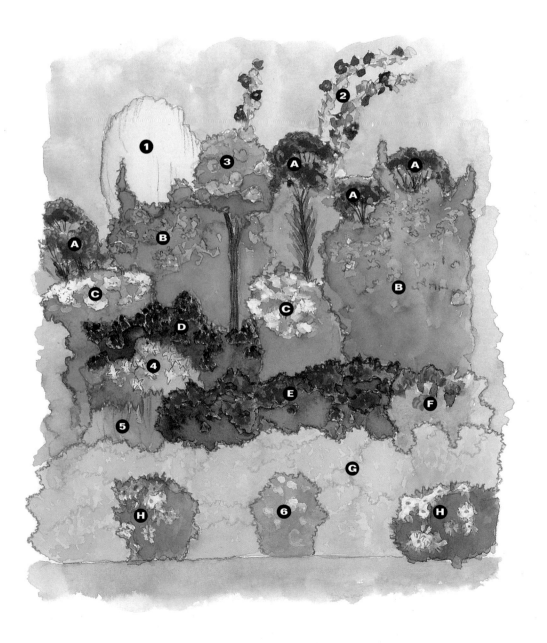

Building a Trellis Planter

This movable trellis provides privacy as well as shade from the hot summer sun—where you want it and when you want it. What's more, the unique, removable, double-planter design allows you to grow twice as many plants as you might on a typical trellis. Just position this trellis so that the planter with sun-loving plants receives at least four to six hours of full sun a day. Put shade plants on the other side, and they'll thrive in the shadows of the plants behind them. (Don't worry if plants such as the impatiens shown below get some morning sun; as the day passes, they'll soon be immersed in shade.)

MATERIALS & TOOLS

- Measuring tape
- Pencil
- Straightedge
- No. 6 decking screws: 1$\frac{1}{4}$", 1$\frac{5}{8}$", and 2"
- Handsaw or circular saw
- No. 2 Phillips-head screwdriver
- Electric drill with $\frac{1}{8}$" and $\frac{3}{4}$" bits
- Coarse sandpaper, or router with $\frac{1}{4}$" roundover bit
- Exterior paint, or stain and sealer
- Paintbrushes

TIPS

- The instructions for this project substitute standard lumber for the milled cedar with which the actual project was built. (Standard lumber is considerably less expensive.) For parts L, M, N, and O, use weather-resistant wood, as standard lumber will rot too quickly, and paints, stains, or sealers may contaminate the soil.
- Predrilling $\frac{1}{8}$" pilot holes for the screws will make screw insertion much easier.

CUTTING LIST

CODE	DESCRIPTION	QTY.	MATERIAL
A	Frame sides	2	1 x 6 x 78"
B	Frame top	1	1 x 4 x 48"
C	Base sides	2	1 x 2 x 15"
D	Base front and back	2	1 x 4 x 46½"
E	Base divider	1	1 x 2 x 45"
F	Crosspieces	3	1 x 2 x 46½"
G	Vertical lattices	3	1 x 2" x 53"
H	Vertical lattices	4	1 x 2 x 35½"
I	Vertical lattices	4	1 x 2 x 25"
J	Horizontal lattice	1	1 x 2 x 34"
K	Horizontal lattices	2	1 x 2 x 17"
L	Planter bottoms	2	1 x 8 x 44½"
M	Planter fronts and backs	4	1 x 8 x 46"
N	Planter sides	4	1 x 8 x 5½"
O	Planter legs	6	1 x 2 x 6½"

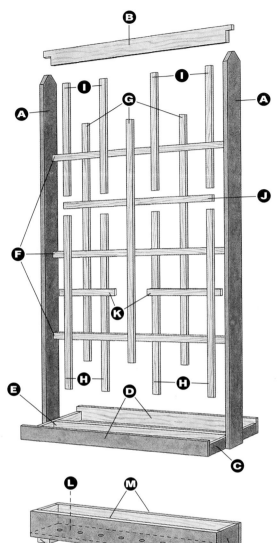

Instructions

1 Cut all the lumber to the lengths specified in the "Cutting List."

2 The top of each frame side (A) has two angled cuts. To mark these cutting lines, first measure and mark two points on the top edge of a frame side, 2¼" in from each long outer edge. Measure and mark two more points, one on each long edge, 2" down from the top end. Then mark lines between each pair of marks, and cut along the angled lines. Repeat with the other frame side.

3 At each short end of the frame top (B), measure, mark, and cut out a ¾" x 2½" notch.

4 Secure the frame top (B) to the angle-cut end of each frame side (A) by inserting a No. 6 x 2" decking screw through the outer face of each frame side, at a point 2" from its top end, into the vertical notched edge of frame top. Also insert a No. 6 x 2" screw down through the top edge of the frame top, into the top end of each frame side.

5 To make the trellis's base, first form a rectangle by arranging the base sides (C) between the base front and back pieces (D). Then secure each corner of the rectangle by inserting two No. 6 x 2" screws through the faces of the longer boards.

6 Center the base divider (E) within the rectangular base frame and fasten it in place by inserting two No. 6 x 2" screws through the outer face of each base side (C).

7 On a flat work surface, position the base between the frame sides (A), with all bottom edges flush and the frame sides centered on both ends of the base. Then fasten the two assemblies together by inserting two No. 6 x 1⅝" screws through the outer face of each frame side.

8 Position one of the crosspieces (F) between the frame sides (A), centering it 40" up from the frame sides' bottom ends and across their widths. Attach this middle crosspiece by inserting two No. 6 x 2" screws through the outer face of each frame side.

9 Attach the remaining crosspieces (F) in the same fashion, centering one 20" up from the middle crosspiece and one 20" below it.

10 Position one vertical lattice (G) across the three crosspieces (F), centering it between the frame sides (A) and allowing it to extend 4½" below the lowest crosspiece. Fasten this lattice piece in place by inserting a No. 6 x 1¼" screw at each intersection. (Note: All the remaining lattice pieces are attached with No. 6 x 1¼" screws.)

11 Fasten the two remaining vertical lattice pieces (G), leaving 10" between the outer edge of each one and the inner face of each frame side (A).

12 Using the illustration and photo as guides, carefully position and attach all the remaining lattice pieces (H through K). Exact placement measurements aren't critical, but do be careful to attach the pieces to the correct side of the trellis frame.

13 To begin building each of the two planters, first attach the planter front and back pieces (M) to the two planter sides (N), using three No. 6 x 1⅝" screws at each corner.

14 Mark and drill a line of centered, ¾"-diameter drainage holes, spaced 5" apart, along the length of each planter bottom (L).

15 Place a planter bottom (L) inside each planter frame (M and N), and secure it with No. 6 x 1⅝" screws, spaced 6" apart and inserted through the faces of the planter frame boards.

16 Center the wide face of one planter leg (O) across a planter bottom (L), and fasten it in place with two No. 6 x 1¼" screws. Fasten two more legs across the planter bottom, positioning each one 3" in from an end. Repeat to attach the remaining three legs to the other planter bottom.

17 Using a router and roundover bit, or coarse sandpaper, round over all the edges of the planters and the frame.

18 Finish your completed trellis with exterior-grade paint or stain and sealer as desired. Don't, however, finish the planters' interiors.

10 Container Plants

for Shade

- **Dead nettle**
  Lamium

- **Fuchsia**
  Fuchsia

- **Impatiens**
  Impatiens walleriana

- **Wax begonia**
  Begonia

- **Wishbone flower**
  Torenia

for Sun

- **Dahlberg daisy**
  Dyssodia

- **Indian borage**
  Plectranthus

- **Narrowleaf zinnia**
  Zinnia angustifolia

- **Petunia**
  Petunia

- **Scented geranium**
  Pelargonium

Vines for Trellises

COMMON & BOTANICAL NAME	HARDINESS ZONES	SOIL & LIGHT CONDITIONS	DESCRIPTION
Black-eyed Susan vine *Thunbergia alata*	10–11	*Moist, well-drained, fertile* FULL SUN TO PARTIAL SHADE	3 to 6 feet; twining, tender perennial with small, trumpet-shaped flowers in shades of yellow, orange, and cream, usually with a dark center, blooms throughout the summer; triangular, mid-green leaves
Clematis *Clematis*	5–9	*Moist, well-drained, fertile* PARTIAL SHADE TO FULL SUN	4 to 30 feet; perennial climber with showy flowers in white, pink, or purple, spring to summer; leaf form varies greatly; prefers shade for roots but full sun for the rest of the vine
Honeysuckle *Lonicera*	4–11	*Moist, well-drained* PARTIAL SHADE TO FULL SUN	4 to 20 feet; perennial climber with small, fragrant yellow, white, pink, or red flowers spring to fall, depending on species; medium green foliage, some varieties evergreen or semi-evergreen; attracts bees and hummingbirds; can be invasive
Mandevilla *Mandevilla*	10–11	*Rich, moist, well-drained* PARTIAL SHADE	10 to 20 feet; tender perennial; woody, twining climber with pink or white, trumpet-shaped flowers in summer; often shiny, mid to dark green leaves; the flowers of some species are very fragrant
Morning glory *Ipomoea tricolor*	annual	*Well-drained, sandy* FULL SUN	15 to 20 feet; annual, twining climber with wide range of colorful, saucer-shaped, tubular flowers in summer; mid-green, heart-shaped leaves; *I. alba* (moonflower) has large, fragrant, white flowers that open at night
Passion-flower *Passiflora*	6–10	*Well-drained* FULL SUN TO PARTIAL SHADE	15 to 25 feet; tender perennial climber with multiple-colored flowers from spring to autumn, depending on species; usually three- to five-lobed, mid to dark green leaves; colorful, edible fruit; heavy growth requires sturdy support
'Jeanne Lajoie' rose *Rosa 'Jeanne Lajoie'*	5–10	*Rich, well-drained* FULL SUN	up to 8 feet; climbing miniature rose with lightly fragrant, two-toned pink blossoms borne in clusters from spring to fall; glossy, dark green leaves; must be trained to climb trellis
Sweet pea *Lathyrus odoratus*	annual	*Moist, well-drained* FULL SUN TO PARTIAL SHADE	6 inches to 6 feet; hardy annual bush or twining vine that bears fragrant, puffy flowers in a variety of colors in spring and summer; mid to dark green leaves; mulch to keep soil cool
Wisteria *Wisteria*	5–9	*Moist, well-drained* FULL SUN	up to 30 feet; perennial, woody, climbing twiner with white, pink or purple panicles of flowers in spring; bright green foliage provides dense shade; needs sturdy support; can be invasive

A Backyard Oasis

Water has an amazing range of effects. Gentle trickles and still pools of water soothe our spirits, while refreshing sprays invigorate them. Install a water garden, and you'll find yourself visiting every day to watch birds drinking at its edge, frogs singing in the rushes, and the aquatic ballet of water lilies unfolding on its surface. A few modern innovations make it easy to construct your own backyard oasis, even if your budget and available space are limited.

SELECTING A SITE

Before you decide what kind of pond you want, you'll need to choose a site. A water feature that you can see from indoors will provide more pleasure than one set away from the house, but if this kind of site isn't available, choose one close to a patio or low deck.

Water lilies and other aquatic plants require at least six hours of full sun each day. For pumps, fountains, and lighting features, the site should be close to outdoor electrical outlets. Avoid areas near trees, especially deciduous ones; they'll cast shade, send out marauding roots, and scatter falling leaves. Avoid low-lying areas, too; runoff may pollute your pond with pesticides and fertilizers. Finally, if children will be present in the area, either make your pond inaccessible to them or delay installing one until they're older.

WHAT KIND OF POND?

Most small backyard pools consist of either rigid fiberglass preformed shapes or flexible butyl liners. Preformed ponds are usually easiest to install, but liners allow you to determine a pool's shape and can be placed over large, smooth rocks, which you must excavate when installing a preformed pond.

Let the style of your house and yard help you select a design for your pond. Formal pools feature straight lines or geometrical shapes, while more natural-looking pools are curved and irregularly shaped. If you're installing a liner, use a hose to outline the size and shape of your pool. Before you start digging, view this imaginary pond from several perspectives and at various times of day.

The pond's size should be proportional to the landscape, but the larger

the pond, the less vulnerable it will be to pollution and temperature extremes. The water should be at least 18 inches deep, and—if you want to overwinter hardy fish—must include an area at least 24 inches deep.

Adding a waterfall to your pond is surprisingly easy. Waterfalls look best installed in naturally sloping areas. For flat sites, a few large rocks or boulders added to a mound of the excavated dirt can provide the slope for falling water. You'll need butyl lining for the waterfall portion, flat rocks and pebbles to hide the lining and provide the falls, and a pump to recycle and lift the water through a concealed pipe or tubing. Even if you don't include falls, your pond water may need a recirculating pump and filter to keep it healthy.

AQUATIC FLORA AND FAUNA

Most water gardens contain two types of plants: underwater ones (such as wild celery), which contribute oxygen, provide spawning nests for fish, and reduce algae growth by competing for nutrients; and floating ornamental plants, such as water lilies. Most floating plants prefer still water; situate them away from fountains and waterfalls. Many nurseries and home-improvement centers now stock a variety of water plants; ask for advice about which ones to choose, and beware of species that are invasive in certain parts of the country.

Birds, dragonflies, frogs, and snails will all be drawn to your water garden, but the sight of a bright orange fish darting beneath a lily pad is hard to resist. Fish also dine on mosquitoes and other insects. (Before introducing fish to your pond, you'll need to treat the water with a chlorine neutralizer.) You'll find that these surprisingly attentive pets can become longtime companions. Goldfish can live for 10 to 15 years, and koi can live for decades.

Water Plants for Small Ponds

COMMON & BOTANICAL NAME	HARDINESS ZONES	DESCRIPTION
Chromatella water lily *Nymphaea 'Chromatella'*	3–11	hardy perennial; blooms abundantly over a long season, with canary-yellow petals surrounding deep yellow stamens; very fragrant; olive-green lily pads mottled in shades of chestnut-maroon
Pygmy water lily *Nymphaea tetragona*	4–11	hardy perennial (frost tolerant, but languishes in hot weather); 1½- to 2½-inch, white, star-shaped flowers; 3- to 4-inch lily pads
Siberian iris *Iris sibirica*	4–9	perennial; blooms from mid-spring to early summer, in deep blue, violet, white, or yellow; sword-shaped leaves; grows 2 to 3 feet tall; boggy iris for margins of small ponds
Tulip lotus *Nelumbo 'Shirokunshi'*	4–11	perennial; spectacular white, tulip-shaped, fragrant flowers on stems 18 to 24 inches tall; broad leaves, shaped like wide, shallow bowls, on separate 18- to 24-inch stems
Water hyacinth *Eichhornia crassipes*	8–11	potentially invasive perennial, controlled by state and federal laws; keeps water clear; showy violet-blue spikes, 4 to 9 inches tall; fine roots dangle from glossy green leaves
Water poppy *Hydrocleys nymphoides*	9–11	tender perennial; 2- to 2½-inch, lemon-yellow blossoms; slightly fragrant; small, oval green leaves; can overwinter in an aquarium in a sunny window

Making a Backyard Pond

Ponds and pools are age-old sources of sights, scents, and sounds that bring a sense of peace to the garden. A carefully planned pond complemented by a cascading waterfall creates a dramatic effect as well as endless possibilities for your gardening pleasure. (See "A Backyard Oasis" on pages 64–65 for tips on selecting a site and choosing the right kind of pond liner.)

- Any garden center that carries water features and accessories can help you select a pump and an appropriate filter. (For the small waterfalls described in this project, a low-voltage pump is adequate.) Non-oil pumps are best for the health of your pond, especially if you intend to stock the pond with fish.

- For safe pump operation, be sure you plug it into a moisture-proof electrical outlet with a Ground Fault Circuit Interrupter (GFCI).

- Ponds look much smaller once you've added rocks and plants around them, so choose a pre-formed pond that is twice as large as you think you'll need.

- Sustain the health and beauty of your pond by stocking it with fish and oxygenating plants. Fish enhance the pond's health (and yours!) by dining on mosquitoes and bugs. Remember that pond depth is critical to growing aquatic plants; water lilies need 15"- to 36"-deep water.

- The three basins that form the small waterfalls in this project must be created in soil that is above the pond itself. If your yard has no natural slope to it, form a berm of mounded soil by heaping the soil that you remove as you excavate the pond hole.

MATERIALS & TOOLS

- Preformed pond (3' x 4', reinforced plastic or fiberglass)
- Shovel
- Wheelbarrow
- 2 straight boards, 35" and 5' long
- Tape measure
- Carpenter's level
- Trowel
- Three 50-pound bags of sand
- Submersible pump (200 to 300 gallons per hour capacity) with filter
- Heavy-duty PVC conduit (see step 9)
- Hacksaw
- Scissors
- Top-quality PVC liner for waterfall pools
- Stones, rocks, and plants for landscaping edges
- Aquatic plants
- Mulch

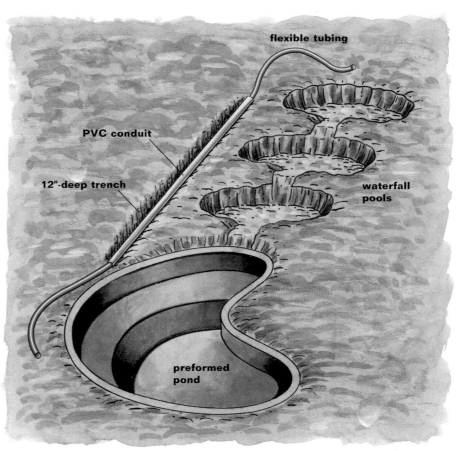

flexible tubing

PVC conduit

12"-deep trench

waterfall pools

preformed pond

Instructions

1 Place the preformed pond, right side up, on the selected site. Trace the perimeter of the pond's top rim onto the soil by dribbling handfuls of sand to make an outline. Set the preformed pond aside. (Be sure to trace the outline of the top rim and not the bottom of the pond; the rim will be larger in diameter.)

2 Carefully dig a hole within the traced lines, making it 2" deeper and 2" wider than the actual pond form. Pond forms often include ledges and are smaller in diameter at the bottom than they are at the top, so as you dig, be careful to shape the hole as closely as possible to the contours of the pond form, leaving shelves of soil to support the built-in ledges. Reserve some of the soil that you remove; you'll need it to backfill the hole once the pond form is in place. To check the depth of the hole, place the 5'-long board across the top of the hole. Then measure from the bottom of the hole up to the board with a tape measure. (Be sure not to continue unless the hole is at least 2" deeper than the depth of the pond form, or you'll have to repeat some arduous steps later!)

3 Using your shovel and trowel, scrape the bottom of the hole to make it level, removing any large or sharp rocks, and any roots or debris. To check the bottom of the hole for level, set the 35"-long board across it, and place the carpenter's level on top of the board. (Remember: If the bottom of the hole isn't level, the water in your pond will be higher at one end than it is at the other.) Reposition the board and level several times in order to check for level in several different positions.

7 Install the submersible pump, with its flexible tubing—and the filter —according to the manufacturer's instructions. (The pump must be raised above the pond bottom, usually by setting it on bricks, so that debris won't clog its intake valve.)

8 As shown in the illustration on page 67, the water in the pond will eventually be pumped up through the flexible tubing to the uppermost waterfall basin. To disguise and pro- tect the tubing, you'll bury it in a 6"- to 12"-deep trench that runs along one side of the three basins and up to the top of the site. Before digging the waterfall basins, dig the trench, setting aside the soil you remove.

4 Spread a 2"-thick layer of damp sand across the bottom of the hole. This will cushion and protect the bottom of the pond form once you've filled the form with water. Smooth the sand by running one edge of the 35"- long board across it. Then check the layer of sand by setting the board on it and placing the carpenter's level on top of the board. Repeat to check for level in several different positions.

5 Set the pond form in the hole; its rim should be at ground level. Then check the rim for level by plac- ing the 5'-long board and the carpen- ter's level across it at various places. To correct the pond form's positioning, remove it from the hole, level the sand

again, and replace the shell. You may have to repeat this step several times, so be patient! Removing a water-filled pond to make readjustments later is a task you'll want to avoid!

6 Add 4" of water to the pond form. Next, in your wheelbarrow, mix some of the reserved soil and the sand. Then firmly pack this mixture around the outer wall of the pond form, up to the water level inside. Continue this process, gradually adding water and then backfilling with sand and soil, until the pond is filled with water and is firmly supported around its exterior. As you backfill, make sure there are no gaps under the shelves or around the sides of the pond form.

9 To protect the pump's flexible tub- ing, you'll encase it in a length of rigid PVC conduit before you bury it. Measure the length of the trench, and then use a hacksaw to cut a piece of PVC conduit to that length. Slip the flexible tubing into the conduit, leav- ing several feet of exposed tubing at the top end. Then place the conduit and tubing in the bottom of the trench and refill the trench to bury them. (Alternatively, you may fill the trench with mulch. If the tubing ever needs repairs, you'll find that remov- ing the mulch from the trench is easier than removing heavy soil.)

10 To begin making the waterfalls, scoop out three basins above the pond, as shown in the illustration on page 67. Each basin should be approximately 2' to 3' in diameter (the depths may vary) and 3" to 1' higher than the one beneath it. Be careful to slant the floor of each basin slightly backward so that the water in it won't automatically flow out. At the front of each basin, shape a 4"- to 6"-long sill (the pathway through which water flows as it drops to the basin below).

11 Measure and cut a separate sheet of PVC liner for each basin, allowing for the diameter and depth of the basin and sill, a generous overlap from basin to basin, and plenty of extra liner (at least 6" in all directions) to overlap the soil surrounding the basin. Starting with the bottom basin, line each basin and sill, pressing the liner into each hole firmly. Then trim the excess liner so that at least 6" overlaps the edges of each basin. Cover these edges with soil.

12 Arrange the loose upper end of the flexible tubing in the uppermost basin (you'll need to trim it if it's too long). Then arrange stones, rocks, and plants around the pond and basin sites. Use only smooth, rounded stones on any exposed portions of the liner, as sharp stones may tear the plastic.

13 Turn the pump on and continue to add water to the pond until both the pond and basins are full. Now comes the fun part: Create the series of small waterfalls by positioning smooth stones and rocks in the basins and on their sills. Experiment as much as you like by arranging the stones and rocks to create ripples and rapids. Rearranging stones at the edge of each fall will produce changes in the sound of the water as well as its appearance.

14 Add soil around and between the rocks at the edges of the pond and basins, and put in some plants. You won't want to plant anything directly over the buried PVC conduit and tubing, as you may need to uncover them if the tubing ever needs to be repaired or replaced. To disguise the trench line, make an arrangement of rocks on top of it, or cover it with an attractive mulch.

15 Now you're ready to think about stocking your pond with aquatic plants and fish. Wait a week or two before bringing fish to their new home; the water will need to settle.

Water Elements on a Porch or Patio

Haven't got the room for even a small backyard pond? Not quite ready to take the splash into full-scale water gardening? Add a small water feature to your porch, deck, or patio, and you can still enjoy the enchanting effects of water.

You'll be amazed by all that water can do for even the smallest outdoor living space. Moving water weaves patterns as hypnotic as a flickering fire. Still water in a container garden will reflect blue sky and stars. Falling water, whether a trickle or a cascade, soothes as it blocks out distracting street noises.

CONTAINER WATER GARDENS

Container water gardens are the perfect feature for decks, patios, and porches. Almost any watertight, 10-gallon or larger container can become a miniature pond. For most aquatic plants, you'll also need a spot that receives at least four to six hours of sunlight a day. Half whiskey barrels and plastic liners for just this purpose are now available at many garden centers.

Along with water lilies, any number of handsome bog plants, floating ornamentals, and grasses are suited to container water gardens. Fish will help control mosquitoes and other insects. Semitropical varieties such as gambusia (mosquito fish) and guppies can best survive the heat of a container garden in full sun.

MOVING WATER

Moving water will bring both music and motion to your outdoor living space. Features with moving water can be as elegant or rustic as your setting dictates. They can also vary in both size and complexity. Create a small raised pool with a waterfall on your patio or place a ready-made fountain in your porch corner or on a patio wall. Make your own whimsical tabletop fountain from a small bowl, a submersible pump, plastic tubing, and the decorative material of your choice. (Many small fountains can even be moved indoors and enjoyed during the winter.) Just be sure to replace the water that evaporates from fountains, as the pumps will burn out if they're allowed to run dry.

Container Water Garden

Maybe you're not quite sure you want a water garden. At least, not sure enough to go out and start digging a large, deep hole in your yard. Why not get your feet wet with a small water garden in a container? This project uses a half whiskey barrel with a plastic liner (available at many gardening centers), but almost any clean, watertight container that will hold at least ten gallons of water will do. The chart on page 65 lists other aquatic plants suitable for a container water garden.

MATERIALS

- ■ Half whiskey barrel
- ■ Rigid plastic barrel liner
- ■ Water
- ■ Chlorine neutralizer (optional)
- ■ Clean rocks or bricks
- ■ Aquatic plants (see list)
- ■ One or two small semitropical fish (optional)

WATER DEPTHS FOR PLANTS SHOWN

- ■ Parrot feather (*Myriophyllum aquaticum*), 3–12 inches
- ■ Pickerel rush (*Pontederia cordata*), 1–12 inches
- ■ Umbrella palm (*Cyperus alternifolius*), 1–6 inches
- ■ Lizard's-tail (*Saururus cernuus*), 1–6 inches

Instructions

1 Rinse out both the barrel and the liner to remove any residue; then put the plastic liner inside the barrel. Position the barrel in the desired location, making sure it will receive at least six hours of sunlight a day. (The container will be very difficult to move once you've filled it with water.)

2 Fill the liner with water to within two to three inches of the liner's top. Let the water stand for two or three days; any chlorine in it must be allowed to evaporate. (Alternatively, add chlorine neutralizer as recommended by the manufacturer.)

3 Set your potted plants in the liner, using clean rocks or bricks to raise each plant so that its crown is submerged at the required water depth. (The list above gives the water depths for the plants shown in the photo.)

4 After ten days (or at least one hour if you've treated the water with chlorine neutralizer) add one or two small semitropical fish, such as guppies or "mosquito fish" (gambusia), to help control mosquitoes and other insects. (The water in container gardens can get too warm for cold-water fish such as goldfish or koi.)

5 Be sure to replace any water lost to evaporation. If you don't have fish you can add up to five percent of untreated new water at a time. If you do have fish, you'll need to use chlorine neutralizer each time new water is added.

Backyard Fountains

The relaxing and restorative powers of moving water are amazing. A few moments spent watching and listening to even the simplest of fountains can slow the pace and still the soul. These captivating effects date all the way back to 4000 B.C., when water gardens were created in Iran. Cascading fountains were common features in Roman courtyards and medieval gardens as well, and Renaissance gardens were marked by their theatrical and architectural waterworks. During the seventeenth century, in the grand gardens of Versailles, more than one thousand fountains greeted the guests of Louis XIV.

While your bank account may not support the elaborate elegance enjoyed by Louis XIV and his friends, your garden will come to life on a smaller scale with the peaceful ambiance of a backyard fountain. The steady sound of rhythmic splashes, sprays, gushes, or gentle gurgles will enhance your experience of relaxing outdoors.

SITES FOR FOUNTAINS

The location of your fountain will depend on several factors: the direction of the prevailing breeze, the height and spread of the spray, the position of the sun during the day, and the location of an available electrical outlet. Sunny spots make the best homes for

fountains, while shady areas are best for viewing them. Place your fountain near a favorite seating spot to ensure optimal listening and viewing pleasure.

When deciding whether to install a fountain in a pond or pool, consider the effects of moving water on plants and fish. Water lilies won't survive the effects of constant splashing or strong underwater currents. You'll need to make sure that aquatic plants with surface flowers are out of the range of splashing water and that underwater currents don't disturb the water's surface. On the other hand, aerated water that is pumped and filtered enhances the health of fish. Creating the proper balance to allow both plants and fish to thrive is critical.

It's best to locate the fountain near an existing outdoor outlet (the pump operates on a normal household current), or have an electrician run an underground wire to the site and install an outlet there. Wires and cables leading from the outlet to the pump can be hidden beneath a layer of soil and stones. Be sure to use Ground Fault Circuit Interrupter (GFCI) circuitry and avoid using extension cords.

Either have the fountain installed by a landscape architect or (a less expensive alternative) install one yourself. The process can be fun and is much easier than you might think. You'll find most of the materials you need at garden centers, aquatic nurs-

eries, and hardware stores that have knowledgeable staff to give you advice on pumps and other equipment.

SELECTING A FOUNTAIN DESIGN

From the tiny trickle of a tabletop fountain to the shooting spray of a fountain in a large formal pool, moving water can be an enchanting addition to any garden. Keep in mind, however, that the water is a feature only when the pump is running, so choose a fountain design that is appealing even when the water isn't flowing. Pay close attention to the fountain's quality and sturdiness, as well as to its aesthetic appeal.

A fountain is a powerful focal point in any yard; however, it need not be extravagant in design. Carefully

selecting a fountain that will look at home in your landscape is a key consideration. As you investigate the fountain designs available today, you'll find that you have literally hundreds of possibilities from which to choose, ranging from the subdued gurgling of a rustic millstone set on a jumble of river rocks to the dramatic effect of a geyser bursting from a bed of stones. Try to imagine how a given fountain will fit into your garden setting. For a classical look, you might select a tall spray centered in a round, formal pool or with water that spills over a dish and splashes down into a pond. To create an intimate, contemplative atmosphere, choose a simple, unadorned bubbling fountain. Or perhaps you'd prefer a fountain inspired by a Greek ruin, one that provides an archaeological link with the past. Play around with ideas to achieve an effect that harmonizes with your landscape and the architecture of your house.

When planning your design and installation, be aware of the potential hazards of water features. If your family includes young children, consider a trickle fountain or a small bubble fountain with an underground reservoir. Both offer the soothing sound of moving water and are virtually free of hazards, but remember to avoid using decorative materials that can be swallowed, such as marbles or small stones.

SELECTING A FOUNTAIN JET

The glimmering spray of a fountain creates a kind of aquatic sculpture, the form of which is determined by the type of fountain jet you choose. Jets come in a wide range of types and patterns, including bubble jets, geysers, multi-tiered jets, tulip jets, and water-bell jets. Some have interchangeable heads that allow you to vary the spray

pattern. If you have aquatic plants, geysers and bell jets are good choices, as they create minimal water disturbance. The simplest jets connect to a cone-shaped outlet or to a T-piece provided with most small and medium-sized pumps.

When choosing a jet, you'll need to consider the size of the fountain and the height of its spray in relation to the dimensions of your pond. You don't want excess water from an oversized fountain splashing onto a patio full of guests! As a general rule, the spray should be no taller than half the pond's width or diameter.

For a playful touch, shop for a fountain ornament—a gushing gargoyle, a spouting fish or frog. Many ornaments are available in garden centers and catalogs. Before buying, be sure to find out what kind of pump is required to achieve the desired result. Most ornaments are made from concrete or reconstituted stone, but other choices include bronze, terra-cotta, carved stone, and fiberglass.

SELECTING A PUMP

Like it or not, every fountain must be powered by a pump, and selecting one can seem a little daunting. The key is to buy a pump that is suitable for the fountain you have in mind. You'll need to know how many gallons per hour it will pump to create the desired spray, as well as the distance that the water will be pumped. The pump should circulate half the volume of a pond or pool every hour. Always choose a model that produces a flow rate greater than you think you'll need—the extra capacity allows you to enhance features later on without having to buy a new pump.

There are two basic types of water pump—submersible and surface (externally mounted). Submersible pumps sit in a pond or pool and pump water out through a fountain jet or along a piece of tubing to a fountain elsewhere in the pond. For simple installations, the jet is fitted directly on top of the pump by a T-piece that has a flow adjuster and an outlet for a waterfall. A surface pump

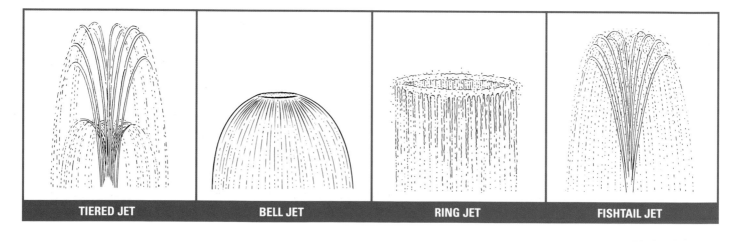

TIERED JET   **BELL JET**   **RING JET**   **FISHTAIL JET**

must be housed in a separate chamber aboveground, usually to the side of the pond. A reinforced inlet hose "feeds" water from the pond to the pump. The pump then sends water through a return pipe to the fountain.

In most cases, a submersible pump will meet your needs when installing an ordinary fountain in your garden. Consider a surface pump only if you plan to install a very large water feature with a spray higher than seven feet. Submersible pumps are available at most garden centers, in sizes and price ranges to match whatever fountain design you've chosen. The pumps are self contained, easy to install, require no priming, and often come in a handy kit complete with a T-piece, flow adjuster, and jet.

Keep in mind that the experts at garden centers can help you decide on a pump once you've determined the size, style, and location for your fountain. That's why they're there—so let them make your job easier by doing theirs!

SMALL FOUNTAINS

If you don't have room for a pond, but you'd still like to add the calming sight and sound of a fountain to your garden, consider a self-contained fountain ornament. With the advent of small submersible pumps, these have become increasingly popular. The lower bowl of the ornament acts as a reservoir from which water is

pumped, or if you prefer, the reservoir can be concealed underground and covered with a layer of decorative materials. A host of charming themes abound—a millstone fountain on a bed of cobblestones centered in a country cottage patio, a stone basin transformed into a fountain reminiscent of ancient oriental rituals, or the elegant lines of water over hand-carved granite complemented by smooth obsidian stones around its base.

If you're limited by space, budget, or time (or maybe all three!)—not to worry. There's a fountain design for anyone who enjoys the magical effects of moving water. Tabletop fountains are an emerging trend, perfect for a porch or patio during warm weather and easy to move inside during the colder months. Inside your home, they make handsome displays that will

stimulate your senses throughout the winter season until spring rolls around again. Just sit back, relax, and let the natural sounds of moving water nurture your spirit all year round.

Tabletop fountains are incredibly easy to build. A creative spirit and a few basic materials from a garden center will get you started; within a few hours, your fountain will be up and running. You'll need a decorative container to serve as a reservoir, a small submersible pump, rubber tubing, and materials such as stones or marbles to cover the hardware. You'll be surprised by the versatility of tabletop fountains, too. If you tire of a particular container, you can simply replace it with a new one that suits your mood. Or you can modify an existing fountain by choosing a different assortment of surrounding plants and decorative materials.

Backyard Seating

For many of us in the workaday world, the outdoors is an area we experience when we trudge from the house to the car, or when we take out the trash. Sitting outdoors—actually remaining still long enough to let the natural world around you come into focus—is a particular pleasure, whether you're relaxing alone in a secluded garden nook or joining friends and family for an outdoor meal.

Outdoor seating—a swing beneath a rose-covered arbor or a wooden chaise beside a reflecting pool—becomes a part of the backyard architecture, what

remains steadfast in a continually changing scene. A bench and a small table placed in just the right spot become more than a convenient place to relax; they create an instant tableau that's a part of your overall landscape design.

SELECTING SEATING

When selecting outdoor seating, consider both its form and its function. Attractive but uncomfortable chairs just won't be used. Delicate, whimsical furniture that's primarily garden decoration is fine, but seats intended for

actual use should wear well and feel good when you're in them. Wood furniture should be well constructed from a rot-resistant or finished hardwood and should be properly joined—not glued. Hardware should be adequately sized and rustproof. Inspect all furniture before purchasing to make sure it's free of cracks or other flaws. (Crashing backwards onto the patio just as you're chomping into a ear of corn is definitely not relaxing!) Make sure, too, that your seating is sturdy enough not to topple over in high winds.

The color, material, style, and size of your outdoor furniture should complement rather than clash with your house and yard. An ornate, wrought-iron bench that looks stately in the formal gardens of a brick Colonial may look inappropriate in a bungalow's informal cottage garden. When it comes to color and style, remember that what seems trendy today may well appear dated a few years from now or may no longer be

appealing to you. Of course, if you paint wooden furniture, you can always change the color with little effort or expense, but the safest way to experiment with color and patterns is with pillows and cushions.

Gardening centers usually carry a variety of outdoor seats and benches, as do some department stores. Shops specializing in outdoor furniture will generally have the largest selection in a wide range of prices. Consider, too, mail-order catalogs, which sometimes offer build-it-yourself kits for everything from arbor seats to Adirondack chairs. Antique stores, junk shops, yard sales, and flea markets are all potential sources of unique or unconventional outdoor furniture. Never underestimate the power of a can of bright paint or a few cheerful throw pillows!

WHAT GOES WHERE

Once again, consider both the appearance and function of your seating when deciding where to place your outdoor furniture. A single lounge chair or bench tucked away in a private backyard corner is ideal for quiet relaxation. Hammocks are more enjoyable in shady spots, and if they catch the occasional breeze, so much the better. A bench at the end of a path provides a destination that encourages strolling; and seating backed by tall plants, shrubs, a fence, or a wall satisfies our very human need to feel protected and secure when we're relaxing.

Small backyard pools, evening gardens, and aromatic beds are all best appreciated from seat level. Place a bench or a few chairs beside any of these features, and your yard will become a place for leisurely watching fish swim and fireflies dance, instead of just a path to the trash can.

Building a Rustic Bench

A charming rustic bench offers a surprisingly comfortable place to enjoy the fruits of your labor and will look as if it grew right in your backyard. Either cut fallen wood on your property, or make use of the tree branches that power companies, builders of new houses, and road construction crews often leave in their wake. (See "Tips" for special instructions.)

MATERIALS & TOOLS

- Tape measure
- Pencil
- Handsaw
- 4d and 16d galvanized nails
- Hammer
- Rope or twine (optional)
- Sandpaper

TIPS

- Try to use wood that is resistant to decay. Black locust, walnut, hornbeam, sassafras, cherry, cedar, and white oak all work well.
- Trees that have been felled in the fall and winter tend to hold their bark much better than trees cut in the spring or summer.
- Do avoid wood that's been lying on the ground too long; it's probably already on its way to decomposing and is best left to the bugs.
- For added stability, when you fasten any two pieces of wood together, hammer in each nail at an angle.

Instructions

1 Cut all the branches to the lengths specified in the "Cutting List." As long as the various parts are thick enough to be sturdy, exact diameters aren't important.

2 Lay two legs (A) flat on your work surface, 40" apart. Position one stretcher (B) across both legs, 2½" down from the top of each leg. Attach the stretcher to the legs with 16d nails. Repeat with the other stretcher and the other two legs.

CUTTING LIST

CODE	DESCRIPTION	QTY.	BRANCH DIAMETER X LENGTH
A	Legs	4	2¼" x 21"
B	Stretchers	2	2" x 48"
C	Long top end support	1	1½" x 25"
D	Long bottom end support	1	2" x 25"
E	Short top end support	1	1½" x 15"
F	Short bottom end support	1	2" x 15"
G	Bottom stringer	1	2" x 43"
H	Top stringer	1	1½" x 40"
I	Angle braces	4	¾" x 17"
J	Seat branches	27 (approx.)	½" to ¾" x 25"

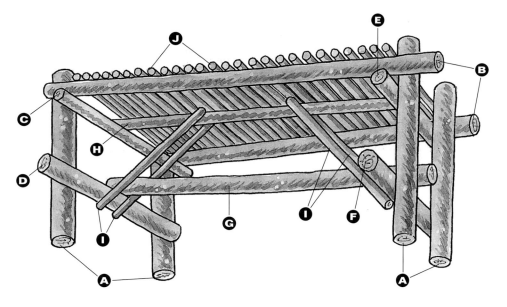

bottom end supports (D and F) and fasten it in place with 16d nails. Repeat to attach the top stringer (H) to the top end supports (C and E).

10 Position one angle brace (I) at a 40-degree angle so that it contacts one bottom end support (D or F), the bottom stringer (G), and the top stringer (H). Make sure the top of the angle brace doesn't rise above the top stringer, or the seat branches (J) won't rest flat on top of the stretchers (B).

11 Using rope to hold the angle brace (I) in place if necessary, attach it to the bottom end support (D or F) and the bottom and top stringers (G and H) with 4d nails. Repeat with the remaining three angle braces, turning the bench assembly as required.

12 At the widest end of the bench, use 4d nails to attach a seat branch (J) to both stretchers (B) and to the top stringer (H). Attach all the seat branches in the same manner, leaving ½" gaps between them.

13 Using the stretchers (B) as guides, cut the seat branches (H) so their ends are flush with the outer edges of the stretchers.

14 Lightly sand all cut branch ends if desired. This bench grows more beautiful as it weathers, so no protective treatment is necessary.

3 To begin assembling the wider end of the bench, first position one leg-and-stretcher assembly so that one leg (A) is flat on your work surface and the stretcher (B) and other attached leg stick up in the air. (To get the leg to rest flat on the work surface, you'll need to let the 2½"-length of protruding stretcher hang off the edge of the surface.)

4 Position the second leg-and-stretcher assembly similarly, 17" away from the first assembly and parallel to it. Have your friend hold the two stretchers upright for you.

5 Position the long top end support (C) in the interior corner formed by the legs (A) that rest on the work surface and the stretchers (B) that rise from them. Then fasten the long top end support to both the legs and the stretchers with 16d nails.

6 Place the long bottom end support (D) across the legs (A), 6" down from the long top end support (C). Attach it to the legs with 16d nails.

7 To assemble the narrower end of the bench, first turn the frame over carefully so the other two legs (A) are flat on your work surface, and both stretchers (B) extend upward. (Have your friend hold the frame in place again.) Pull the two legs on your work surface in toward each other until they're 6" apart. (Doing this will create the xylophone shape of the bench.)

8 Repeat steps 4 and 5 to fasten the short top end support (E) and the short bottom end support (F) to the legs (A) and stretchers (B).

9 Set the assembled bench frame on its feet. Center the bottom stringer (G) on top of and across the

Paths and Walkways

It's easy to focus so intently on the separate plots and patches you're planting in your yard that you lose sight of the overall design. In addition to serving a practical purpose by connecting point A to point B, a path is the perfect way to create visual coherence by drawing together individual garden components.

DESIGN CONSIDERATIONS

No matter where your path will lead, plan its design before you start the work. Outlining specific design strategies now will save labor down the road. Will your path lead to or run beside a building? If so, it must slope away from the structure, either along its length or across its width, in order to prevent water damage. Will the roots of trees or other large plants extend beneath the path? Depending on the root sizes, you may be able to use a paving material that is heavy and strong enough to withstand any upward force they exert. Consider the climate of your area, as well. Is the annual precipitation above average? Unless you incorporate a drainage system under your path, a heavy rainfall may turn it into a rushing stream. And if your area experiences frequent ground freezes or other temperature extremes, you will need to take extra care with the pathway's base.

You don't have to be an expert to devise a good layout; you know your backyard better than anyone. Experimenting on paper is much easier than hauling around piles of stone, so start by making some sketches, taking the shapes and lines of your outdoor space into account. Are they sharp and angular? You may want a gentle, curving path to give contrast and balance. Study your home and any existing structures in your backyard, too, and select a pathway material that will complement them. When you're ready to transfer your design to the ground, outline the future path site with lengths of rope or garden hose, both of which are easy to shape into curves.

DOING THE WORK YOURSELF

Simple stepping-stone paths are easy to make. Dig a hole for each stone, place an inch or two of sand in the bottom, set the stone in the hole with its flattest side up, and pack some more sand around it. Setting other pathway materials can be challenging, however, especially if your soil doesn't drain well. That's not to say you shouldn't attempt a pathway project; just be sure to consult several good books on the topic before beginning.

A drainage pipe set on one inch of gravel in the trench's bottom helps carry away water.

CREATIVE PATHWAY PAVERS

If you're looking for a fun, inexpensive paving option, consider enhancing ordinary concrete pavers with mosaic *tessarae*. (Tessarae are small objects that are arranged to form a larger mosaic design.) Almost anything small and solid can be attached to a manufactured concrete paver or tile, including buttons, bottle caps, broken glass, terra-cotta shards, and pebbles. (If you lack a collection of colorful tessarae, just visit your local thrift store, buy an armful of patterned dishes, and break them into pieces with tile nippers.) Before creating your pathway, arrange the tessarae on the pavers in any way you like; the final effect can be smooth or tex-

tured, careful or crazed, colorful or subdued. Then use a cement-based mortar to affix the tessarae onto the pavers. When you're finished, apply grout to fill the cracks.

SELECTING MATERIALS FOR PATHS

Pathway materials vary widely. Organic materials, such as pine needles, are attractively informal and well suited to level, dry areas that aren't traveled frequently, but they decompose quite rapidly and tend to wash away on slopes. Gravel or crushed-stone paths are easy to create, drain well, and are relatively inexpensive, too. Just be sure to spread landscape cloth over the base beneath them, or you'll face a continuous battle with weeds. Brick or stone paths are time-consuming to construct and can be quite expensive, but if they're properly laid out, they'll last for years.

THE PATHWAY BASE

Pathways made with bricks, stones, and concrete pavers should rest on a base that will ensure good drainage and prevent frost heaving. The standard base is created by first digging a six-inch-deep trench that's the same width as the intended pathway. Three inches of washed gravel are spread in the bottom of the trench, and a layer of landscape cloth (available from garden centers) is spread across the gravel in order to inhibit weed growth. At this stage, edging materials such as upright bricks are sometimes placed along both edges of the trench. Stones or bricks are set on a one- to two-inch-thick layer of sand that's spread over the landscape cloth, and the gaps between the pavers are then filled with sand. In areas where drainage is exceptionally poor, the base should be deeper and V-shaped.

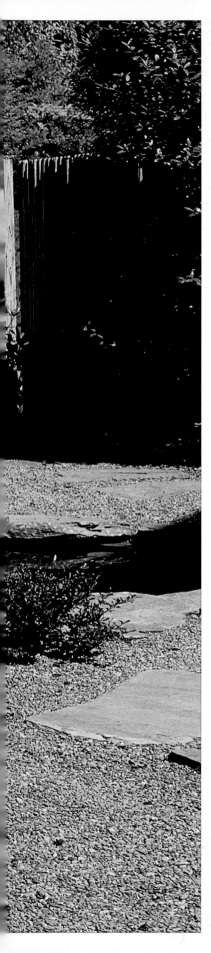

Sunlight & Shade

Are you one of those people who yearns all winter long for the return of the warm summer sun? Who can't wait to lounge on a favorite patio chaise, wearing a floppy sun hat, comfortably loose clothing, and dark glasses? Or do you head straight for the coolest and shadiest spot you can find when the sun starts to climb in the sky? People—and the plants in their yards—have definite preferences when it comes to sun and shade.

The most comfortable backyard designs include areas to satisfy both inclinations. During the summer, bright, open spaces offer warmth and light for sun-loving flowers and people. During the spring and fall, plants that need simultaneous exposure to sunlight and protection from cold air and soil nestle happily inside greenhouses, cold frames, and cloches.

Shade-loving plants, on the other hand, thrive beneath the spreading branches of broad-leafed trees, or in containers under vine-covered pergolas. And what about shade-loving people, who crave outdoor light but who can't stand the heat that sometimes comes with it? You'll find them sipping iced tea in their garden gazebos or relaxing under garden umbrellas.

Sunlight

A great landscape architect once named the rays of the sun among the gardener's essential raw materials. Right he was. Both the practical and aesthetic success of your garden space depend largely on natural light. Step into your yard on a summer's day, and observe the greens: the neon chartreuse, the soothing celadon, the deep hunter. All these colors owe their vibrancy to active chlorophyll, which channels the sun's energy for food. The sun provides a feast not only for plants, but for your eyes as well.

SUNLIGHT AND PLANT GROWTH

You'll need to consider your garden plants' lighting needs as well as their light-catching characteristics. The next time you're diagnosing ailing plants,

look for the one sure sign of sunlight deprivation—long, spindly growth. When a plant receives insufficient light, day after day, it will begin to look as if it's reaching for the sun. The leaves will be elongated, and the entire plant is likely to be thin, pale, and watery in color. Eventually, light-deprived leaves will turn yellow and fall away. Excessive light, on the other hand, will stunt a plant's growth. The leaves will curl under, as if they were shrinking away from the sun's severe glare.

To prevent either of these scenarios, always find out how much light a plant requires before you set it out—not after. Also study the light and shade patterns in your yard. (Monitoring the exact amount of available sunlight would require advanced scientific equipment and isn't at all necessary; just estimate the hours of direct sunlight that each section of your yard receives.)

A little research will go a long way toward keeping your plants thriving. Many gardening books offer descriptions of light requirements for individual plants, as do the labels or tags that often come with plants from garden

THE AESTHETICS OF SUNLIGHT

Using the sun as a design element allows you to expand your outdoor canvas right up to the sky. Even the tiniest patch of land, porch, or rooftop can feel boundless when you invite a bit of sunlight into your space. You can do so in any number of ways—by scattering bits of polished, colored glass throughout garden beds, by dangling beautiful suncatchers from tree branches, or by stretching iridescent cloth across a folding screen.

All too often, though, we forget that some of the most colorful suncatchers are actually plants. It's clear that the sun is responsible for the screaming oranges, smooth bright yellows, and lush violets of the flowers in our garden beds, but what about those underrated foliage plants and ornamental grasses? Nature offers a host of living suncatchers year-round, including ornamental grasses, trees, shrubs, and perennials. In the springtime, for example, the delicate parts of the silverbell tree (*Halesia*) are set aglow by sunlight and moonlight. Autumn highlights their foliage, especially during the early morning and late afternoon, when shadows arc long. Come winter, bright sunlight lends a stunning architecture to bare tree branches and tall, dried grasses, and gleams through the lace of winged seeds and paper-thin leaves.

centers and nurseries. If a plant needs "full sun," make sure that it will receive at least six hours of sunlight a day. Plants that will grow in "partial shade" need two to six hours of direct sunlight, and those that thrive in "full shade" don't require much direct sunlight at all.

SUNLIGHT AND PEOPLE

Gone are the days when sun-tanned bodies, glistening with coconut oil lotions, were envied. Today, wise sun-lovers lather their skin with lotions that will protect them from the sun's dangerous ultraviolet radiation. If you're a shade lover, you may not harbor any nostalgia for the days in which tans were admired, but do keep in mind that exposure to sunlight has its advantages, too. A few minutes of sunlight every day help the body to synthesize vitamins, and may help fend off depression and sleep disorders.

Daylilies and purple coneflowers

Cold Frames, Cloches, and Greenhouses

COLD FRAMES

A cold frame is a wooden or metal box with a cover (known as a light) made from a transparent material such as glazed glass or clear plastic sheeting. Cold frames may either sit directly on the soil, right in a garden bed, or be placed on a deck or patio and used to protect container plants. These simple, covered box structures allow you to extend the growing season and prolong summer harvests by protecting plants well into the winter. They're also used to start seedlings in the early spring.

Maintaining growth in cold frames is simple. Keep a thermometer inside the frame to monitor the interior temperatures, which should be kept at about 70°F (21°C) in the spring and 65°F (18°C) in the fall. Closing the light will raise the temperature by trapping warmth created by the sun. To lower the internal temperature, just open the light and prop it up. (Some cold frames come with built-in temperature gauges that raise and lower the lights automatically.)

In most instances, cold frames need no ventilating during the coldest months of the year, and because the groundwater table is higher during these months, the plants within the frame will probably need no watering. During very early spring and late fall, only the occasional check-in is necessary. The transition months, during

While extremely cold or hot weather can damage plants, sudden changes in temperature are actually much more dangerous to them. In many areas of the continental United States, particularly in mountain and desert climates, extreme temperature swings can destroy a plant's chances of survival. Temperature, wind, and moisture changes are all factors that affect a plant's stability, but there are protective measures you can take to guard your garden and container plants from them. The most effective step you can take is to create a microclimate for your plants—one that will stabilize the temperature, prevent excess moisture from freezing on stems and leaves, and shield delicate plants from harsh winds. Cloches, cold frames, and greenhouses are all used for this purpose.

the spring and early fall, when temperatures can fluctuate dramatically, are the ones during which you should keep a close watch on plants. Raise and lower the lights as necessary to keep temperatures stable, and water when you water the rest of the garden. In the summertime, open the lights completely.

CLOCHES

For protecting individual container plants from frost, traditional glass cloches are wonderful garden devices. These small, bell-shaped covers ("cloche" is the French word for bell) are made to be placed right over the plant and container whenever frost is predicted. Unlike traditional cloches, contemporary versions are made with materials ranging from plastic and fiberglass to paper. These provide the same basic services and are sometimes easier to find. Available from gardening centers and antique

shops, traditional cloches have no competition when it comes to beauty; their smooth, domed surfaces catch sunlight from all angles.

GREENHOUSES

Greenhouses are best for year-round container gardening and for starting garden plants from seed.

Don't be overwhelmed by the thought of the huge commercial greenhouses that you see being used at nurseries; these just aren't necessary or economical for backyard gardens. Many smaller models are available, however, from shed-sized kits that can

be assembled over a weekend and inexpensive plastic "tunnels" that arch over rows of plants to very small, portable conservatories that fit over individual container plants. Let the size of your garden—and budget—guide you as you select an appropriate plant-protection system.

To protect large planted areas in the garden, tunnels work best. They're assembled right where they're needed, by bending fiberglass rods into arches over the soil and covering them with plastic sheeting. Portable, one-plant conservatories, which consist of platforms with glass covers, are similar to cloches and come in all shapes and sizes. They're most often used to protect delicate potted plants and seedlings.

Decorative Garden Sundial

A lovely addition to any area of your yard that receives full sun, this easy-to-make sundial will keep you in touch with the time whenever you're within sight of it. Do keep in mind, however, that making a truly accurate sundial is a relatively complex undertaking, involving calculations too time-consuming for most backyard hobbyists. Use this simplified version to remind you when to start cooking dinner, but don't try to time your roast beef or baked potatoes with it!

SUNDIAL FACTS

The major difference between an accurate sundial and a watch or clock is that a sundial tells time as it actually is. A watch or clock, on the other hand, is designed to satisfy the human need for predictability. Because we'd like every day to pass in exactly twenty-four hours, we've invented a system in which every day does—it's called *Mean Time*. In reality, the time that passes between noon on one day and noon on another varies throughout the year—and "real" noon (when the sun is at its peak) in one region of a country is different from noon in another.

Until transportation improved during the Industrial Revolution,

and until the telegraph was invented, people in a given region had no reason to care whether their local time matched the time in another region. (It made no difference to anyone that noon in one village might occur several minutes earlier or later than noon in another village several hundred miles away.) Establishing a time-keeping system that would be consistent internationally only became important when people could communicate quickly over long distances.

MATERIALS & TOOLS

- 10 curved sections of scalloped brick edging
- Several cups of white flour
- Shovel
- Trowel
- Landscape fabric
- Scissors
- 18 bags (½ cubic foot each) of pea gravel
- Garden rake
- Compass
- 1 triangular slab of granite, with one 90° angle and two 45° angles
- 12 granite scraps or stones

TIPS

- The hour markers of this horizontal dial rest on a flat gravel portion known as the *dial plate*, which can be as large or as small as you like. The diameter of the dial shown on the opposite page is approximately six feet.

- As well as containing the gravel, the edging material will help define the area clearly so that you won't scatter the gravel when you mow the lawn. Any type of edging that is sturdy enough to support the gravel and to survive any minor encounters with a lawn mower will work.

- Landscape fabric is available from garden centers. It's used in this project to help prevent weeds from growing up through the gravel.

- The *gnomon* (or shadow-casting part) of this sundial is a slab of scrap marble. You may use any waterproof material you like, as long as it forms a triangle with one 90-degree angle and one 45-degree angle.

Instructions

1 Position the curved edging sections to form a circle, adjusting each section as necessary.

2 To mark the area for digging, trickle a line of white flour around the outside of the circle formed by the edging sections.

3 Remove the edging sections and set them aside.

4 Using a shovel, strip the sod from within the marked circle and dig out the soil to a depth of 2" or 3". (Make sure that you don't remove too much soil, or the edging sections will be so low they'll be obscured by the lawn surrounding them.) Scrape the soil at the bottom to make it level.

5 Cut a circle of landscape fabric to fit inside the circle, and position it on top of the soil. This will help prevent weeds from growing up through the gravel once the circle is filled, but will also permit rainwater to drain away properly.

6 Position the edging sections around the interior perimeter of the circular hole, scraping more soil from the hole if required. Make sure the sections are upright and are supported by the outer edges of the holes; backfill with soil if necessary.

7 Fill the hole with pea gravel, and spread it evenly with a garden rake. Be careful not to add too much gravel, or it will spill over the tops of the edging sections. Scoop out some gravel in the center to make space for the gnomon.

8 For real timekeeping accuracy, a gnomon in the northern hemisphere should be parallel to the earth's axis, or point at the Pole Star. (If you live in the southern hemisphere, your gnomon should point to the southern celestial pole.) This decorative sundial, however, makes no pretenses to complete accuracy; its gnomon will face magnetic north. Stand inside the gravel dial plate, and use your compass to locate magnetic north; then position the gnomon with its vertical edge facing in that direction.

9 Level the gravel around the gnomon. (If the gnomon seems unstable to you, bury its base in the soil beneath the gravel.)

10 To set the granite hour markers, you'll need to set aside a sunny afternoon and a sunny morning. At noon on the first day, set the noon marker on the gravel dial plate, locating it on an imaginary line extending from the point of the shadow that the gnomon is casting to the perimeter of the dial plate. At one o'clock in the afternoon, place another marker in the same fashion. Continue placing markers, every hour, on the hour, until the sun sets. You'll notice that the markers will run clockwise, away from the noon marker.

11 The next sunny morning, get up early and place the remaining markers, from sunrise to 11 a.m. These will run clockwise toward the noon marker.

Shade Trees

Planting a tree is not the quickest way to get shade in your yard, but it may be the smartest. Did you know that the temperature beneath a shade tree can be a full 15°F (8°C) degrees cooler than in a sunny site? Did you know that as few as three properly situated trees can cut your air-conditioning bills in half?

No other plant can perform so many functions at one time. A well-tended tree gives your home a feeling of permanence and actually increases the value of your property when you sell your house. It can hide unattractive views while buffering traffic noise. It will absorb carbon dioxide and replenish oxygen. Its roots will combat soil erosion while acting as a natural filter for pollutants. A tree's leaves (which also filter pollution) will add organic nutrients to your soil. Trees provide habitats for wildlife and at the same time add vertical elements to your landscape design. Without a doubt, the right tree in the right place is a wonderful addition to your yard, but the wrong tree in the wrong place can be a costly mistake, so it pays to plan carefully before planting.

CHOOSING A SHADE TREE

The best shade trees are round or vase shaped, deciduous, and deep rooted. Deciduous trees block the hot summer sun but allow the warming sun of winter through. Deep-rooted trees, such as honey locusts, oaks, and loblolly pines won't compete with nearby plants. If you're planning on growing plants beneath the tree, avoid trees with dense canopies of large leaves. Instead, choose finer-leaved trees such as honey locusts; these cast dappled shade in which plants can grow.

While fast-growing trees (such as poplars) provide shade quickly, they tend to be short-lived, and their wood is more vulnerable to damage from insects, diseases, and storms than the wood of slower growing trees. Local nurseries or your Cooperative Extension Service should be able to tell you which shade trees grow best in your climate and your particular site.

PURCHASING SHADE TREES

Trees are among the costliest plants to purchase (and the larger they are, the more expensive they'll be), but think of them as long-term, low-maintenance investments. Select healthy, vigorous trees, at least five to six feet tall, with a two-inch caliper (the perimeter of the stem six inches above the ground). Avoid trees with damaged bark. You can purchase trees as bareroot, with balled roots wrapped in burlap, or in containers. Make sure you leave the

nursery with specific planting instructions for your type of tree.

PLANTING AND CARE OF SHADE TREES

To find the best site for your shade tree, study the movement of the sun across your yard, keeping in mind that the pattern will change throughout the year. If you'd like to shade a specific part of your yard, such as a terrace, be sure to plant the tree so it will shade that spot during the hottest time of day (or during the time you're most likely to use the area). In general, shade trees should be located on the south or southwest side of your house or yard. If you plan to grow flowering plants near your tree, situate the tree so that your flowers will receive morning sun and afternoon shade. As you select a site, consider the spread of the mature tree's roots and branches, too; make sure they won't interfere with overhead or underground utilities.

How you should plant your tree will depend, in part, on whether you purchased the tree bareroot, burlapped, or in a container; get detailed instructions from the nursery or your Cooperative Extension Service. In general, start by digging a hole as deep and at least twice as wide as the root ball. Then set the tree at the same depth that it grew in the nursery (the soil line should be obvious on the tree trunk); spread the roots out; and prune back

any broken ones. Fill the hole halfway with topsoil, and water well. Refill the hole entirely and water until the soil is moist to a depth of 12 to 18 inches. Cover the bare dirt with a two- to three-inch layer of mulch, but don't let the mulch touch the trunk.

Most trees only need to be staked if they're more than eight feet tall, are top heavy, or are being planted in a windy location. To protect tree trunks from gnawing animals, sun damage, and nicks from lawnmowers, place a loose-fitting plastic tree wrap or wire guard around the trunk.

Your new tree will need regular deep watering for one full year after planting. A topdressing of compost (see page 18) is all the fertilization most trees require.

Umbrellas and Awnings

One of your first decisions will be to choose the fabric: cotton or acrylic. Well-made acrylic fabric manufactured with a solution-dyeing process will prove far more resistant to fading and mildew than cotton, which—while less expensive—will quickly prove itself to be a fair-weather friend. Solution-dyed acrylic repels moisture at the surface, while cotton fabrics (even when waterproofed) will usually allow some moisture through. With both acrylic and cotton, mildew can grow on dirt and other organic material that attaches itself to the fabric, so spot washing your umbrella regularly is a good idea.

Of course, you'll also want to pick a style and color of umbrella that complements, rather than clashes with, your home and yard. Standard patio umbrellas tend to come in solid colors or stripes. More expensive umbrellas offer you a wider choice of sizes and patterns.

When purchasing umbrellas, look for sturdy frames made from heavy-gauge aluminum or hardwoods such as ash and mahogany. If you buy a foreign-made product, make sure the wood is an equivalent of the American hardwoods. Poles that are constructed by screwing together separate pieces may be easier to ship, but they're also less stable than solid ones. If you want the pole to fit a standard umbrella table, make sure it's two inches or less in width.

All through the spring, you've dug, planted, and weeded around your patio, spurred on by visions of alfresco dinners in your beautiful backyard. Now summer is in its fullness, the yard is indeed lovely, and yet you find yourself choosing to eat most meals indoors because "it's just too hot out there." Consider the solutions to this problem; they're easier than you might think.

UMBRELLAS

A patio umbrella will cast shade where you want it—when you want it—while adding a splash of color to your yard. The typical patio umbrella extends from five to nine feet in diameter above a pole that runs through a hole in your tabletop and is anchored by a weighted aluminum or concrete base. A crank usually raises and lowers the umbrella. Patio umbrellas can also come free-standing for use without a table, and some are as large as 20 feet in diameter.

An umbrella with a tilting mechanism will allow you more sun-blocking options, but make sure the model you select is well built and stable. (The hardware, cable, pins, and screws of all umbrellas should be steel or brass.) Umbrellas raised with rope cords rather than steel cables and those held together with flimsy hardware may only see you through a few summers. Umbrellas raised and lowered with double pulley systems will usually outlast all others.

Whatever final product you select, insure a longer lifetime for your umbrella by keeping it closed when it's not in use and storing it inside during rainstorms and colder seasons.

AWNINGS

If you'd like to shade more than just a table or small area, consider adding an awning to your home. An awning can transform the look of any patio or deck, while providing a visual transition between indoors and out and filtering out harmful ultraviolet radiation. But the primary reason you might opt for an awning is energy efficiency. On a hot summer day, an awning can reduce temperatures of adjacent rooms by a whopping 15°F (8°C). If you typically pay high air-conditioning bills, one of these more expensive sun shields could eventually pay for itself.

Unlike umbrellas, awnings have a very real impact on your house's architecture—make sure you choose a style that enhances both your house and yard. A brick red awning on a Spanish-style house will place it firmly along the Mediterranean coast. A candy-striped awning will lend a cheerful touch to your home. Remember that you will probably be able to see the inside of the awning from at least part of your home, so consider, too, the style and colors of those rooms when choosing your awning.

Since an awning is usually a much larger purchase than an umbrella, it's even more important to determine the quality of an awning's fabric, frame, and mechanisms. Make sure all materials are weatherproof and sturdy and the construction is solid. Before you buy your awning, familiarize yourself with the warranty the manufacturer provides and the options available to you for replacing the fabric.

Typically, awnings must be left exposed to the elements; one alternative is an awning that can be retracted (either manually or with a motor) to avoid inclement weather or when sun is desired. Some even come equipped with sun and wind sensors that automatically activate the lifting mechanisms.

Pergolas

Oh, dear. Have you made your yard so lovely that now you can't bear to be away for even a couple of weeks? Don't worry. Why not sip iced cappuccinos in the leafy shade of your own backyard pergola—and buy more plants with the money you save on airfare to Italy?

Pergolas (sometimes called arbors) are structures with open roofs supported by columns. As well as casting shade, pergolas provide a place to grow all manner of climbing, twining, rambling, and scrambling vines. Built over a path, a pergola creates a covered walkway; sheltering a patio or deck, it provides an outdoor "room" for dining or entertaining. Though pergolas range in style from stately to rustic, sitting or strolling beneath one will make you feel as if you're vacationing in a private Mediterranean villa.

CHOOSING A PERGOLA

If your yard includes a walkway that might benefit from the play of light and shade or the addition of a vertical element, a tunnel-like pergola may be in order. If you'd like a shady bower beneath which you can dine or relax, a larger pergola (either freestanding or attached to one wall of your house) will work well.

Like all garden structures, pergolas are both functional and ornamental.

While choosing one that won't collapse in a windstorm or buckle under a heavy snow should be your first priority, you'll also want to choose one that won't clash with the style or color of your house. (This is especially true if the pergola will actually be an attached extension to the house.) A cedar-sided home surrounded by native plants might call for a rustic pergola made with locust poles.

A more formal house would be enhanced by a white wooden pergola with classic lines and columns. The materials—whether wood, brick, stone, or metal—should match or be compatible with those of your house. Lattice, wood 2 x 2s or 2 x 4s, woven reed, bamboo, and even canvas are all possible roofing options. When it comes to choosing roof materials, remember that the size and spacing of the materials will affect the type of shade beneath.

Although it's possible to build a pergola that's too large and that overwhelms the house or yard, don't be cowardly when it comes to "thinking big." You'd be surprised by how much a space will seem to shrink once you set up a table and a few chairs. And any pergola-covered pathway will be much more user-friendly if two people can walk abreast along the path without being scratched by rose thorns or swatted by wet leaves. No matter what size pergola you choose, before you progress too far with your plans, check with local officials regarding building codes that might apply to your new structure, and find out whether or not a building permit is required.

SELECTING A SITE

A pergola should cast shade where and when you want it most, so familiarize yourself with the sun's path across your yard. And as you study the path, remember that the sun's position and angle change continually throughout the year. If you're planning to construct a pergola to shelter a path, try to place it so that an attractive goal, such as a bench or small pond, will be visible at the path's end. Strollers will be much more likely to use the path if there's something that draws them along it.

The open "walls" of a pergola that covers a terrace or deck will form visual frames for your yard, so make sure you like the pictures at which you'll be gazing. Also, take care that any pergola attached to your house doesn't block a lovely view from indoors or prevent desired sunlight from reaching your home's interior.

PLANTS FOR PERGOLAS

Few experiences can match the opulence of relaxing beneath a canopy of fragrant wisteria in full bloom or sipping wine on a terrace as clusters of grapes dangle overhead. So many wonderful plants can grow up and over pergolas that you may find yourself building a few more for your yard!

For pergolas located close to a house, deciduous climbers are best; their leaves will provide summer shade, but will die back to allow light and warmth to filter through in winter. Perfumed plants, such as jasmine and honeysuckle, can be lovely overhead, but too much of a good thing *is* possible, especially near dining areas—floral perfumes don't always mix well with the aromas and flavors of food. Also, make sure the vines you choose will actually grow tall enough to climb up the posts and over the top of your shelter. Your choice of plants will sometimes be determined by the sturdiness of your pergola. Wisteria and trumpet vine, for example, grow too vigorously for all but the most substantial of supporting structures.

Wisteria

10 Plants for Pergolas

- **Clematis**
  Clematis
- **Climbing hydrangea**
  Hydrangea petiolaris
- **Climbing roses**
  Rosa
- **Grape vine**
  Vitis
- **Jasmine**
  Jasminum
- **Malabar gourd**
  Cucurbita ficifolia
- **Moonflower**
  Ipomoea alba
- **Scarlet honeysuckle**
  Lonicera sempervirens
- **Trumpet vine**
  Campsis radicans
- **Wisteria**
  Wisteria

Gazebos

Few garden features are as romantic as gazebos. Even the word itself (thought by some to be a combination of *gaze* and *about*) sounds whimsical. But there is a practical side to these poetic structures: A gazebo can become an extra room for your home. Picture yourself reading in its shade on a lazy summer afternoon—or lingering over dinner with friends inside a screened gazebo as the children dance after fireflies in the yard.

PLANNING

A gazebo is a structure that will alter the whole character of your yard, so it's important to plan thoroughly before installing one. Research legalities such as building codes, zoning ordinances, and your property deed. Then consider your needs. Do you want an extra space for entertaining or do you just need a place to rest in the shade while gardening? Do you want to be able to use the gazebo on rainy days?

Look in magazines and books for pictures of gazebos that appeal to you. Most are round or octagonal, but some are rectangular or three-sided. Pick a style that blends in with the design elements of your home and garden. For example, if you have a shingle roof on your home, tie in the gazebo by roofing it in shingles. If you live in a timber frame home, complement the structure by building a gazebo crafted with dovetailed joinery and wooden pegs.

Next, take some graph paper and create a map of your house and yard drawn to scale. Include trees, garden areas, and the property line. Show where the windows and doors are on the house. Indicate the direction of the sun and the location of utility lines and any wet spots in your yard.

Now use this map to determine the best position for a gazebo. Place tracing paper over the map and draw in the gazebo rooftop, experimenting with different locations. It should be accessible to foot traffic and should not block desired views from any of your windows. Gazebos work best as a design element when they are positioned at the edges of gardens, defining a boundary and leaving the middle open for planting and recreation. A gazebo built in the center of a yard can sometimes look exposed and out of place. It will not seem as inviting as it would if it were placed to the side and landscaped into the yard with shrubbery and climbing vines, appearing as though it had always been there.

Plan the site carefully, taking water drainage into account. You may need to consult a soil engineer and a structural engineer before the foundation is built if you live on an unstable slope or in a windy region. They can insure that the foundation is well matched to the soil it rests upon.

Once you've settled on the site, you can gauge the gazebo's dimensions. A general rule is to build a gazebo as large as possible while keeping it balanced with its surroundings.

BUILDING THE GAZEBO

Use only the finest materials, and build a sturdy gazebo meant to last. If you try to cut corners on quality, you'll end up with an expensive eyesore. The most popular material for gazebos is wood, but other materials include glass or plastic for roofs and windows; tiles, shingles, and aluminum for roofs; steel, stucco, and concrete for posts.

If you decide to hire a professional builder to construct your gazebo, get recommendations from gazebo owners or ask a trade association for names. Some gazebo builders will let you customize their stock designs.

Many people opt for gazebo kits, which range quite a bit in price. Before purchasing a kit, it is wise to look at a finished model and to scrutinize the instructions for clarity. You should also find out what kind of wood is in the kit and how it needs to be finished. Make sure you know exactly what is included in the kit, such as screening and flooring, and who is to cover the cost of delivery.

If you hire a carpenter to assemble the kit, the project will still be less expensive than if you had the gazebo designed and constructed by a builder. You can also have the carpenter tailor the kit to your own design.

PLANTING THE GAZEBO

One of the best ways to blend the edges of a gazebo into its surroundings is to plant vines or climbing plants around it. Consult a nursery to see which ones would do best in your region. Consider wisteria, grapes, clematis, climbing roses, trumpet vine, or bougainvillea, depending on the microclimate of your gazebo's site.

Shade Gardening

Perhaps those trees you planted a few years back grew a little taller a little faster than you'd anticipated. Or perhaps you've bought a house blessed with mature plantings and a lot of shade. Does this mean you'll have to give up on gardening? Certainly not: A surprising number of plants can glorify your shady spots with myriad shapes, heights, textures, and a rainbow of colors.

MADE IN THE SHADE

While it's true many flowering plants need full to partial sun, it's also true that there's plenty to be grateful for if you're gardening in shade. You can get away with less watering, mulching, weeding, and pruning than when gardening in full sun. Some garden pests, such as slugs and snails, prefer shade, but many of the most damaging insects (aphids, mites, and caterpillars, for instance) will number far fewer in shade gardens. And come late July, you'll find yourself much more willing to be out maintaining shade gardens than toiling beneath the scorching sun.

Gardeners in warm climates can grow many "full sun" plants in afternoon shade. Shade will also turn you into a more sophisticated gardener. Because fewer flowering plants grow in shade, you'll need to concentrate on texture, size, and shape when choosing plants—all elements essential to a well-designed garden. Once you discover the elegant beauty of a fern frond unfolding or the handsome composition a planting of stately hostas can offer, a whole new world of gardening will open up to you.

GARDENING IN THE SHADE

Okay, you're convinced there's a sunny side to shade gardening; now, how do you go about doing it? Well, the first thing you need to figure out is just what kind of shade you are dealing with. Full shade areas receive no direct sunlight at all. Areas with partial shade receive sun for four to six hours a day. Gardens with dappled shade usually get only sunlight that filters through the foliage of trees. It *is* difficult to grow a large variety of plants in full shade, but many plants thrive in partial or dappled shade.

Of course, the shade in your yard will shift continuously as the sun moves from east to west each day, as the sun's position in the sky changes throughout the year, and as the tall plants in your yard grow or die.

You can usually alter at least some of the shade in your yard. Large trees can be pruned to thin their leafy canopies, and dark walls may be painted white or another light color to better reflect light. If you have the advantage of choosing your planting areas, remember that morning sun and afternoon shade is a better combination for plants than morning shade and afternoon sun. (Morning sun will help dry the dew from plants, and afternoon shade will provide relief from the harshest sun of the day.)

PLANTS FOR SHADE

A large assortment of flowering shrubs grows in shade. The enchanting blue blossoms of a lace-cap hydrangea will cheer up any dark corner of your yard, while the electric orange blooms of a flame azalea will practically shout. Many shade shrubs also offer

Astilbe

berries or variegated foliage, and some, such as witch hazel and daphne, will scent your yard with their wonderful fragrances.

You'll probably run out of room in your shaded areas well before you run out of varieties of perennials that would grow there. Many woodland wildflowers, such as cardinal flower and lupine, thrive in partial shade. Plants such as Jack-in-the-pulpit and Solomon's seal add their own unique beauty to any garden. And gardeners in warm climates with partial or dappled shade can try out a host of perennials that are sun-lovers in colder climates.

Of course, when it comes to shade annuals, the old stand-bys, impatiens and begonias, are readily available at most gardening centers, but you can also liven up your dark spots with the colorful wishbone flower (*Torenia*),

fragrant flowering tobacco, or the tall spires of foxgloves (usually biennial). Fuchsia, ageratum, and evening primrose are all flowering annuals that perform well in shade.

The hardest part of growing ground covers in shaded sections of your yard may be selecting from among the many choices available. Periwinkle, pachysandra, ajuga, ivy, and moss are just a few of the many low-growing, fast-spreading plants that prefer shade.

When you buy plants for your shade areas, choose the fullest ones you can find, since plants tend to grow leggier in shade. Purchase the earliest blooming varieties of annuals, perennials, and bulbs if you will be planting them under deciduous trees. And finally, look for varieties with variegated foliage to add even more bright highlights to your shade gardens.

A Shade Garden Plan

Work with, rather than fighting, Mother Nature to let the shady sections of your yard add their own charm and beauty to your property. All of the plants in this garden will thrive in partial shade. The plants' flowers, though subtle, will embellish this shade bed off and on from spring to fall; while the hues, textures, and variegations of the plants' foliage brighten the shady spot all season long. Because this bed is planted beneath a deciduous tree (in this instance, a birch), early-flowering bulbs could also be added to the bed.

A WOOD FERN
Dryopteris

Hardiness zones 4–8

1 to 2 feet tall

Leathery green leaves used for textural accent; moist, well-drained soil; filtered sun to full shade

B 'FRANCEE' HOSTA
Hosta 'Francee'

Hardiness zones 3–9

24 inches tall

Funnel-shaped, lavender-blue flowers in summer; large, heart-shaped, puckered, green leaves with irregular, white margins; fertile, moist, well-drained soil; partial to full shade

C 'GOLD STANDARD' HOSTA
Hosta 'Gold Standard'

Hardiness zones 3–9

24 inches tall

Funnel-shaped, pale lavender flowers in summer; heart-shaped, chartreuse leaves with irregular, dark green margins; fertile, moist, well-drained soil; partial to full shade

D BISHOP'S WEED
Aegopodium podagraria 'Variegatum'

Hardiness zones 3–10

up to 12 inches tall

Flat clusters of white flowers late spring to early summer; deep green leaves with irregular, creamy white margins; tolerates dry or moist, poor soil; partial shade to full sun; can be invasive if not contained

E 'ELEGANS' HOSTA
Hosta 'Elegans'

Hardiness zones 3–9

36 inches tall

Funnel-shaped, lavender-white flowers in summer; large, heart-shaped, dark blue-green leaves; fertile, moist, well-drained soil; partial to full shade

F BLEEDING HEART
Dicentra spectabilis

Hardiness zones 3–8

up to 48 inches tall

Heart-shaped, pink and white flowers dangling from arched stems late spring to early summer; lacy, pale green leaves; moist, well-drained soil; partial shade

G GRAPE-LEAVED ANEMONE
Anemone vitifolia 'Robustissima'

Hardiness zones 3–8

up to 36 inches tall

Clusters of small, mauve-pink flowers held high above foliage in late summer and early autumn; dark green leaves are white and woolly underneath; fertile, moist soil; sun or partial shade

H OAKLEAF HYDRANGEA
Hydrangea quercifolia

Hardiness zones 5–9

up to 6 feet tall

White flowers in conical clusters early to late summer; large leaves, resembling oak leaves, turn crimson in autumn; moist, well-drained soil; partial shade

A Moonlight Garden

A poet once said that the two most beautiful words in the English language are *summer evening*. For many of us, especially during the week, our time to relax or entertain starts just when the sun is ready to set. There is a bright side to being outdoors after dusk: The heat of the day has faded, the air feels softer, the weeds don't show, and—if you plant an evening garden— you can enjoy luminous and fragrant flowers by moonlight.

Gardens designed for night viewing have been cultivated since medieval times. Moon gardens were quite common during the Victorian age and have been key features in some of this century's most famous gardens—in particular, Sissinghurst Castle, home of the writer Vita Sackville-West. You don't need to own a British estate or employ a full-time crew of gardeners to experience your own bit of twilight magic. Even the most modest planting of white and pale-colored flowers, paired with silver, grey, or blue foliage, will look elegant in daylight and enchanting at night.

Night-blooming flowers, pollinated by moths, wait until late afternoon or twilight to unfold their blossoms and

Evening primrose

release their perfumed fragrances.

Tuck a small bed of such plants beside your patio, in containers on your deck, along the path to your front door, or even in a window box outside your bedroom window. If you choose a spot that gets full sun during the day, which most evening bloomers require, the plants will be in the path of moonbeams at night.

Flowers that open at night tend to be summer bloomers—a real advantage since, for most of the country, that's when it's actually warm enough to sit outside after dark. Of course, you don't have to include

only night-blooming flowers—any plant with grayish silver foliage or with pale-colored blossoms that remain open after dark will look lovely in moonlight.

LIGHTS FOR THE NIGHT GARDEN

Keep in mind when planning your evening garden that you'll need a source of illumination for moonless nights. A few well-placed luminaries, tiki torches, or lanterns will provide the most romantic light. Use a citronella (or other insect repellent) candle or torch, and your lighting can serve two functions at the same time.

A more permanent solution is to install a landscape lighting system. These are now widely available and affordable, and many are simple enough to be installed by the homeowner. If you do choose to use electric lights in your garden, use low-wattage bulbs to create the effect of soft moonlight. Glaring lights will take away from the magical effect of the pale flowers and will also attract bothersome insects.

Play around and have fun when placing the lights in your evening garden. Lights perched in the branches of trees can create the effect of moonlight, while spot lighting best accents a particular plant or small bed. Diffused lighting (bulbs covered with frosted material) gives an appropriate level of light for viewing night-blooming flowers, and the effects of shadowing (positioning a light so the shadow of a plant is cast upon a flat surface) can be stunning.

WATER IN THE NIGHT GARDEN

No night garden is complete without at least a bit of water. The smallest tub of water, if strategically placed, will mirror the moon, while the simplest fountain will provide soothing night music. Artificial waterfalls look lovely (and often more natural) by moonlight, and a small pond will encourage frogs to stop by to serenade you.

Water will allow you to grow even more night-blooming plants. Imagine sipping a cool drink on your terrace as exotic water lilies in a nearby pond open slowly and release their heady perfume. (Many tropical lilies of the genus *Nymphaea* bloom at night.) White irises, white turtleheads, and light-colored grasses are all plants that look lovely at the water's edge at night. (See pages 64 through 75 for more information on backyard water features.)

MOTHS

Viewing the moth (plain-Jane cousin of the elegant butterfly) with pity or scorn is easy. We plant entire gardens with dazzling, bright blooms to lure butterflies to our yards, but we mine our closets with chemicals to keep moths from snacking on our winter woolens.

In truth, the moth, which has 13 times as many species as the butterfly (its fellow member of the order Lepidoptera), is a pretty impressive insect. Butterflies must feed on erect, brightly colored flowers with clearly marked centers that are open in the daylight. But the moth comes equipped with complex, light-gathering eyes; antennae that provide both balance and a highly developed

sense of smell; and a *proboscis* (or tongue) up to six inches long. All these features allow the moth to gather nectar from fragrant flowers that open at night and hide their sustenance in deep, tubelike blossoms.

Planting even one or two evening-blooming flowers will encourage moths to visit your backyard. Evening primroses and honeysuckles are favored by a species commonly called "hawk" or "sphinx" moths. Strong fliers with rapid wingbeats (some can fly up to 30 miles an hour), these moths are often mistaken for hummingbirds because they feed by hovering in front of flowers while sipping nectar through their long proboscises.

Families

Family backyards aren't always picture perfect. Their garden beds may contain a few weeds, their lawns may boast badminton sets instead of elegant koi ponds, and their sunflowers may outnumber their exotic plants. Nevertheless, these backyards can be places where the entire family relaxes and plays.

You'll grow your flowers in beds you've protected from cavorting children, while your children play in specially designed areas. Songbirds will nest comfortably in houses that you've provided for them, and even the family pets will be welcome outdoors—once you've learned how to protect your plants (and the birds) from them.

As your yard becomes a more inviting place, you'll find your children leaving the T.V. behind to play in treehouses, soar on swings, or draw pictures in their garden journals—perhaps of the monarch butterflies that you've lured to your butterfly garden. Or maybe they'll be trying out their trowels in the first garden they've so proudly planted. And you may or may not be pulling those weeds. After all, backyards—like families—aren't meant to be perfect: They're meant to be loved and enjoyed.

Designing Yards for Children

secret to designing yards that children will enjoy is to first remember what it was like to be a child.

ROUGH AND TUMBLE

Just as it would make no sense to outfit a child's playroom with precious oriental carpets, fine lace, and fragile china, it would also be foolish to expect children to romp happily in a yard with weak, finely textured grasses; narrow paths; and delicate plants. Kids need to run, jump, skip, and climb outdoors. They need open spaces for games—preferably areas carpeted with tough, resilient grasses. They require sturdy-limbed trees to climb and swing from; and wide, well-marked paths to trample. Children want plenty of sunshine, but they also need adequate shade. They don't care if your yard wins awards from the local gardening club. Overgrown shrubs provide them with secret forts; problem muddy spots become mysterious swamps to muck about in.

SETTING LIMITS

Does this mean you have to give up your dreams of dazzling, well-designed flower beds? No, because children also need boundaries. Just as you might

No matter how perfectly landscaped your yard, to any small child, it's a wild place, filled with crawling, climbing, slithering creatures; leafy secret passages; vast savannahs of grass; towering trees; and dirt (glorious dirt!). What adults see as a weed's bothersome seed head is—to a child—a magical puff ball to blow upon. A branch knocked onto your manicured lawn by a summer storm can become—for a child—

a pen, a sword, a galloping horse, a conductor's baton, or a flying broomstick. And rocks. What makes children so crazy about rocks? Do your children sometimes seem to have more rocks in their indoor collections than could possibly have existed outside?

Gardening and rearing young children have something important in common. They both force us to slow down, to kneel, and to see the world up close through new/old eyes. The

teach your children to treat a special room in your house with extra care, so, too, can they learn that certain sections of the yard are ball-, bat-, and frisbee-free zones. Boundaries such as fences and hedges can help reinforce this idea, while simultaneously hiding some of the less attractive aspects of the kids' areas. Keep such borders low enough to let you keep an eye on the children's play, but high enough to serve as visual demarcations.

Limits also need to be set for safety reasons. Teach children never to put plants in their mouths unless you say it is okay (the list to the right names some of the poisonous plants that can be found in backyards).

BUDDING GARDENERS

No matter how fascinating a play area, children may want to do what you're doing—try their hands at gardening. If so, help them start their own small patch of easy-to-grow plants. (You'll find a plan for a child's garden on pages 108–109.) Keep this starter garden small, and site it in a sunny spot close to a water source. Also remember that a kid's garden should be fun. If gardening instills a little horticultural knowledge or encourages a child to taste broccoli, treat these as bonuses, *not* goals.

PLAY THINGS

While children can usually pass many happy hours playing with nothing but plants, dirt, bugs, sticks, and rocks,

you'll probably wind up providing them with outdoor play things anyway. Just remember to purchase items that can stand up to both your children's rambunctious play and the elements.

Climbing structures allow children to do all the things you keep trying to get them to stop doing on your furniture indoors. Remember how quickly children grow, though; select structures that are not only safe and well constructed, but that will also continue to be used a few years down the road.

Swings will not only be swung on; they'll probably be twisted tight and spun wildly, stood upon, and hung upside down from. Make sure they're well made and safely attached, and that the ground below them is softly cushioned. Slides should be sturdy. The metal ones can get terribly hot, so plastic is often a better choice.

Most young children love digging in sandboxes; unfortunately, most cats also find them convenient. Get or make one with a lid to keep out both rain and felines.

And don't forget about playhouses. Can you remember how magical it felt to be a child in your own small, private hideaway? Playhouses can range from free and simple (a cardboard box from an appliance store or vines planted to climb a tepee of bamboo poles) to elaborate and quite costly ar-chitecturally-designed play palaces.

Yards are places for exploration and discovery, and kids—fascinated by

things we overlook or hurry past—treat them that way naturally. Rather than spoiling their fun by telling them that the yard is an educational haven, encourage your budding scientists and poets by providing them with magni-fying glasses, field guides, telescopes, star charts, containers for collections, and journals.

10 Poisonous Backyard Plants

- **Angel trumpet**
  Brugmansia arborea

- **Castor bean**
  Ricinus communis

- **Daffodil bulb**
  Narcissus

- **English yew**
  Taxus baccata

- **Foxglove**
  Digitalis purpurea

- **Glory lily bulb**
  Gloriosa superba

- **Jimson weed**
  Datura stamonium

- **Lantana**
  Lantana

- **Lily-of-the-valley**
  Convallaria majalis

- **Oleander**
  Nerium oleander

A Plan for a Child's First Garden

For a child, planting a garden like the one shown below can be a tremendously exciting experience. First, there's the chance to get as dirty as you like while you dig up the garden bed. Then there's getting to buy all those colorful seed packets and baby plants from the nursery. Once they're tucked into their new home, there's the joy of spotting the first tip of an emerging green shoot, and the wonderful taste of that first ripe strawberry. Of course, a garden is an education in itself—a class in patience ("When will those seeds finally sprout?"); in decision-making ("What kind of flowers should I plant?"); in gardening science ("You mean that dead leaves are sort of like food for the food I'm growing?"); and in paying attention ("Whoops! That sunflower looks thirsty! I'd better start remembering to water it").

A PEPPERMINT
Mentha x piperita

Hardiness zones 3–7

12 to 36 inches tall

Whorls of lavender flowers in summer; fragrant, green leaves; rich, moist soil; full sun; can be invasive

B BELL PEPPER
Capsicum annuum Grossum Group

Annual

2 to 3 feet tall

Sweet, bell-shaped, green peppers, ripen to yellow, red, or deep purple; matures in 50 to 75 days; fertile, evenly moist, well-drained soil; full sun

C PLUM TOMATO
Lycopersicon esculentum 'Roma'

Annual

4 to 10 feet tall

Plum-shaped fruits all summer; matures in 70 to 80 days; fertile, evenly moist, well-drained soil; full sun

D ALPINE STRAWBERRY
Fragaria vesca

Hardiness zones 3–7

6 to 10 inches tall

Small white or pink blossoms turn into small, flavorful fruits early summer to frost; starts very slowly from seed (buy plants); fertile, well-drained soil; full sun

E SNAPDRAGON
Antirrhinum majus

Hardiness zones 5–9

6 to 36 inches tall

Tubular, double-lipped flowers in many colors all summer; lance-shaped, deep green leaves; average to rich, well-drained soil; full sun

F SWEET POTATO VINE
Ipomoea batatas 'Blackie'

Hardiness zones 9–11

up to 20 feet tall

Tender perennial vine with large, purple-black leaves; grown as ornamental for foliage; well-drained soil; full sun

G GLOBE AMARANTH
Gomphrena globosa

Annual

12 to 24 inches tall

Cloverlike flowers in many colors summer to frost; oblong, hairy, mid-green leaves; moderately fertile, well-drained soil; full sun; flowers dry well

H SCARLET RUNNER BEAN
Phaseolus coccineus

Annual

6 to 10 feet tall

Bright scarlet, pea-like flowers cover vine early to midsummer, then 4- to 12-inch pods with seeds speckled black and red; dark green leaves with three leaflets; moist, well-drained soil; full sun; both flowers and seeds are edible

I SUNFLOWER
Helianthus annuus

Hardiness zones 4–9

2 to 10 feet tall

Large, yellow, daisylike flowers with yellow, brown, or purple disk florets; large, heart-shaped mid- to dark green leaves; moderately fertile, moist, well-drained soil; full sun; seeds are edible

Swings

Feeling a little too grounded? Maybe all you need is a little liftoff—Tarzan-style. Nothing is more liberating than hurtling headlong into the wind. If a more sedate swing is what you have in mind, sit back and relax in a glider. Generations of Southerners—for whom centuries of gossip, courtship, war, and peace have risen and fallen to the gentle swaying of porch swings and gliders—swear by their therapeutic qualities. Whether recreational, functional, or both, swings and gliders are simple and well-deserved garden luxuries.

ROPE AND TIRE SWINGS

The simplest style of swing is the rope swing—just a strand of freedom dangling from a single point. What's unique about rope swings is that instead of just taking you back and forth like plank swings do, they spin, whirl, and twirl, too. Traditional rope swings are made from heavy hemp with a large knot at the free end to support the rider's feet. Hemp tends to chafe a bit, but it does offer a superior grip. Most nylon ropes are slightly more comfortable to grasp, but they're also more difficult to hang on to, as nylon tends to be slippery. Nylon rope works well if you're planning on creating a more evolved and secure version of the rope swing—one that features a wooden disk for the rider to sit or stand on as he or she grips the rope.

Tire swings usually fall into the rope-swing category as well and are remarkably easy to make. Just hang a tire by attaching a rope to it. (Instructions for attaching ropes securely are provided on page 113.)

PENDULUM SWINGS AND GLIDERS

Pendulum-style swings may not take you around the world, but their almost 180-degree thrust can provide plenty of excitement. A plank swing like the one featured on page 112 is a breeze to build and can be safer than the more primitive rope swings. This type of swing can offer a gentle ride or a wild one, depending on the length of rope you use—and the courage you exhibit.

A more subtle way to stay in motion is to integrate a swing or glider into your garden furniture collection. The porch swing is a timeless classic, but make sure that the ceiling of your porch is stable enough for safe attachment. If you aren't blessed with a sturdy porch ceiling, consider hanging the same style of swing from a freestanding A-frame structure, as shown in the photo to the right. A glider such as the one shown on the opposite page is also a good alternative. This smooth-riding piece of furniture is a cross between a rocking chair and a swing, but its gentle back-and-forth motion can be even more relaxing. The hammock, another universal source of rest and recuperation, has a history that stretches back to ancient times, when a student of Socrates' invented it. Since then, the hammock has inspired laziness in anyone snared by its net. Another version of the hammock is the "monkey chair," which offers the traditional hammock's cocoon-like comfort while allowing you to sit upright.

SAFE LAUNCHING

Before you go airborne, you'll need to start with a steady and secure launching point. Engineering a swing isn't difficult, but a vital step before the fun begins is to ensure passenger safety. Consider where to site your swing, keeping in mind the importance of a pleasant view and a soft landing.

Examine the vegetation beneath your chosen site. Then bid it farewell, as it will inevitably be trampled if a swing is hung above it.

If you plan to hang your swing from a tree, choose a strong one—maple, oak, and ash work best. The branch you select should be alive, healthy, and at

least six inches in diameter (or larger if the tree is a less hardy variety). Don't loop the rope around the branch; this common suspension method actually suffocates the limb, thereby posing a threat to the rider's safety. Instructions for safe attachment of swings are provided on the next two pages.

Making a Plank Swing

What is it about swings that's so captivating? Feeling your hair sweep back in the wind as you rise through the air? The rush of excitement as your feet leave the ground? The almost irresistible challenge of seeing just how high you can go? Throughout the ages, the basic plank swing has delighted passengers both young and old. From the open-air picnics of France to the religious festivals of India, this simple type of swing has played a starring role in cultures worldwide. And unlike many of the other "toys" you may remember from your childhood, swings are never outdated. Maybe that's because adults enjoy them just as much as children.

MATERIALS & TOOLS

- ¾" x 10" x 24" poplar
- Sandpaper
- Electric drill
- ¼" and ⁵⁄₁₆" drill bits
- ½" wrench
- Pliers
- Tape measure
- Sturdy ladder
- Tool apron
- Two ⅜" eyebolts (for the tree)
- Four ¼" eyebolts (for the swing)
- Four ¼" washers
- Four ¼" locknuts
- 6 quick-link joints, ¼" in diameter
- Eight ⅜" cable clips
- 2 lengths of strong chain, each 18" long
- 2 lengths of heavy nylon or oiled hemp rope (see "Tips")
- Polyurethane sealer
- 3" paintbrush

TIPS

- The tree limb you select for your swing should be at least 6" in diameter.
- The lengths of the rope you use for this swing will depend on the height of the tree limb you choose. Cut these at least 18" longer than you think they need to be; you can always trim them later.

■ A safe way to attach ropes to a swing is to use devices known as cable clips. You'll find these at a hardware store. One warning here: Cable clips can loosen over time, so check and tighten them frequently!

Instructions

1 The 10" x 24" piece of poplar will serve as your swing seat. Measure and mark a point at each of its corners, 2" in from a short end and 2" in from a long edge.

2 Using the electric drill and the ¼" bit, drill a hole through the seat at each of the four marked points.

3 To smooth all the sharp edges on the seat, sand them thoroughly.

4 To preserve the wood from the elements, apply a couple of coats of polyurethane sealer, letting the first coat dry thoroughly before applying the next.

5 Insert a ¼" eyebolt into each hole in the seat, with the eye on the top face of the seat. Secure each bolt with a ¼" washer and locknut.

6 Attach a quick-link joint to each eyebolt. Then link the ends of each chain to the quick-link joints so that each chain runs from the front of the swing to the back.

7 Attach another quick-link joint to the center of each chain.

8 To attach the rope to the tree branch you've selected, set your ladder against the tree, and have a friend hold it steady. Put on your tool apron: You'll need to bring your drill, the 5⁄16" drill bit, a tape measure, the two 3⁄8" eyebolts, a pair of pliers, four cable clips, the wrench, and the two lengths of rope when you climb up the ladder. Take a good look at the illustration to the right before you make your ascent!

9 Measure 30" out from the trunk of the tree and drill a 5⁄16" hole in the bottom of the limb. Measure out another 20" and drill a second 5⁄16" hole, also in the bottom of the limb. Then insert an eyebolt into each hole, using the pliers to twist them in.

10 Slip one end of a length of rope through two cable clips, through one of the eyebolts in the branch, and back down through the cable clips. Adjust the clips, one beneath the other, so they face in opposite directions. Then use the wrench to tighten the nuts on the cable clips so they'll secure the rope firmly. Repeat to fasten the other rope to the second eyebolt.

11 Once you're back on the ground again, use the technique described in step 10 to attach the other ends of the rope to the quick-link joints on the swing-seat chains.

Treehouses

Perching atop a tree isn't just for the birds. Humans have demonstrated a hunger for heights since ancient times, when the Roman emperor Caligula held banquets in the enormous limbs of a plane tree. During the Italian Renaissance, the Medici family held competitions to see who could build the grandest treehouse. Unfortunately, since those times, treehouses have been regarded largely as kids' stuff. Recently, however, they've undergone a renaissance of their own, gaining a foothold in contemporary alternative architecture. People live, work, and even vacation in treehouses and treehouse resorts. You may not want to go so far as to install a hot tub in the limbs of your backyard oak, but you don't have to stop at nailing a few flat boards to its branches. A little forethought will go a long way toward giving you a cozy, raised room with a view.

PLANNING YOUR TREEHOUSE

First, decide whether you'll build the house yourself (you'll need some basic construction experience if you do) or have someone else do it for you. Then decide what purpose your treehouse will serve. Who will use it? Will they eat, sleep, read, or play in it? Do you want to locate it conveniently close to your house or nestle it far away in a hidden corner of the yard?

Make sketches of both your dream palace and of realistic alternatives. Consult books on treehouses for inspiration, and use your sketches as you work toward a final design. With these sketches in mind, choose a tree in which to build. Maple, oak, and ash have the best reputations for strength and hardiness, but obviously your choices will be limited to what's grow-

ing in your backyard. The truth of the matter is that almost any type of tree of the right size can support a properly engineered structure. When in doubt, though, check with an arborist and an architect.

Once you've chosen a tree, determine the height at which you'll place the treehouse. This is a vital safety consideration: Walls erected at extreme heights in unprotected areas will act as sails that catch the wind, and will threaten the stability of the structure. And do you really want your small child climbing that high? Even if you plan to construct a simple platform-style structure, which will fare better than more complex designs at higher branch levels, proceed with caution.

Branch thickness is another important consideration. Locate the places on the tree where you'll need to fasten supports and measure the circumference at those points. Depending on the type of tree you've chosen, and the weight of the structure, look for branches at least eight to twelve inches in diameter. Ensure the safety of the future treehouse inhabitants by carefully considering these factors and by consulting a treehouse construction manual.

TREEHOUSES FOR KIDS

Your child, of course, needs a getaway as much as you do. Kids are rarely out of the range of watchful adult eyes, and treehouses are famed for the sense of privacy and refuge they offer. Very few activities offer children a better sense of ownership than involvement in the planning and building process. In a note to his carpenter, a president once scrawled "Please have this [treehouse] built. [My daughter] will help...To be placed as directed by her." Allowing children a role in the decision-making process and a hand in the construction will enhance their appreciation for the structure and the personal space that it provides—not to mention their carpentry skills!

LOFTY LIVING

All sorts of things that are fun to do inside are even more delightful when they take place up in the leafy canopy of a tree!

Napping Nook. Snuggling into the limbs of a century-old oak provides an unparalleled sense of sweet security. Whether you actually build a sleeping structure into your treehouse or just store a blanket and pillow up there, you'll sleep like a baby in your treetop retreat.

Studio. Do you have a secret yearning to try your hand as a painter? Is your child determined to master the tuba, but your family unable to tolerate one more note wailing through the house? No matter the art form, a treehouse can liberate the creative spirit while providing the solitude necessary for artistic endeavors.

Dining Perch. Whether the kids are having a tea party with their teddy bears or you're hosting dinner for that special someone, dining on high can be a special treat. Spread a picnic blanket and some cushions if floors are coarse, or consider adding a small table and a few chairs to your treehouse.

Reading Refuge. A good book always provides an escape for weary minds. Reading in a treehouse, however, will really send your imagination soaring. Try some of these great treehouse reads:

Baron in the Trees	Italo Calvino
Swiss Family Robinson	Robert Louis Stevenson
Walden	Henry David Thoreau
Meetings with Remarkable Trees	Thomas Pakenham

Making a Garden Journal

A free hour or two and a few supplies are all you need to make this lovely, leather-bound garden journal. Fill its pages with photos and sketches of your garden and family, pressed flowers and leaves, and other garden memories. Once you've learned the stitching technique with which the signatures (or folded paper sheets) are attached to the cover, you'll be able to make as many journals and albums—in as many sizes and shapes—as you like.

MATERIALS & TOOLS

- One 12" x 15" sheet of leather
- Utility knife
- Pencil and ruler
- Awl or sharp nail
- 4½ yards of waxed linen thread or dental floss
- 31 sheets of 11" x 14" paper (90 lb. weight)
- Five 4" x 5" pieces of colorful fabric

Instructions

1 Using a utility knife—and the photo as a guide—cut out a 1½" x 3" window in the center of the leather sheet.

2 To make the first signature, stack three sheets of paper on

top of each other and fold the stack in half to make six 7" x 11" pages. Repeat to make nine more signatures.

3 Using a pencil and ruler, draw a vertical line down the center of a sheet of 11" x 14" paper, dividing it into two 7" x 11" sections.

4 Spread out the leather cover and center the paper under it. Mark two dots on the paper at the center top and center bottom of the window in the cover. This marked paper will now serve as a hole-punching template.

5 Reopen one of the signatures, and place the template on top of it. Using an awl, punch through each dot in the template to make holes through the open signature. Repeat to punch holes in each of the remaining signatures.

6 Now you'll wrap pieces of fabric over the spines of five signatures. Cut the template down to 4" x 5" and use it as you punch two holes in each piece of fabric to ensure that these holes align with the signature holes.

7 Refold a signature, and wrap a piece of fabric around its spine, aligning the holes in the fabric and paper. Repeat with four more signatures. Then stack the folded signatures, alternating those with fabric and those without.

8 Open signature #10 (the top signature in the stack) and position it flat inside the opened cover. Thread the needle and tie a knot on one end. Run the thread in through the signature's top hole and out through the window in the cover. Bring the thread over the top of the spine, back through the same top hole, and out again through the window.

9 Refold signature #10 inside the open cover. (These pages will be in the back of the journal.) Open signature #9 (the next from the stack) and place it inside the cover, on top of signature #10. Holding the journal in one hand, turn it over so the cover faces up and pass the thread back down through the window and through the top hole in signature #9. Turn the journal cover side down. The thread should be coming up from the top hole of signature #9.

10 Bring the thread up over the spine and turn the journal cover side up. You'll see a small horizontal stitch at the top of the window. Pass the thread down under that

stitch, pull it up toward the top of the journal, and turn the journal so the cover faces down.

11 Refold signature #9 to close it, open signature #8, and place it inside the cover. Turn the journal so the cover faces up, and pass the thread back down through the window, into the top hole in signature #8. Turn the journal cover side down. The thread should be coming up through the top hole of signature #8.

12 Bring the thread up over the spine and turn the journal so the cover faces up. Bring the thread down under the next small horizontal stitch, pull it up slightly to tighten it, and turn the journal cover side down.

13 Continue adding signatures in this way until the tops of all the signatures are stitched. After bringing the thread under the last horizontal stitch, pass it through the window and back through the top hole in signature #1.

14 Bring the thread down through the bottom hole of signature #1 and out through the window. Bring the thread down the outside of the spine and back around to the inside of signature #1. Then pass the needle back through the bottom hole again and out through the window.

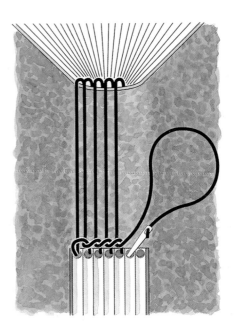

15 Refold signature #1 and open signature #2. Bring the thread through the window and back through the bottom hole in signature #2. Repeat the same stitching technique as you used for the top holes, using the same butterfly stitch to secure each signature.

16 After stitching the last signature, feed the needle back through the window and into the bottom hole of signature #10. Then run the thread underneath the top stitch inside the signature and knot the thread to it. Trim the remaining thread.

17 To make the place marker, wrap a small rock with thread, leaving two long, loose thread ends. Bring the loose thread ends together and tie them to one of the signature stitches on the journal's spine.

Pets in the Garden

Is it possible to have both a wonderfully landscaped backyard and happy pets? The answer, as evidenced by countless pet-loving gardeners across the country, is a resounding *yes!* Just as children and gardens can peacefully coexist, so, too, can pets and plants. Gardening does, however, pose special challenges for pet owners and their pets. Toxic plants and poisons and even wildlife can be dangerous to your pets, and, without training, your animal companions may decide your garden beds make perfect litter boxes. Your dog will wag its tail with delight at the digging pits you've so thoughtfully cultivated, and your cat may think it most kind of you to be luring those birds to the yard with feeders. But with a little care and planning you can keep both your pets and your garden safe.

KEEPING YOUR GARDEN SAFE

For some cats, a garden is one grand litter box. Surprising cats with a quick squirt of water from a spray bottle can sometimes discourage such unwanted behavior. For particularly willful cats, consider laying chicken wire on the soil before planting, or purchase a pet-deterrent spray or powder from a pet store. (Check the safety of such products before using them near edible plants.) Never use soiled litter as a fertilizer; it's not only a health hazard, but it will also attract other cats to your yard.

The main challenge posed by dogs in the garden is digging. Dogs dig for a variety of reasons. Sometimes they are hunting rodents beneath the ground; sometimes they're creating a "den" (remember dogs are descendants of wolves). But dogs also dig for the sheer joy of it—digging is fun! If your dog digs trenches, it's probably hunting moles or other small rodents. Taking steps to eliminate this prey from your yard will help curb this activity. If your dog seems to be digging holes and then lying in them, make sure you are providing shelter that is cool in summer and warm in winter. Dogs that dig as a recreational sport need to be given plenty of exercise and attention. Try teaching your pet the command "No digging," filling holes with things the dog won't enjoy pouncing on (chicken wire and water balloons work well), or providing a doggie sandbox (burying your dog's toys and treats there will encourage its use).

Cats and dogs often eat grass, sometimes to add nutrients to their diets and more often to provide a stomach irritant that will help them eliminate something they've ingested. To discourage this behavior, try feeding them other vegetables. Raw broccoli, cauliflower, and carrots are good choices, but avoid onions and potatoes. Alternatively, you could grow a container of grass just for your pet on your patio or even indoors.

KEEPING PETS SAFE

If you notice your pet eating vegetation other than grass, don't assume it's harmless. Various parts of many common plants, such as morning glories, daffodils, rhododendrons, azaleas, rhubarb, and tomato plants, can be toxic. If your pet seems disoriented, is salivating excessively, or has an upset stomach after eating a plant, take the animal to

a vet, and bring along a sample of anything you think your pet may have ingested. Do not allow your pets onto lawns that have been recently treated with fertilizers or pesticides. Take special care whenever you apply insecticides, weed killers, and fertilizers.

KEEPING WILDLIFE SAFE

Domestic animals and wild animals rarely coexist peacefully without human intervention. Remember, your cat is

not a natural part of your backyard ecosystem. Install bird feeders at least five feet above ground level and in an area clear of brush. Try to keep birdseed off the ground, too, as fallen seed makes birds easier prey for cats, and ingesting birdseed can be harmful to your pets. Try using a suet feeder instead of a seed feeder or surrounding your seed feeder with chicken wire. Unfortunately, bell collars on cats are probably less effective than you think. Cats stalk slowly and then pounce. By the time a bird hears the bell, it's often too late.

Finally, don't overlook your pets when planting your garden. Easy-to-grow catnip and valerian root are both harmless kitty intoxicants. Just make sure you start the seedlings someplace safe from your cat! And unless you want your cat to play in a garden bed, plant catnip away from it. Because catnip spreads easily, it's best to keep it in a pot, buried to the rim. Once the plant is mature, just pinch off the leaves and buds for your cat to play with, or dry and store them for a special treat. If you have birds, consider growing your own seed. Rabbits, hamsters, and gerbils will appreciate all sorts of treats from your garden.

Backyards for Birds and Butterflies

Entire families, from toddlers to grandparents, will enjoy a yard where birds sing from the tree branches (or perhaps even raise a brood), and butterflies flutter from flower to flower. With just a bit of planning and planting, you can easily turn your backyard into a beautiful sanctuary for birds and butterflies.

SHELTER FOR BIRDS

From a bird's-eye-view, your backyard is appealing if it offers a place to hide, a place to escape harsh weather, and a place to nest, feed, and drink. The more of these requirements you can fulfill for a particular type of bird, the more likely that species will be to reward you with a visit or perhaps a long-term stay.

Birds need to be able to hide from predators. Many will look for cover in thorny shrubs, such as hollies, rhododendrons, and roses. Birds that tend to remain low to the ground will seek cover in berry thickets or even ivy.

Evergreen trees will attract birds because they provide both cover from predators and shelter from the cold, wind, rain, and hot sun. Plant pines, firs, hemlocks, or junipers, and you'll soon see a rise in your bird population.

To encourage birds to nest and raise their young in your yard, make sure you provide a variety of plants: grasses, thickets, shrubs, and taller trees. Birds will be especially attracted to these if they're located in a quiet part of your property. Hollies, dogwoods, hemlocks, and oaks are all trees that encourage nesting.

FOOD AND WATER FOR BIRDS

A variety of birds can coexist in one place because they feed (as well as nest) in separate niches in that area. Just as with nesting, diversity is the key to planting a backyard bird banquet. By including tall, medium, and low-growing food plants for birds, you'll ensure that many different birds will feed in your yard.

It's also important to choose a mix of plants that will produce food throughout the year. Maples offer a feast of seeds in the spring, dogwoods produce berries in the summer, grasses set seed in autumn, and winterberries (as their name indicates) provide berries in winter. Other plants that produce seeds for birds include spider flowers, cornflowers, cosmos, and snapdragons.

Growing native plants is a great way to attract birds. To entice a specific type of bird, refer to a field guide (or contact a local conservation group) to find out what plants that bird feeds on. A bird's beak will usually provide some clues to its diet. Hummingbirds use their long thin beaks to probe nectar from funnel-shaped flowers, while woodpeckers' strong, sharp beaks puncture trees to find insects. And speaking of insects, remember that when you use pesticides to kill off all the bugs in your garden, you'll be eliminating an important food source for many birds.

The birds dining in your yard will also need fresh, clean water. If you already have a small pond or stream, you're set; otherwise, a birdbath should suffice. Because different birds are happiest with different water depths (chickadees and goldfinches like fairly shallow water, while robins and blue jays prefer deeper water), consider adding a couple of small rocks to your birdbath.

A wet bird is hindered in its ability to fly and escape enemies. Therefore, it's important to position your birdbath in an area open enough that cats can't launch surprise attacks, yet close enough to shrubs or trees that birds can wing it to cover quickly.

BUTTERFLIES

As luck would have it, most of the plants that attract butterflies are plants we humans find attractive, too. Your butterfly garden can be one of the most colorful, sunny spots in your yard. Butterflies, like other insects, are cold blooded; in order to fly, they need the sun to warm them. Most of the plants that butterflies rely on are also sun-lovers. Butterflies frequent gardens with large splashes of color, as colors help them find the nectar they feed on. As you plant a butterfly garden, group together flowers with similar colors instead of scattering them.

Try to have butterfly-friendly plants blooming continuously from spring through fall. For instance, you might plant lilac for spring blooms, butterfly bush for the summer, and chrysanthemum for autumn. The list of plants that attract butterflies is so extensive (sunflowers, zinnias, heliotrope, lantana, and verbena are but a small sample) that you'll easily find flowers to suit your site conditions and landscape plans.

Along with providing the flowers that offer nectar for adult butterflies,

your garden should also contain the plants that caterpillars feed upon. Different species of butterflies choose different plants as the host plants upon which to lay their eggs. Black swallowtails lay their eggs on parsley, while monarchs use milkweed as a host.

Along with food, butterflies will need a water source. A shallow dish sunk into the ground and filled with water can serve this purpose. Add a few very small rocks or a cluster of pebbles to provide landing pads.

Flat rocks can serve another purpose in your garden if you set them in spots that receive a lot of light. Butterflies like to sunbathe on them and warm themselves up before flying.

Bird-Watching

Bird-watching, believe it or not, is one of the most popular hobbies in the world. More than one-third of the population of the United States feeds birds, and bird-watching is the fastest-growing outdoor activity in the country. Why? Perhaps because birds are a delightful source of year-round entertainment and can be found wherever food and water are available to them—including in the smallest of backyards.

BIRDING BASICS

If you're new to bird-watching, you'll want to pick up a good bird-identification book. The best of these are organized so you can quickly identify birds by one or more categories: their shapes, colors, markings, habitats, and niches. (While different bird species often live in the same habitat, each does best in a particular niche of that habitat—on the forest floor or high in the treetops, for example.)

Most bird-watchers keep lists of their sightings. If you're providing food at a feeder, your list is bound to grow as your food supply becomes better known to all the different birds in the area. The entire family can have fun adding new birds to the list. You could also keep a more detailed

Summer tanager

notebook in which you record the date, weather conditions, activities, and exact locations of birds you spot in your yard.

WHEN TO WATCH BIRDS

Dawn and dusk—when birds are most active—are the best times of day for bird-watching. Good bird-watching opportunities exist year-round and in almost any location. In the leafless woods and yards of winter, birds are easier to see. When spring arrives, large numbers of birds migrate north, singing loudly to establish their breeding territories and flaunting bright

plumage to attract mates. By midsummer, some birds begin their winter migration, and by the fall, these flocks have swelled with new offspring.

BIRD-WATCHING TIPS AND ETHICS

Remember, as an appreciative and caring audience, your role is to be as unobtrusive as possible while bird-watching. Never flush birds out of hiding or disturb their nesting sites by approaching them too closely. Birds are keenly aware of the presence of humans, so the less visible and audible you are, the more birds you're likely to see. Either situate yourself in a comfortable, stationary spot, or—if you'd rather walk through your property—move in as nonthreatening a way as possible (as carefully and quietly as a cat).

If you're in the company of friends, avoid talking loudly. And when you take a break to go indoors, don't dash—and don't let the door slam behind you. Sudden movements, such as pointing or grabbing for your binoculars, will drive birds away. While you probably won't want to turn your patio table on its side and use it as camouflage, it will help to stay as hidden as possible.

Keep an eye on the weather, too. Strong winds can tire migrating birds, causing them to land in unexpected places. When the weather lightens up, they resume their flight. Low-pressure zones and cold fronts drive migrating birds ahead of them.

To bring an elusive bird into view, try making a "ch-ch-ch-ch-ch-ch" sound; some birds will respond by flying closer and answering with their own chatter. It's important to stop this tactic as soon as you glimpse the bird, however, as this particular sound can cause birds undue stress.

Playing tapes of bird calls has a similar effect, but again, play the tape only briefly; tapes played for long periods of time may disrupt nesting and cause other problems. (For these reasons, playing tapes has been banned in some refuges.)

BIRDS OF A FEATHER

One of the fastest ways to learn about birding is to join one of the many organizations that sponsor outings and tours. Your local library or conservation organizations can put you in touch with a group of birders in your area.

Eastern bluebird

BEGINNING BIRD-WATCHER'S TOOL KIT

Field Guide. Buy an up-to-date field guide to birds. A little practice using it will help you narrow your search when you're trying to identify a bird. If you're a beginner, start with a field guide that covers only the birds in your region.

Binoculars. Binoculars are numbered to indicate their magnification power and their brightness. The 7 in binoculars that are 7 x 40, for example, indicates that the viewed object will be magnified 7 times, while the number 40 represents the diameter (in millimeters) of the front lenses. The wider the front lenses, the brighter the object—and the heavier the binoculars. The binoculars you select should be between 7x and 10x.

Clothing. If you're watching birds during the winter, be sure to wear warm clothing—sitting still on a porch or patio in the cold can be agonizing unless you're dressed properly! To attract hummingbirds during the summer, wear red! A hat will offer protection in any kind of weather.

Spotting Scopes. Best for long-range viewing of nesting birds, feeder birds, or shore birds, spotting scopes are most useful in the 25x to 30x range and come in two eyepiece styles: one aligned with the barrel, and the other elevated at a 45-degree angle.

Pack. For bird-watching expeditions out of your yard, a day pack will keep your hands free while protecting your gear from the elements. A birding vest, with pockets tailored to hold a field guide and binoculars, will also come in handy.

Birdhouses

You may already have a bird feeder, a birdbath, and an abundance of flora to encourage feathered folk to feast and flourish in your garden. Why not beckon the birds to stay awhile and raise a family? Imagine the delight of discovering a tiny pile of delicate eggs, the pleasure of seeing hatched nestlings, and the final excitement of watching the fledglings take flight on their wobbly wings. With a bit of inspiration and planning, you'll soon have your own backyard bird sanctuary.

About 80 species of North American birds are "cavity nesters" who find natural homes in the hollows of decaying trees (now in short supply due to logging practices). But you don't have to transplant a hollowed tree to your backyard—though some people actually have!—to invite their company. Many cavity nesters are easily attracted to conventional birdhouses, or nest houses, including bluebirds, chickadees, nuthatches, wrens, kestrels, and purple martins. Whether you choose to buy or build a house for nesting birds, you'll have the pleasure of sharing their family life while helping to protect and preserve bird populations whose natural habitats are increasingly threatened.

BUYING A BIRDHOUSE

Shopping for a birdhouse can be a lot like choosing your own house plan. A vast array of possible designs awaits you—from miniature barns, log cabins, and hollowed-out gourds to replicas of Frank Lloyd Wright homes. You'll find a wide variety of birdhouses at garden and hardware stores, at gift shops, and in mail-order catalogs.

The first step is to decide what kinds of birds you'd like to have as neighbors. The next is to select a house (or multiple houses) that will be safe and functional for your birds of choice. The dimensions of a birdhouse and the manner in which it's sited are important; each type of bird has its own requirements (see "Birdhouse Specifications" on page 127). The entrance hole, for example, should be large enough to admit the bird, but small enough to keep out unwanted guests. If you're limited to only one house, choose one with an entry hole 1½ inches in diameter; it will accommodate the greatest variety of birds.

Hardy houses made from well-insulated materials will protect birds and their eggs from extreme heat and cold. Wood is always a reliable choice; however, some of the newer composite materials offer comparable quality. You'll also find houses made of glazed ceramic, plastic, and terra-cotta. With the exception of aluminum martin houses, avoid metal birdhouses. Even a wooden house with a metal roof will overheat in direct sun. Also avoid other materials that might be harmful to birds, such as lead-based paint and creosote- or pressure-treated lumber. And keep in mind that although houses with authentic architectural appeal and colorful paint jobs make delightful garden decorations, they're often more fanciful than functional.

To protect the house (and the birds) from rain and to prevent water damage, make sure the front edge of the roof overhangs the entrance hole by at least two inches, and that the sides are nailed to the edges of the floor rather than to its top. Holes or slits in the bottom of the house will allow for proper drainage and help prevent rotting caused by accumulated water. Birdhouses should also have ventilation holes or slits. If your favorite house lacks these, either drill two ⅝-inch-diameter holes or cut a horizontal slit near the top of each side wall.

You'd think that perches on birdhouses would always be desirable features, as they are on feeders. Not true! Cavity-nesting birds don't usually need them, and the only birds that prefer them are house sparrows and European starlings—two species that fall into the "unwanted guest" category.

You'll also want to choose a house that's easy to clean after each nesting. A hinged side or roof (not the bottom) works best, but be sure to keep the hinged section securely closed. Crafty raccoons are persistent predators, and may figure out how to unlatch hook-and-eye fasteners.

BUILDING A BIRDHOUSE

If you'd like to try your hand at building your own birdhouse, your best bet is to begin with a simple project, such as the bluebird house featured on page 128. If you're not quite ready to tackle building a house from scratch, try transforming an ordinary birdhouse into a whimsical work of garden art with a few creative touches of your own. Let your imagination lead the way with mosaics, acrylic paints, or polymer clay.

MOUNTING A BIRDHOUSE

Birds like their homes to feel safe and secure. Many prefer a house mounted on a vertical surface, such as a tree, fence post, or wall. A house placed on a tree or post near a wooded area makes a cozy spot for cavity-nesting birds such as chickadees, titmice, and nuthatches. Mounting the house on a metal garden post makes siting easy, but do follow the siting specifications for the given type of house (see the chart on page 127).

While hanging doesn't offer the stability of a stationary mount, it works well for designs such as hollowed-out gourds, which make great homes for a variety of birds, including house wrens, purple martins, and bluebirds. If you plan to hang your house from a tree, make sure you choose a branch that will provide solid support. To prevent damage to the branch, pad it with fabric or inner-tube rubber where you plan to attach the wire.

Posts vary in style and durability; they can be metal or wooden, and square or round. If you prefer wood, always use either pressure-treated lumber or a rot-resistant wood such as cedar. When mounting a house onto a tree trunk, first attach the house to a batten (a board about twice the height of the house) and then attach the batten to the tree. Do keep in mind that hardware can harm smaller trees. Some "tree-friendly" alternatives include fitting a wire around the trunk and attaching the house securely to the wire, or simply nailing a wooden crosspiece to the back of the house

and situating it firmly among several branches. Just be sure to balance your efforts to protect the trees with wise measures to deter predators.

DETERRING UNWANTED GUESTS

Along with nurturing and protecting feathered friends with food and shelter comes the responsibility for keeping competitors and predators at bay. Sparrows and starlings are the most aggressive competitors. They'll nest almost anywhere, and they begin building their homes earlier in the season than most birds (usually in late winter). The good news is that their nests can usually be cleaned out before your intended tenants arrive to claim their new home. Another way to deter sparrows and starlings is to purchase or make a house with a slotted entrance opening rather than a round hole (see pages 128–129), or simply plug the entrance hole during the winter months. (Remember to unplug the hole in early spring when other birds are ready to begin nesting.)

As nature would have it, eggs and nestlings are vulnerable to the appetites of predators such as cats, raccoons, snakes, and squirrels. Your birds will enjoy a more peaceful home life if you install protective barriers that prevent uninvited guests from visiting them.

A conical metal barrier (or baffle) attached to a post or pole will block squirrels and raccoons from climbing up to the birds' front door. Baffles can be constructed to fit both round and square posts, and should be installed at least five feet above ground level. If you have a hanging birdhouse, be sure to use heavy wire instead of rope; it's harder to climb. For added protection, metal pie pans make great homemade baffles and are easy to install on the wire.

Placing a metal guard around the entrance hole keeps squirrels from chewing their way inside. For protection against raccoons, try framing the entrance with a one-inch-thick block of wood. (Simply drill a hole the same size as the entrance opening through the block of wood and attach it over the entrance opening.) Spreading chicken wire just above the ground beneath the birdhouse considerably compromises a cat's ability to carry out a surprise attack. Bear in mind, however, that one of the most effective ways to deter intruders is to follow closely the recommendations for proper dimensions and siting for your house.

Unfortunately, birdhouses also make attractive home sites for nest-building insects such as wasps and bees. Don't despair. Coating the inside of the house with bar soap or Vaseline can discourage these tiny nesters. If you use an insect spray instead, be sure to choose one that is safe for birds.

CLEANING

Birds don't enjoy coming home to a messy house any more than you do. You'll need to clean out the birdhouse after each nesting and again in early spring. Beware of wasps, and protect your hands with gloves. First remove and discard old nesting materials (a kitchen spatula or paint scraper works well), along with any uninvited tenants such as mice or insects. Then clean the inside of the house with a stiff brush and soapy water. Be sure to rinse thoroughly. Ridding the house of pests and parasites will make it fresh and inviting for the next family. Your newfound friends will appreciate your kind attention to their homes, and the reward will be yours when they return the following year.

Birdhouse Specifications

SPECIES	FLOOR (INCHES)	INTERIOR HEIGHT (INCHES)	ENTRANCE DIAMETER (INCHES)	ENTRANCE ABOVE FLOOR (INCHES)	HEIGHT ABOVE GROUND (FEET)
American Kestrel	8 x 8	12–15	3	9–12	10–30
Ash-Throated Flycatcher	6 x 6	8–10	1½	6–8	8–20
Barn Owl	10 x 8	15–18	6	0–4	12–18
Bewick's Wren	4 x 4	6–8	1¼	4–6	5–10
Bluebird (Eastern, Mountain, Western)	4 x 4	8–12	1½	6–10	3–6
Carolina Wren	4 x 4	6–8	1½	4–6	5–10
Chickadee	4 x 4	9	1⅛	7	4–15
Downy Woodpecker	4 x 4	9	1¼	7	5–15
Finch (House, Purple)	5 x 5	6	2	5–7	8–12
Flicker	7 x 7	16–18	2½	14–16	6–30
Great Crested Flycatcher	6 x 6	8–10	1¾	6–8	8–20
Hairy Woodpecker	6 x 6	12–15	1⅝	9–12	12–20
House Wren	4 x 4	6–8	1–1¼	4–6	4–10
Nuthatch	4 x 4	9	1⅜	7	5–15
Purple Martin	6 x 6	6	2¼	1	10–20
Red-Headed Woodpecker	6 x 6	12	2	9	10–20
Robin	6 x 8	8	2	2	6–15
Screech Owl	8 x 8	12–15	3	9–12	10–30
Titmouse	4 x 4	9	1¼	7	5–15
Wood Duck	12 x 12	22	4	17	10–20

Making a Bluebird House

To foil the English sparrows and starlings that have displaced bluebirds in so many of their natural habitats, this easy-to-make bluebird house has a special, slotted entryway—one which helps prevent invasions from unwanted visitors. You may either build the house with a rot-resistant wood such as cedar and leave it unfinished, or use a standard softwood such as pine and apply an exterior finish.

MATERIALS & TOOLS

- Measuring tape
- Pencil
- Straightedge
- Circular saw or handsaw
- Table saw or ripsaw
- Clamps
- No. 2 Phillips-head screwdriver
- Electric drill with ⅛" bit
- Sandpaper
- No. 6 decking screws, 1¼"
- 3/32 x 1⅜" screw hook

TIPS

- You'll need a 4'-long 1 x 6, and a 6½"-long piece of 1 x 8 to make this project. As you shop for this lumber, remember that a 1 x 6 is ¾" thick and 5½" wide, and a 1 x 8 is ¾" thick and 7½" wide.

- The sides (A), floor (B), door (C), and roof (E) are ripped (cut to make them narrower) from 1 x 6 and 1 x 8 lumber. The easiest way to rip boards is with a table saw, but if you don't own one, you can use a handheld ripsaw. Be sure to clamp the boards securely before ripping.

CUTTING LIST

CODE	DESCRIPTION	QTY.	MATERIAL
A	Sides	2	¾" x 4¾" x 9½"
B	Floor	1	¾" x 4" x 4"
C	Door	1	¾" x 4" x 7¾"
D	Back	1	1 x 6 x 12"
E	Roof	1	¾" x 6½" x 6½"

Instructions

1 From the 1 x 6, measure and cut the following lengths: 17¾", 4", and 7¾". Then rip the 17¾" piece to 4¾" in width, and the 4" and 7¾" pieces to 4" in width. Rip the 6½"-long 1 x 8 to 6¾" in width. If you have access to a table saw, bevel cut one end of this 6½" x 6½" board to 17 degrees. (Don't worry if you can't make this cut.)

2 To cut the two sides (A), first set the 17¾"-long piece flat on your work surface, positioning it vertically. Then measure down 9½" from the upper left-hand corner and mark the long edge at this point. Next, measure up from the bottom right-hand corner, and mark the other long edge at 9½".

3 Join the two 9½" marks by drawing a diagonal line across the face of the board. Then cut along this marked line to create the two sides (A).

4 Place the two sides (A) flat on your work surface, with their short edges facing each other and their long edges facing outward. On each side, mark two pilot-hole positions: one ⅜" up from the short bottom end and 2" in from the longest side, and another 5¼" up from the short bottom end and ⅜" in from the short edge. Using an electric drill and ⅛" bit, predrill pilot holes at these marks.

5 To provide for drainage through the 4" x 4" floor (B), cut off the tip of each corner of this piece. Remove only a small amount of wood as you make these cuts.

6 To fasten the floor (B) to one side (A), position the side on its long edge, and place an edge of the floor against it so that the bottom face of the floor is flush with the bottom end of the side. Insert a 1¼" screw through

the pilot hole to fasten the parts together. Repeat to fasten the other side to the opposite edge of the floor.

7 Fit the 4" x 7¾" door (C) between the sides (A); its outer face should be flush with the sides' front edges and its top end should be 1⅛" below the top front corners of the sides. Fasten the door in place with a 1¼" screw inserted through the pilot hole in each side. Then back the two screws out slightly so the door will swing freely outward from the bottom.

8 Position the box with the door (C) face down. Place the back (D) on top of the sides (A) so that its bottom end hangs over the bottom ends of the sides by 1". Predrill four pilot holes through the back, placing each hole 4" from an end of the back and ⅜" in from a long edge. Then drive four 1¼" screws into the pilot holes.

9 Drill two ⅛" holes in the back (D) for mounting the birdhouse, each ½" in from an end and centered across the back's width.

10 Drill four pilot holes through the 6½"-square roof (E): two holes each ⅞" in from an edge and 1½" down from the bevel-cut end; and two holes, each ⅞" in from an edge and 4½" from the bevel cut end. (If you didn't bevel cut the roof, you may take these measurements from either end.)

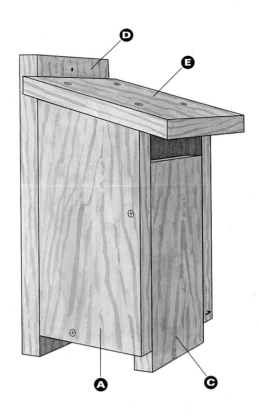

11 Center the roof (E) on top of the angle-cut ends of the sides (A), with a ½" overlap at each edge, and the bevel-cut end of the roof pressed against the front face of the back (D). Secure the roof in place with four 1¼" screws.

12 Insert the screw hook into the front edge of one side (A), ⅝" from the side's bottom end. To prevent the door (C) from opening, turn the screw hook to a horizontal position. When it's time to clean out the birdhouse, turn the screw hook up or down, and pull the bottom edge of the door upward and outward.

Health & History

Imagining your backyard garden as a florist's shop or as a grocery store stocked with fresh produce is easy. Just picture yourself arranging a bouquet of fresh-cut flowers or plucking a sun-warmed tomato from the vine. But what if one corner of your garden were a pharmacy offering free prescriptions for good health? And another boasted a botanical museum—filled with descendants of centuries-old plants? And yet another included a collection of wildflowers and native plants?

While you may not want to learn the fine points of herbal medicine, there's no reason you can't turn to your own backyard for the stimulating scent of lavender or a soothing cup of chamomile tea. And why not bring touches of history and local interest to your yard by setting out a few heirloom and native plants? Wildflowers and native plants provide almost maintenance-free pleasure all season long. Heirloom flowers and vegetables—grown from seed that's been carefully harvested and passed along through the centuries—offer the rich flavors, vivid colors, and perfumed scents that our ancestors enjoyed.

Heirloom Gardening

Any seed holds an almost magical potential, but if it is an heirloom seed, then it also holds a vast store of history. Passed down from generation to generation of gardeners, heirloom seeds provide a rare opportunity to see and taste and smell the world as our ancestors did—long before technology began genetically altering the food and flowers we grow.

HEIRLOOM AND HYBRID PLANTS

Most of the fruits and vegetables offered in our supermarkets' produce sections (and most of the seeds offered by large commercial seed companies) are hybrids. They come from plants that have been genetically engineered to produce fruits and vegetables that ripen uniformly, can be mechanically harvested, have tough skins that will survive shipping, and have a long shelf life.

Heirloom plants, on the other hand, are plants that have been passed (usually by seed) from gardener to gardener for years—sometimes even centuries. Some heirlooms, such as 'Pink Hopi' corn, are natives, but others came to this country as seeds in the pockets of immigrants, who brought their favorite varieties from their homelands.

Hollyhock

One reason these antique plants have endured is that they are open-pollinated, that is, they reproduce from seed and the resultant plants come back true to type. Hybrid plants (the offspring of a cross between two parent varieties that are genetically different) produce seed that either won't grow or that grow into plants that revert back to one of the parent plants rather than remaining true to type.

THE VALUE OF HEIRLOOM PLANTS

In the last several years, interest in heirlooms has blossomed as more and more gardeners discover the rewards of growing purple-skinned carrots and 15-pound cabbages or the same flowers that decorated their grandmothers' backyards. Their appeal is not solely historic. Heirlooms often boast richer flavors and fragrances than hybrids. Because of this, restaurants are beginning to serve dishes that feature heirlooms,

Great blue lobelia

and antique roses and other heirloom flowers are making a comeback.

Many advocates of heirlooms are also worried about the fact that we have lost so many of the food plants that were once available in this country. It's estimated that 75 percent of the native food plants growing when Columbus first set foot on our soil are now gone forever. And today we have only a tiny fraction of the plant varieties cultivated 100 years ago.

The value of diversity in plant varieties isn't just a matter of having a wide range of tomatoes to choose from when we make a dinner salad. Lack of genetic diversity can have serious repercussions. Because most of the potatoes grown in Ireland during the 1840s were of only one variety, a fungus was able to spread and wipe out the entire crop. More than one million people died in the resulting famine.

ACQUIRING AND GROWING HEIRLOOM PLANTS

A network of seed collectors all over the country is now intent on preserving the cultural heritage and diversity of our plants. Probably the largest single resource accessible to enthusiasts is the Seed Savers Exchange, a non-profit organization with its own 170-acre farm and seed bank, in Iowa. More and more of these seed exchanges are springing up across the country (some can be found listed in magazines; many are listed on the Internet).

TOMATOES: **'Yellow Pear,' 'Red Pear,' 'Yellow Perfection,' 'Riesenstraube,' and 'Slava'**

Seed companies specializing in or including heirloom seed in their offerings are also on the rise.

If you'd like to try your hand at growing a few living antiques—perhaps a lobelia that's been gracing gardens since the fifteenth century or a yellow pear tomato—keep in mind that heirloom seeds are sometimes slow to germinate. In fact, some will shoot up even after you've given them up for dead.

SAVING HEIRLOOM SEEDS

After you've enjoyed your heirloom plants' sumptuous flavors or perfumed blossoms, you'll want to save some seed for next year's crop or for a gardening friend. Complete information on saving seeds from different plants is available from many seed exchanges, but the process is usually quite simple.

One trick is to collect seeds only from plants that are isolated from other varieties; the seeds of different varieties will hybridize if the plants are grown too close together. Another is to let the seed grow to maturity, which in many instances means allowing the vegetable or flower to mature long past the time you would normally harvest it. The seeds are then separated from the fruit or vegetable, and if they're moist, are sometimes sun-dried for a brief period of time. Then they're stored in a cool, dry place (often the refrigerator) until the next growing season.

By saving heirloom seeds, you'll become one more link in the valuable chain that helps us protect and preserve some of our most valuable inheritances.

Passalong and Commemorative Plants

Hens and chickens

Peony

As much as we gardeners are a competitive bunch (peeking over the neighbors' fences to see if their tulips will open before ours this spring), we are also a generous group. Folks who truly love plants are happy to spread the wealth; after all, flower beds grow crowded, and who could bear to toss an old friend onto the compost heap?

PASSALONGS

In their book, *Passalong Plants,* Steven Bender and Felder Rushing define passalongs as plants that are easy to propagate yet hard to find commercially. Just as heirloom plants have survived despite the big nurseries' and seed companies' push for hybrids, passa-long plants have also endured, thanks to gardeners with generous hearts (and crowded flower beds). Even plants that are readily available from nurseries can be fun to pass along—just be sure they are easily propagated.

Typically, plants get passed along in the most informal of manners. You express admiration for a certain perennial, and the proud gardener digs up a clump with a few good roots and says, "Here, have some." Or your daylilies need dividing so you offer the extras to your neighbor (who reminds you that she gave them to you in the first place when she thinned her own overgrown clump three years ago). Sometimes local garden clubs hold plant swaps (each person comes with a plant to give away and leaves with a new one). Gardeners interested in preserving and sharing heirloom or other specialty seeds have begun organizing groups, and more and more seed exchanges are taking place in magazines and on the Internet.

These humble plants have much to recommend them. Not only are they easy to propagate from seed, cuttings, or division; they also tend to be self-sufficient. While catalogs from the other side of the country offer all sorts of horticultural temptations, paying close attention to what grows for your

Trumpet vine

neighbors is a golden rule of gardening. If the eighty-year-old woman next door has a peony she remembers playing beside as a child, you know it's a plant with staying power that likes your climate.

In fact, the local climate will influence just which plants are most commonly passed along in your region. Hens and chickens (the succulent you might remember from your grandmother's rock garden); spider flower (a tall, reseeding annual with large, whiskery flower heads); and money plant (a biennial with flat, translucent seedpods that resemble coins) are just three examples of the hundreds of plants that have made their way into countless yards by being passed over the back fence from gardener to gardener.

COMMEMORATIVE PLANTS

Cut flowers have long been used to mark special occasions, but living plants can serve as gifts or memorials that only become more meaningful with the passage of time. Plant a sapling to celebrate your child's birth, and his or her grandchildren may one day swing from its branches. Present newlyweds with a fragrant shrub in June and it will flower for countless anniversaries to come. Helping to tend to a small shrub planted in remembrance of a pet that's passed away can let children express their grief while instilling respect for the natural cycles of life.

Commemorative plants should be easy to care for and long-lived. Daylilies, bearded iris, peonies, and Asiatic lilies are examples of flowering plants that will last for many years (and in some cases multiply) in the right conditions. Weeping cherry or dogwood trees will flower each spring for years to come, while dwarf evergreens will brighten the winter landscape without ever growing too tall.

Special care should be taken when giving a plant as a gift. The recipient's local climate and specific soil and sun conditions should be taken into account. For plants as substantial as a shrub or tree, it is best to ask for personal preferences. Purchase healthy, disease- and insect-free plants, and make sure you include instructions for planting and care.

10 Passalong Plants

- **Cosmos**
  Cosmos bipinnatus

- **Corn poppy**
  Papaver rhoeas

- **Hens and chickens**
  Sempervivum

- **Hollyhock**
  Alcea rosea

- **Honesty**
  Lunaria annua

- **Lamb's-ears**
  Stachys byzantina

- **Larkspur**
  Consolida ajacis

- **Rose campion**
  Lychnis coronaria

- **Spider flower**
  Cleome hassleriana

- **Trumpet vine**
  Campsis radicans

Spider flower

Native Species and Wildflowers

Many gardeners have discovered a series of valuable secrets right before their eyes: Native plants (plants indigenous to the areas in which they grow) thrive in local backyards, attract native wildlife, are relatively pest-free, typically require less water than non-native plants, and boast a beauty all their own.

Native plants are sometimes referred to as wildflowers, but not all wildflowers originated where they now grow. Wildflowers are simply plants that have naturalized (or gone wild); one of their benefits is that they grow easily with little or no care. The only problem is when a non-native wildflower grows too well. Then it can become invasive and threaten native plants and wildlife.

Claret-cup cactus

GARDEN HISTORY

Traditionally, gardens in the United States were (and often still are) recreations of the homeland gardens of the immigrants who settled here. While the plants in these gardens grow well in their countries of origin, they're sometimes not suited to their new homes. The green, manicured lawns so common in the United States, for example, originated in England, where ample rainfall keeps lawns lush. Maintaining lawns as luxurious in the desert regions of the southwestern United States requires massive amounts of water and fertilizer. Enlightened desert gardeners have turned instead to the beauty of native plants such as blue gamma, native buffalo grass, prickly poppy, and claret-cup cactus, to name just a few—all plants that are perfectly suited to their desert environments, both in their growth habits and in their appearance.

FINDING NATIVE PLANTS AND WILDFLOWERS

To locate native plants and wildflowers adapted to your region, contact your local Cooperative Extension Service or a wildflower society. A growing number of nurseries specialize in native plants, and even those that don't will frequently offer a few native species. Botanical gardens are also good sources. When purchasing a native plant, find out where it came from by looking for

Jack-in-the-pulpit

the term "nursery propagated" (not "nursery grown") in the nursery catalog or on the plant label. Buying a nursery-propagated plant ensures that the plant wasn't simply removed from its natural habitat—a practice that endangers plant communities. (In North America, there are hundreds of endangered species, all threatened by reckless collecting.) Many wildflowers are easily propagated from seed, which more and more seed companies are offering, often as a mix of various wildflowers.

One of the best ways to decide which native plants or wildflowers you'd like to try in your garden is to observe what's growing in the wild or along roadsides. Which of these plant combinations pleases your eye? North America is particularly rich in its variety of native plants, and there are countless ones to choose from, whether you live in a desert or tropical environment.

LANDSCAPING

In natural areas, different plant species grow together in a community. These, in turn, create the perfect environment for other types of plants. To emulate this rich harmony in your own garden, plant many individuals of a given species and then blend in at least one other compatible type of plant.

When gardening with native species, it's often more appropriate to enhance the natural lay of your land than it is to force a level surface by creating a flat bed as you might for non-native flowers. If you live in a desert region, you might want to shape the uneven surface of your yard into a creek bed—a desert arroyo—which can serve as a walkway when dry and an irrigation canal for plants when it carries water from a thunderstorm.

If you live in the eastern woodlands and have a perpetually wet spot in your yard, try planting a combination of cinnamon fern, cardinal flower, and bee balm. Then sit back and enjoy the hummingbirds that will seek out the brilliant cardinal flowers.

If your yard is too small for much gardening, plant natives in containers. Ageratum, trumpet honeysuckle, Christmas fern, celandine poppy, and blueberry will all do well in small spaces.

AN INSTANT NATURAL AREA

An easy way to start a wildflower and native plant garden is to stop mowing an area of your yard. Let the grass grow, and it will gradually create an environment for pioneer plants that are planted by birds, small animals, and the wind. Over time, the new plants will shade out the grass. To speed the process along, you can pull the grass and introduce more wildflowers and native plants. But remember, these gardens will never be perfectly landscaped, tidy beds. The emphasis here is on "wild."

Bitterweed

The Healing Garden

Lavender

St. John's wort

In every culture, throughout the centuries, the knowledge of herbal remedies has been recorded and passed down by healers and herb gatherers. Native Americans, for example, honored certain indigenous plants as valued remedies for common complaints, and early immigrants to the New World cultivated non-native healing plants from the carefully preserved seeds they brought with them. Today, many active ingredients in pharmaceutical preparations are plant-based, and medicinal uses for new plants are still being discovered.

Even in the tiniest suburban backyard, a medicinal garden can add a sense of the mystery and magic of traditional healing gardens of the past. One caution, however: Plants are powerful. Never ingest one unless you know exactly what it is and exactly what effects it will have! If you're interested in growing and using medicinal herbs, a variety of helpful books is available.

MEDICINE WHEEL DESIGN

One of the most common medicinal garden designs is the traditional medicine wheel, in which herbs are planted in wedges around a center-point. If you'd like to try your hand at designing a wheel of your own, you may find the following suggestions helpful:

Plant the center of the wheel with the lovely *Echinacea* (or purple cone-flower), which is believed to have cleansing and purifying qualities. Then surround the circle with a hedge of lavender, which will add its uplifting fragrance, as well as headache-soothing blossoms. Try planting a few rosemary shrubs with the lavender; they're reputed to dispel melancholy.

A wedge of the apple-scented, daisylike flowers of chamomile and a spot of lemon balm will both yield calming teas. Peppermint will aid digestion, and sage—when it's transformed into a gargle—will soothe sore throats.

Yarrow is valued for its antiseptic and wound-healing qualities; and bee balm, with its scarlet blossoms, can relieve nausea. Calendula will soothe irritated skin, and St. John's wort will calm the nerves.

WILD MEDICINAL GARDEN

If your gardening style is informal, just set aside a wild area of your yard, mow a path through the center, and wait to see what herbal allies will emerge. Herbs as common as dandelion, chicory, curly dock, the bold burdock with its deep root, and the downy-leafed mullein with its tall stalks of golden flowers are all powerful plant remedies. Early in spring, notice the blue violets (which are high in vitamin C) and the creeping, star-like flowers of chickweed. Plantain leaves, bright red clover blossoms,

Purple coneflower

purslane, self heal, wild strawberry, and blessed thistle are all medicinal herbs. If you take along a good reference book to help you identify these common allies and companionable healers, each excursion into the wild spaces of your backyard can become an adventure of discovery and joy.

ONE-OF-A-KIND MEDICINAL GARDENS

The only real limits to the way in which you design a medicinal herb garden should be the amount of space you have, the time available to you for garden care

Rosemary

and maintenance—and a healthy concern for safety.

People who believe that herbs release their healing properties through their colors and scents will often design medicinal gardens for these qualities only. Other gardens have plants selected for their specific medicinal properties. The thousands of herbs known for their healing capacities will provide you with a myriad possibilities for garden designs. And researching the folk wisdom and lore surrounding each of these plants will add another dimension of interest to a wonderful backyard project.

A Medicinal Garden Plan

The plants in this small medicinal garden are among the hundreds that herbalists have recommended through the centuries for complaints ranging from fatigue to headaches and indigestion. (You'll find descriptions of these herbs' uses on page 145.) In recent years, as natural health-care methods have become increasingly popular, easy-to-grow medicinal herbs are appearing in more and more gardens. Even if you don't want to relax with a cup of home-grown lemon balm tea or soothe a sore throat with a sage-tea gargle, you'll find that the plants' flowers and foliage make lovely additions to any garden bed.

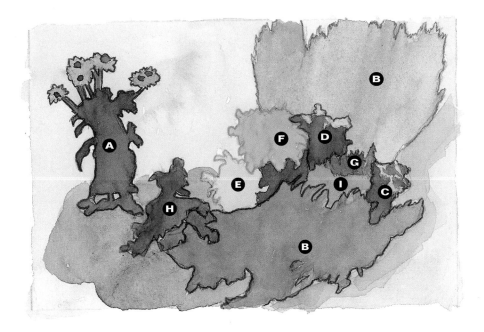

A PURPLE CONEFLOWER
Echinacea purpurea

Hardiness zones 3–9

2 to 4 feet tall

Deep purple to rose to white, drooping petals, with dark brown conical centers midsummer to early fall; lance-shaped, dark green leaves; well-drained loam; full sun to light shade

B ROSEMARY
Rosmarinus

Hardiness zones 8–10

6 inches to 7 feet tall

Tiny pale blue, pink, or lavender flowers mid-spring to early summer; fragrant, needlelike leaves used in cooking; well-drained, alkaline soil; full sun

C ROMAN CHAMOMILE
Chamaemelum nobile

Hardiness zones 6–9

1 to 6 inches tall

Small, white, daisylike flowers with golden centers late spring to early fall; bright green ferny foliage; dry, well-drained soil; full sun to light shade

D CALENDULA
Calendula officinalis

Annual

12 to 24 inches tall

Orange, yellow, or cream, daisylike flowers all summer; oval, deep green leaves; poor to average, well-drained soil; full sun

E GOLDEN SAGE
Salvia officinalis 'Aurea'

Hardiness zones 4–8

1 to 2 feet tall

Small spikes of lavender blue flowers in early summer; fragrant, variegated yellow and green leaves used in cooking; well-drained soil; full sun

F BASIL
Ocimum basilicum

Annual

1 to 2 feet tall

Small, white, tubular flowers midsummer to frost; fragrant, green or purple leaves used in cooking; rich, moist, well-drained soil; full sun

G LAVENDER
Lavandula angustifolia

Hardiness zones 5–10

1 to 4 feet tall

Fragrant, lavender flower spikes late spring to summer; fragrant, woolly, gray-green foliage; well-drained soil; full sun

H LEMON BALM
Melissa officinalis

Hardiness zones 3–7

2 to 4 feet tall

Spikes of yellow or white, tubular flowers in summer; fragrant, wrinkled, light green leaves; well-drained soil; full sun

I PARSLEY
Petroselinum crispum

Annual

up to 32 inches tall

Crinkled bright green to dark green leaves used in cooking; fertile, moist, well-drained soil; full sun

Making Tinctures and Decoctions

In order to render herbs useful as medicinals, various plant parts are included in tinctures, decoctions, infusions, syrups, salves, and poultices. The method of preparation depends on the plant, the part used, and the results sought.

Two recipes are provided here: one for a tincture and one for a decoction. A tincture is a water- or alcohol-based solution that contains an extraction of the essential active ingredients of the plant or plants. Alcohol-based tinctures are usually mixed in a ratio of one part finely-cut herb to five parts 60- to 70-proof brandy, vodka, or gin. A decoction is made by simmering plant parts (often roots or seeds) in water.

Echinacea Tincture

Many health-food stores carry versions of this simple tincture, which has become very popular as a method for battling viruses. Echinacea is also thought to help promote proper digestion and cleanse the blood.

MATERIALS & TOOLS

- Trowel
- Sharp knife
- ½ cup (or 4 ounces by volume) of clean and finely chopped echinacea (*Echinacea purpurea*) rhizome or root
- 1 pint of brandy, vodka, or gin
- 1 quart glass jar with lid
- Dark glass storage bottles with eyedropper lids
- Cheesecloth
- Sieve
- Mixing bowl
- Labels

TIPS

- No matter what herbal preparation you're making, gather your herbs on a sunny morning, after the dew has dried. Fresh herbs usually yield the most vital and effective remedies, but if you don't have access to any, purchase dried herbs at a health-food store.
- Dark glass bottles with dropper lids are available at many health-food stores.
- A safe dosage for this tincture is 15 to 20 drops diluted in water or orange juice, taken three times daily.

INSTRUCTIONS

1 Echinacea is a perennial. Harvest the roots and rhizomes during the autumn, when the flowers and leaves have died back, or in the spring, before the plant begins to grow again. Dig up the roots carefully, removing only as much as you need for your tincture and leaving plenty of undisturbed roots for the next growing season.

2 Clean the root thoroughly under cold running water. Then chop it finely.

3 Place ½ cup of chopped root in a clean glass jar. Add one pint of brandy, gin, or vodka, and cover the jar tightly.

4 Place the sealed jar in a cabinet or dark corner for two weeks, shaking well at least once a day.

5 After two weeks, line a sieve with several layers of cheesecloth, and place the sieve over a mixing bowl. Pour the solution through the sieve, and then pour the strained tincture into dark glass dropper-top bottles.

6 Label each bottle with the tincture name and preparation date, and store the bottles in a cool, dark place. Because the alcohol acts as a preservative, the tinctures will keep for up to two years.

Dandelion Decoction

The common dandelion (*Taraxacum officinale*) is a traditional favorite in many folk remedies for aiding digestion. The medicinal part used in this decoction is the long taproot.

MATERIALS & TOOLS

- Trowel
- Sharp knife
- Enamel or glass saucepan
- Filtered water
- ½ cup of clean, chopped dandelion roots
- Cheesecloth or muslin
- Sieve
- Mixing bowl
- Dark glass jars for storage

TIPS

- Decoctions don't stay fresh for very long, so make only what you'll drink in a few days' time.
- Take one tablespoon of this decoction three times daily. (If you suffer from persistent stomach ailments or from gallstones, do not use the decoction at all; consult your physician instead.)

INSTRUCTIONS

1 Dig the dandelion roots in the fall, after the plants flower, or use whole plants in early spring.

2 Clean the roots thoroughly and then slice them into thin rounds.

3 Place the rounds in a saucepan, and add two pints of filtered water.

4 Bring the water to a boil, turn down the heat, and simmer gently until the liquid has been reduced to one pint.

5 Allow the mixture to cool. Line a sieve with several layers of cheesecloth and place the sieve over a mixing bowl. Pour the decoction through the cheesecloth.

6 Store the strained decoction in a dark glass jar, and keep the jar sealed and refrigerated between uses. Decoctions will stay fresh for only a few days.

Making an Herbal Foot Bath

TIPS

- Any of the following herbs may be used in an herbal footbath: basil (invigorates and deodorizes); bay (relieves aching); bergamot (invigorates and relieves itching); chamomile (soothes irritated skin); horsetail (refreshes); hyssop (relaxes and relieves stiffness); lavender (invigorates and refreshes); lemon balm (invigorates and refreshes); lovage (deodorizes); marjoram (soothes aches); meadowsweet (relaxes); mugwort (eases fatigue and restores flexibility); peppermint (refreshes); rosemary (relieves aching); sage (soothes); thyme (cleanses).

- Decoctions may be stored in the refrigerator for a few days, but they're most effective when fresh.

- Fresh herbs are always more potent than dried ones, but if your garden isn't home to any of the herbs suggested above, visit your local health-food store and purchase dried ones instead.

MATERIALS & TOOLS

- ½ cup of fresh herbs or ¼ cup of dried herbs
- 6 cups of water
- Large enamel or stainless steel saucepan
- Sieve
- Cheesecloth
- Large glass or stainless steel mixing bowl
- 5 teaspoons of sea salt
- Mixing spoon
- Large bowl or small foot tub

W hether you've been turning the soil in a garden bed or digging holes for your new apple trees, an hour or two of active gardening can be a physical challenge, especially to your feet. Before you start your day's gardening, brew the reward—the herbal decoction described here! Then, when your backyard chores are finished, pour yourself a tall glass of iced tea, find a comfortable chair, and pamper your aching toes and soles by soaking them in a small tub filled with the warm herbal solution of your choice.

Caution: If you tend toward skin allergies, by all means make an herbal decoction for a friend who isn't, but don't use herbal decoctions yourself, as you may have an unexpected reaction.

Instructions

1 Place the herbs and water in the saucepan and bring the water to a boil.

2 Lower the heat, cover, and simmer for 30 minutes.

3 Line a sieve with two or three layers of cheesecloth, and place the sieve over a large bowl.

4 Pour the decoction into the lined sieve, and retain the strained liquid in the bowl.

5 Add the sea salt to the hot liquid, and stir to dissolve.

6 To make the foot-bath solution, pour hot water into a foot bath and then add one cup of the decoction.

7 Soak your feet in the bath for at least ten minutes. (Make sure you're resting in a comfortable chair as you do this.)

8 When you're finished, dry your feet well with a warm, fluffy towel.

Common Medicinal Plants

MEDICINAL PLANT	MEDICINAL PARTS	MEDICINAL USES
Basil *Ocimum basilicum*	*leaves*	tea taken internally to improve digestion and lower fever
Calendula *Calendula officinalis*	*flowers*	tincture applied externally to soothe skin problems; tea taken internally to soothe stomach inflammation
Chamomile *Chamaemelum nobile*	*flowers*	tea taken internally to aid digestion and improve appetite, and as a mild sedative
Lavender *Lavandula angustifolia*	*flowers*	essential oil used externally in baths as an aromatic aid for depression, fatigue, and headaches. Do not ingest essential oil.
Lemon balm *Melissa officinalis*	*leaves*	tea and tincture taken internally to relieve stress, insomnia, and indigestion
Mullein *Verbascum thapsus*	*leaves and flowering tops*	tea taken internally to relieve congestion
Parsley *Petroselinum crispum*	*leaves*	tea taken internally to relieve indigestion and congestion
Peppermint *Mentha piperita*	*leaves*	tea taken internally as an aid to digestion, to relieve headaches, and to reduce symptoms of stress. Do not give tea to infants.
Purple coneflower *Echinacea purpurea*	*roots*	tincture taken internally as an antiviral; should not be ingested by those with autoimmune illnesses or other progressive diseases
Rosemary *Rosmarinus officinalis*	*leaves*	tea or tincture taken internally to relieve headaches and as an anti-oxidant. Do not ingest essential oil.
Sage *Salvia officinalis*	*leaves*	tea taken internally to relieve symptoms of menopause, and as a gargle to alleviate sore throats. Do not use when nursing or running a fever.
Thyme *Thymus vulgaris*	*leaves and flowering tops*	tea taken internally to relieve sore throats, indigestion, headaches, and congestion
Yarrow *Achillea millefolium*	*flowering tops*	tea taken internally to aid digestion; tea applied externally to stop minor bleeding. (Use only on minor scratches.) May increase sensitivity to sunlight.

Aromas & Flavors

A backyard should certainly offer visual delights and provide a sanctuary for quiet relaxation, but what about a yard that also yields a feast of fragrance and flavors? With just a little planning and care, your own backyard can become a private Eden of tantalizing herbs, edible flowers, and homegrown fruit.

Imagine the path from your back door carpeted with aromatic herbs spilling out from between paving stones. Imagine a yard brimming with scented flowers and herbs you'll harvest, dry, and share with friends while your garden sleeps beneath next winter's snow. Or perhaps you'll grow aromatics in a window box, so you can enjoy their fragrance or snip a sprig for dinner simply by opening a window. Plant edible flowers and turn even the simplest meals into something lovely. Start a miniature apple orchard, and in just a few years, you'll be enjoying homemade apple butter and golden-crusted apple pies.

You don't need a ten-acre homestead to realize these dreams. Even the smallest backyard can be lovingly coaxed and tended into a garden that awakens the senses with wonderful aromas and flavorful food.

Planting an Aromatic Pathway

A fieldstone or flagstone path or patio makes a striking design element for any backyard, but keeping the crevices between those stones weed free is time-consuming, back-breaking work. Cut weeding tasks to a minimum and create a fragrant carpet for your feet by planting hardy aromatic herbs between the pavers. The plants will soften the visual effect of the stone path or patio by tying it in with the rest of the landscape and will release their enticing aromas whenever you step on them. Most herbs can grow in dry, unfertile soil, and many varieties stand up to foot traffic remarkably well.

MATERIALS & TOOLS

- Asparagus fork or narrow trowel
- Hardy creeping herbs (see list)
- Water source
- Trowel or gardening spade
- Water-absorbing polymer crystals (available at gardening centers)
- Wheelbarrow or large bucket
- Topsoil
- Compost

TIPS

- Are the materials in your patio or path set too close to accommodate plants? Remove a few of the pavers and plant aromatics in the spaces left behind.
- The gravel bed beneath most stone paths and patios encourages moisture to drain from plant roots quickly, so water new plants deeply and frequently.

Instructions

1 Water all your plants while they're still in their pots. If you aren't planting in the early evening or on an overcast day, set potted plants in the shade until you're ready to transplant them.

2 Use a narrow trowel or asparagus fork to pull up all grass and weeds from between the stones. Make sure you remove the entire root of each weed.

3 Remove any gravel or sand from between the stones. Dig a hole slightly wider and deeper than the root system of the first plant you plan to put in.

4 Sprinkle a small amount of water-absorbing polymer crystals in the bottom of the hole. Mix the topsoil and compost together and add some of this mixture on top of the water-absorbing granules.

5 Set the plant into the hole, making sure its roots are able to spread out without bending or breaking.

6 Add more of the soil-compost mix to fill in around the plant. Press the soil gently to eliminate any air pockets.

7 Repeat steps 2 through 6 until the entire area is planted; leave at least 8 to 12 inches between each plant.

8 Water thoroughly and mulch with a 1"-thick layer of straw, pine needles, or shredded leaves. (The mulch may be removed after the plants are established.)

9 Water new plants frequently and avoid heavy foot traffic until the plants are well established.

10 Aromatic Herbs to Plant Between Pavings

- **Calamint**
  Acinos

- **Chamomile**
  Chamaemelum noblis 'Treneague'

- **Corsican mint**
  Mentha requienii

- **Miniature thrift**
  Armeria juniperifolia

- **Mother-of-thyme**
  Thymus serpyllum

- **Pennyroyal**
  Mentha pulegium

- **Pink chintz**
  Thymus serpyllum 'Pink Chintz'

- **Rock cress**
  Arabis blepharophylla

- **Woolly thyme**
  Thymus pseudolanuginosus

- **Winter savory**
  Satureja montana

Harvesting and Drying Aromatics

D on't spend the winter months pining for the aromas of summer.
Capture the essence of your garden with a holiday potpourri
made from the fragrant lavender or roses you tended so lovingly
back in June. Many fragrant plants retain their scents well after drying.
Some of the more popular categories of scents include citrus (lemon verbena), spicy (star anise), floral (scented geranium), and fresh (lavender).

Winters are also easier to bear with a pantry stocked with culinary and
medicinal herbs. Imagine, for example, sipping a hot, hearty sage-flavored
soup as snow blankets your summer herb garden. The tradition of drying
herbs is thousands of years old and expresses our inseparable connection to
the plant world.

HARVESTING

Gathering aromatics should be a
relaxing, sensory pleasure rather than
a chore. Let the fragrance of the
sun-warmed plants wash over you;
abandon gardening gloves (except,
perhaps, for roses) and let aromatic
oils scent your hands as you work.
The best time of day to collect plants
is on a sunny morning after the dew
has dried and the sun has heated the

plant's volatile oils. Picking plants when they're still wet encourages mold to grow on them, so go ahead and have that extra cup of tea instead. Try to avoid harvesting in the hot afternoon sun, as flower blooms will wilt.

Select plants that are free of insect damage, disease, and discoloration. Pass up plants exposed to pesticides, especially herbs that you intend to use for culinary purposes. If you'll be gathering plants beyond your yard and out in the wild, collect only a small number of any particular plant. Educate yourself as to which plants in your area are poisonous or endangered—leave these untouched—and remember that plants growing along roadsides may be contaminated with toxins.

To collect plants, you'll need pruning shears and a basket. Pruning shears cut plant stems cleanly, and help prevent the bruising and twisting that occur when stems are broken by hand. The basket allows plants to rest loosely in an upright position, so that blooms and leaves aren't crushed by the weight of other plants. It also allows air to circulate among the stems.

When harvesting flowers, cut the stems extra long, as some plants shrink to half their original size by the time they've dried. Most herbs will be at the peak of their flavor if they're gathered just before they bloom. Either hose herbs down gently with water the night before you gather them, or rinse them after picking, and then blot away any moisture. For best results, prepare plants for drying immediately after harvesting.

THE BASICS OF DRYING

To dry properly, plants need circulating air (preferably warm, dry air) and a darkened room, such as an attic, shed, or garage free of car fumes. In a damp, still room, mold will grow on the plants. Sunlight robs petals of their colors and some herbs of their flavors. Drying times range from a few hours to ten weeks, depending on the amount of moisture in the plant and the drying method used. Six days is usually adequate for drying most herbs, as long as the humidity is low and the temperature is between 70°F and 90°F (21°C and 32°C). If herbs are dried much longer, they may lose their flavors.

HANGING

Hanging is the simplest way to dry aromatics and herbs, and it allows them to dry in the most natural position. Just secure several stems of one type of plant together with a rubber band, and then hang the bunch upside down by attaching it to a nail or rope with a paper clip opened to an S-shape or with a clothespin. (Avoid tying the bundles with string; stems shrink as they dry, and unless you retighten the string regularly, the stems will slip out.) To dry large quantities in this manner, mount a length of lightweight chain from one side of your drying room to the other, and hook the paper clips into its links. This will keep the bunches evenly separated. Blooms and leaves are dry when they feel papery and rigid.

SCREEN DRYING

Screen drying is suitable for fragile stems, large flower heads, or loose petals. Window screens work well. Just raise them off the floor or ground by setting them on bricks so that air can circulate around them. Making a screen is easy. Build or buy a wooden frame and staple a piece of hardware cloth across its top. When screen drying, you need to turn your materials every day or two to prevent curling. For large flower blossoms, punch a hole in the screen, remove leaves from the stem, and stick the stem down through the screen, allowing the head to remain flared open against the screen's flat surface. If you're drying loose petals, turn them once every few days.

OVEN DRYING

For flowers with many petals, preheat an oven to 175°F (80°C) and place the flowers—still attached to their stems—directly on the oven racks. To maintain the flavor of culinary herbs, make sure the oven temperature never exceeds 150°F (65°C). Leave the oven door cracked open, and remove the items before they're completely dry. This drying method can take anywhere from three to ten hours, depending on the moisture content of the flowers. After removing the flowers from the oven, place them on a rack or screen to complete the drying process.

PRESSING

To press, you simply place your plant between sheets of newspaper, wax paper, or blotting paper; set the sheets on a hard surface; and weigh them down with several heavy books. In two to four weeks, carefully uncover the plant. The paper will have absorbed the plant's moisture, leaving you a delicate whisper of a plant.

DEHYDRATOR DRYING

For perfect drying, the electric dehydrator is unmatched. These energy-efficient devices circulate heated air evenly, usually through stacked trays, and are particularly useful for drying flowers with numerous petals, such as rose buds. Available through mail-order suppliers and some hardware stores, they're well worth their cost, especially if you'd also like to dry fruits and vegetables.

STORING DRIED PLANTS

Store dried herbs and other aromatics out of the sun, in pottery or darkened glass containers with airtight lids. (Paper bags and plastic containers can leach away desirable oils.) In general, properly dried and stored herbs will keep for 12 to 18 months.

To create a fragrant potpourri, simply blend a mixture of fragrant dried naturals, and add a fixative such as orris root or cellulose fibers—both available from health-food stores—to extend the life of the fragrance. When the aroma begins to fade, leave the mixture in a humid room, where the moisture will release more fragrance.

Golden thyme

Lavender

Golden sage

Drying Aromatics

AROMATIC PLANT	HARVESTING METHOD	DRYING METHODS
Basil *Ocimum basilicum*	harvest stems with leaves before plant blooms	screen drying (turn plant frequently), hanging in small bunches; leaves will shrink 50%
Bee balm *Monarda didyma*	harvest stems with blooms and leaves just as flowers open	hang in small bunches; leaves will shrink 50%
Chamomile *Chamaemelum nobile*	harvest flowers when fully opened; pick leaves at any time	screen drying, hanging, pressing, or upright in a vase
Lavender *Lavandula angustifolia*	harvest spikes at full bloom	screen drying, hanging, pressing, or upright in a vase
Lemon balm *Melissa officinalis*	harvest stems with leaves at any time	screen drying, hanging in small bunches, pressing; leaves will shrink 60%
Lemon verbena *Aloysia triphylla*	harvest blooms when just beginning to open; pick leaves at any time	screen drying, hanging in small bunches, pressing
Rose *Rosa*	harvest when buds are tight or slightly opened	screen drying or pressing (petals), oven (whole flower), or dehydrator
Rosemary *Rosmarinus officinalis*	pick leaves at any time but preferably during flowering	screen drying (small sprigs), hanging (long stems), pressing
Sage *Salvia officinalis*	harvest blooms at their peak; pick leaves at any time	screen drying, hanging, pressing; plant retains 75% of fragrance
Thyme *Thymus*	harvest stems with leaves before plant blooms for best flavor	screen drying, hanging in small buches, pressing; leaves retain much of their fragrance

An Aromatic Window Box Plan

Throw open your window and let the clean, fresh scent of aromatics into your home. Reach out and snip a few stems of thyme to flavor a stew or some fragrant lavender to add to your bath. A window box is the perfect place for a miniature aromatic garden.

Just be sure to situate the box so it receives at least six hours of sun each day. Keep the plants well watered (soil dries out more quickly in containers than in the ground); occasional harvesting should keep them from becoming leggy or overrunning the box.

A ROMAN CHAMOMILE
Chamaemelum nobile

Hardiness zones 6–9

1 to 6 inches tall

Small, white, daisy-like flowers with golden centers late spring to early fall; bright green, ferny foliage; dry, well-drained soil; full sun to light shade; leaves release apple scent when crushed

B SWEET ALYSSUM
Lobularia

Annual

4 to 12 inches tall

Tiny, fragrant, white, pink, or purple flowers from late spring to frost; narrow, lance-shaped, light to mid-green leaves; well-drained soil; full sun to partial shade; flowers release a refreshing honey-like scent

C LAVENDER
Lavandula angustifolia 'Munstead'

Hardiness zones 5–10

up to 18 inches tall

Whorls of fragrant blue-purple, flowers atop long stems in mid to late summer; linear, gray-green foliage; well-drained to dry soil; full sun; flowers release fresh, clean scent

D HELIOTROPE
Heliotropium

Hardiness zones 10–11

up to 18 inches (in a container)

Large clusters of tiny, sweetly scented, deep purple to white flowers in summer; oval to lance-shaped mid- to dark green leaves; well-drained, fertile soil; full sun to partial shade; flowers release a sweet vanilla scent

E ROSEMARY
Rosmarinus officinalis
'Miss Jessopp's Upright'

Hardiness zones 8–10

up to 5 feet tall (if grown outdoors in zones 8–10)

Tiny, pale blue, tubular flowers from midspring to early summer; fragrant, needlelike leaves used in cooking; well-drained, alkaline soil; full sun; buy small plant for window box (may be over-wintered inside in pot on sunny windowsill)

F THYME
Thymus

Hardiness zones 3–9

2 to 18 inches tall

Small clusters of pink, purple, or white flowers in summer; tiny, aromatic leaves used in cooking; well-drained, alkaline soil; full sun; fresh, pungent scent

Edible Flowers

Noshing on flowers may seem trendy, but it's actually an ancient culinary tradition. Flowers have been valued as attractive, flavorful ingredients since before Roman times. Today, flowers are making a comeback as food and can be found snuggled up next to lettuce in restaurant salads and alongside the produce in gourmet grocery stores. Many flowers you may be growing in your backyard are edible (daylilies, Johnny-jump-ups, roses,

pansies, and hollyhocks are just a few). While some are quite bland and valued more for their color than their taste, others are sweet, spicy, or even peppery. Sometimes the taste of a flower varies, depending on both the variety and where and how the plant was grown.

Flower garnishes lend an elegant, festive touch to any meal, but the blooms can do more than sit prettily on top of food. Next time you plan to serve grilled meat or seafood, try

blending a colorful confetti of chopped nasturtium petals with butter to make a delicious spread. In rice dishes, calendula petals make a great substitute for costly saffron. Both lavender and rose are subtle flavor additives for cookie and ice cream recipes. Daylily buds may be stir fried or dipped in batter and deep fried. Raw daylily buds are tasty, especially when they're stuffed with nuts and cream cheese. And don't forget flowers in drinks. Freeze them in ice cubes or float them in the top of a punch bowl to turn any occasion into a party. Candied flowers (brush the petals with egg whites mixed with a little water and then sprinkle on granulated sugar) look lovely on cakes and cookies.

HARVESTING FLOWERS

Harvest flowers early in the morning. Select only blooms that are free of insect damage and disease. Placing the blossoms between damp paper towels in a plastic bag and refrigerating the bag will help keep the flowers fresh for several days, but flowers taste and look best when they're used the day they're picked. Wash harvested flowers in lukewarm water, checking carefully for bugs. Just before you use the blossoms, plunge them quickly into ice water to revive them.

FLOWER SAFETY

Although some flowers are culinary delights, others are downright dangerous to eat, so don't dash outdoors and pop the first flower you see into your mouth. While many flowers are perfectly safe and even nutritious (violets are high in vitamin C and beta-carotene), you do want to take some common sense precautions when eating flowers.

Eat only flowers that you are certain are safe; don't assume flowers are safe just because they're served with food: Even restaurants have made the mistake of serving toxic blossoms.

People with asthma or allergies should not eat flowers. Blossoms from florists, gardening centers, or home gardens that use pesticides aren't safe for consumption, and neither are flowers that grow along roadsides.

Only the petals of most flowers are edible; remove the pistils and stamens before tasting or serving the rest of the blossom. And start with only small amounts of any new flower; eating too much may upset your stomach. If you'd like to cultivate your own crop of edibles, start them from seed and grow them organically. A kitchen window box or container on the patio might be a convenient spot for your first foray into edible flower gardening.

THE FLAVORS OF FLOWERS

Some flowers are fairly bland and contribute mainly color and texture to food while others add a distinct flavor. Tastes are described for the flowers shown below, clockwise, from top left.

Stock *Matthiola incana*	bland, use as garnish
Calendula *Calendula officinalis*	peppery
Bachelor's-button *Centaurea cyanus*	bland, use as a garnish
Snapdragon *Antirrhinum majus*	slightly sweet
Scented geranium *Pelargonium*	flavor depends on variety
Nasturtium *Tropaeolum majus*	spicy, peppery, somewhat like watercress
Pansy *Viola x Wittrockiana*	somewhat like lettuce
Johnny-jump-up *Viola tricolor*	mild wintergreen
Hollyhock *Alcea rosea*	somewhat like lettuce

Miniature Backyard Orchards

When pristine, shiny, red and green apples are so easy to purchase, why should home gardeners consider planting orchards? The answer is simple. The best-tasting apples—and hundreds of varieties exist—are often excluded from produce bins simply because their skins aren't flaming red or flawless green and because they can't be stored for months on end. Selecting and growing your own varieties will introduce you to an entirely new world of apple flavors.

If you thought you couldn't grow apples because you didn't have the space, you'll be delighted by today's mini-dwarf (or miniature) trees, which can be set as close as six feet apart and which rarely exceed six to eight feet in height. These tiny versions of standard-sized trees bear full-sized fruit—at a height that makes harvesting and maintenance a breeze. Just imagine stepping out your back door next spring to a low-floating cloud of delicate, fragrant blossoms.

PREPARATIONS

As you select a site for your miniature orchard, keep in mind that apple trees do best on gentle, sunny, south-facing slopes, where cold air drains down and away from them. Avoid low-lying and shaded areas. Also make sure not to plant within ten feet of sidewalks or

buried water, sewer, or electrical lines.

Although apple trees will grow in a fairly wide range of soil types, they do require a well-drained site and won't survive in heavy clays. Loosen soil with a moderate clay content by adding peat, sand, and plenty of composted organic material. Test the soil first and add amendments as necessary, well in advance of planting.

SELECTING APPLE VARIETIES

The apple trees sold today consist of two parts that are grafted together: An upper portion known as the *scion* (which eventually branches out and bears fruit) and the lower portion— or *rootstock*—which controls the size of the tree. The scion determines the variety of apple that the tree will produce.

Because most apple trees require cross-pollination in order to bear fruit, you must plant at least two different varieties in close proximity to each other. (Make sure that the two varieties you select will blossom at the same time.) A few varieties produce sterile pollen, and so cannot be used as pollinizers; by all means include these in your orchard, but make sure you plant at least two pollinizing varieties as well. Before making your final selections, ask your Cooperative Extension Service or nursery for advice regarding the best varieties for your growing area. Bees transfer pollen from one tree to another, so avoid

using any garden pesticides when your trees are blooming.

PLANTING APPLE TREES

Apple trees are sold in three different ways: Bare-rooted (without soil around their roots), in containers, or with balled roots (the roots and soil are wrapped in burlap). Soak the roots of bare-rooted trees for several hours just before planting.

Remove all sod and weeds from the planting site. Next, dig a hole for each tree, spacing the holes six feet apart and making each one twice as wide as the extended tree roots. If the trees are bare-rooted, make a small, conical mound of soil in the hole—one high enough to hold the tree's graft union about two inches above ground level. Then spread the roots down and around the mound and add topsoil

(don't add fertilizer) until the hole is two-thirds full. Pack the soil firmly, water the tree well, and finish filling the hole with soil. Don't leave a depression around the trunk; water that freezes around the trunk will kill the tree. Water again when you're finished, lifting the tree up and down slightly to settle the soil around the roots. You'll also need to cut the tree back; the nursery that provides your trees should also provide planting and pruning instructions.

If your trees arrive with burlap-wrapped balls of soil around their roots, untie and discard the rope that fastens the burlap to the trunk. Set the root ball in the hole with the burlap loosely around it (no interior mound of soil is necessary), and fill the hole as before. The burlap will gradually disintegrate. Plant trees purchased in containers in the same way, but remove them from the containers first, and follow the nursery's instructions regarding root pruning.

EARLY CARE

Remove any tags, so they won't strangle the trees as they grow. Protect the tender trunks by surrounding each one with a tree wrap or guard, both available at nurseries. To prevent the injuries that result when the trunks absorb too much heat during the winter, paint the trunks with a water-soluble white latex paint diluted with water in a 1:1 ratio.

The rootstocks of miniature apple trees are weak, so you'll need to use permanent stakes. Set each stake about three inches from the tree, and tie it to the trunk. Check the ties frequently and loosen them as necessary to prevent strangling.

Water the newly planted trees once every week when the weather is dry. Water until the soil is moist to a depth of 12 to 18 inches. After their first growing season, the trees won't require much watering unless your region is suffering from drought.

PRUNING

The art of pruning apple trees is one that requires some study, but most nurseries provide instructional brochures with the trees they sell, and your local Cooperative Extension Service can also give excellent pruning advice. The primary goal of pruning is to guide the tree's growth. Each main trunk should have a single upright limb (or leader) at its top, and a series of sturdy, radiating branches known as laterals, which extend out from the trunk in different compass directions, about four to six inches apart on the trunk.

MAINTENANCE

Cultivate the soil each spring, removing all grass and weeds in a three-foot diameter circle around each tree. Cover the soil with several inches of mulch during the summer (don't let the mulch touch the trunks), and remove the mulch during the winter. Unless you choose to care for your orchard organically (a difficult proposition), follow the fertilization and spraying programs recommended by your nursery or extension agent.

HARVESTING

To help the trees direct their energy to the development of laterals until the fourth year, remove all fruit as soon as each apple is the size of a dime. During the fourth season, your orchard will be ready to harvest. Some immature fruit will drop to the ground, usually during June. (This June drop will occur every year once the trees have reached maturity.) Thin out the remaining fruit until the apples are at least eight inches apart on the branches. They'll be ready to pick when their seeds are brown and when they twist easily away from the branches. You can expect to harvest about one-quarter of a bushel of apples per tree.

A Miniature Orchard Plan

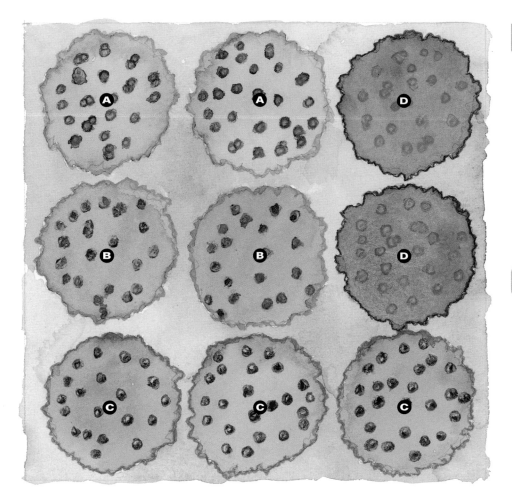

If you plant them six feet apart and keep them pruned to six feet in height, the trees in the orchard plan presented above will take up an area only eighteen feet square. The varieties selected will provide you with apples that are good for eating fresh, for cooking, and for making cider. What's more, each variety will ripen at a different time, so you'll have plenty of fruit from early to late autumn.

A DISCOVERY
Hardiness zones 4–8

Best uses: Best early-season apple for fresh eating and cooking; prolific producer and very reliable
Color: Yellow-tan with splashes of bright pinkish-red
Flesh: Creamy smooth, white with streaks of pink. If well ripened on the tree, can develop to crisp and juicy with a hint of strawberry flavor
Bloomtime: Mid season
Harvest time: Mid August
Resistance: A little to scab

B HONEY CRISP
Hardiness zones 3–8

Best uses: Good fresh eating, cooking, and dessert apple; tremendous keeper—up to 5 months in storage
Color: Mottled red over a yellow background
Flesh: Very crisp, juicy, sweet, with slight acidity
Bloomtime: Mid season
Harvest time: Early October
Resistance: Fireblight and scab

C LIBERTY
Hardiness zones 4–8

Best uses: Fresh eating, cooking, and dessert apple; good keeper; spurs profusely so always produces fruit no matter how badly you treat it
Color: 90% red marble blush over a yellow background
Flesh: Creamy white with a coarse, juicy sweet, slight subacid flavor
Bloomtime: Early season
Harvest time: Early October
Resistance: Immune to apple scab, highly resistant to cedar apple rust, fireblight, and powdery mildew

D GRIMES GOLDEN
Hardiness zones 5–9

Best uses: Dessert, juice, and cider apple; good keeper; good pollinator
Color: Bright golden, yellowish-green fruit
Flesh: Rich golden-yellow color with a sweet, crisp, honeyed, and juicy flavor
Bloomtime: Mid season
Harvest time: Late October

Adding Edibles to Your Landscape

Does your perennial border need a bit of pizazz? Are you looking for ways to add color and texture to your flower beds? Consider the dramatic heads and leaves of a globe artichoke; the brilliant red stems and glossy, crinkled foliage of Swiss chard; or the flouncy blue skirts of a cabbage. There's no need to segregate food crops from ornamentals. If you integrate edible plants into your beds, you can grow a beautiful backyard and eat it, too!

Landscaping a well-designed yard with ornamental trees, shrubs, and flowers is certainly rewarding, but cultivating an equally attractive yard that integrates edibles into its design is an immensely satisfying experience. Sowing seed, growing, and then harvesting food will connect you even more deeply to the rhythm of the seasons. A careful selection of crops and specific cultivars will allow you to gather sustenance almost year-round.

PICK OF THE CROP

As you think about plants to include in your edible landscaping plans, don't limit yourself to nasturtiums and kale. Fruit and nut trees (pear, cherry, apple, peach, hazelnut, and almond) can provide lovely blossoms in the spring, shade in July, and a tasty bounty in the late summer and fall. Consider some of the many fruits and vegetables that grow on vines (grapes, passion fruit, beans, and peas are a few examples); they'll all add a vertical interest to your garden design. Berry-producing bushes (such as blueberries, gooseberries, and currants) can replace some of the purely ornamental shrubs you've grown in the past. The list of edible flowers (see page 157) is extensive, and culinary herbs fit beautifully into almost any garden design. Even ground covers can be edible: Strawberries or herbs such as thyme can add to your meals while reducing your mowing chores.

Edibles do tend to be more labor-intensive than ornamental plants, so you probably won't want to turn your entire backyard into one huge kitchen garden. Start by tucking a few different kinds of lettuce in among the annuals in early spring, or just add a chili pepper plant to one of the containers on your deck. Then, as the inevitable holes in your landscape design appear, move on to other edibles. Instead of planting roses by that newly installed trellis, try raspberry canes or a hardy kiwi vine. If you're a rose lover, the shrub rose *Rosa rugosa* should please you. Its red or orange rose hips have 60 times more vitamin C than an orange and can be made into delicious jams or tea. And the next time you're looking for a plant that combines height with finely-textured foliage, set out some asparagus.

DESIGNING WITH EDIBLES

Vegetables don't have to be propagated in perfectly straight, Farmer MacGregor-style rows. Spring an eggplant from its utilitarian setting, and you'll realize just how exotic and attractive a plant it is. Its satiny, purple-black fruits would look wonderful combined with the silver foliage of dusty miller. Once you get used to the concept of food plants as part of your garden design, all sorts of combinations will come to mind. Violas (which are usually grown as ornamentals, but actually are edible) look lovely lining a path beside swirls of bright green lettuce.

Along with sunlight, soil, and water needs, consider your edible's height, shape, foliage, texture, and color before deciding on its place in your design—just as you would for any ornamental plant. Check seed catalogs carefully; you're sure to find cultivars that are as handsome as they are tasty. Look for herbs with variegated or silver foliage to add interest to your garden.

Even if you devote a separate section of your yard to food crops, there's no reason not to make that space as beautiful as it is practical. Flowers such as marigolds and nasturtiums have long been valued as companions for vegetables; they're natural insect repellents, and some gardeners claim that the strong scent of mari-golds will also keep cats away. Let daisies, corn poppies, and bachelor's-buttons share space with your herbs and vegetables, too; they may not repel insects, but they'll look right at home growing beside your produce.

EDIBLES FOR SMALL YARDS

Even if your back forty consists of little more than a patio and a patch of lawn, you can still raise your own fruits and vegetables. A small, walled yard is often perfect for espalier fruit trees. Even a lilliputian garden should have room for a couple of mini-dwarf fruit trees or a citrus tree in a pot.

Tomatoes, lettuces, cucumbers, beans, and peppers will all thrive in carefully tended container gardens on a patio or deck, as long as sunlight, water, and fertilizer needs are met. Strawberries and cherry tomatoes can even be grown in hanging baskets. Many herbs will be perfectly content in window boxes or strawberry jars.

Just make sure your container-grown fruits and vegetables are in pots with sufficient space for root growth. And plan to feed and water them more frequently than those planted in the ground.

The Backyard Kitchen

Why is it that frying a steak on an indoor range can seem like a tedious chore, but grilling that same cut of meat on the porch or in the backyard is grounds for a social gathering? Part of it is the smell, of course: The smoky aroma of a searing rib eye can lure even the surliest teenager out of his bedroom to linger in anticipation by the grill. And, of course, there's the opportunity to escape a stuffy summer kitchen. Long summer evenings and crisp fall afternoons spent outdoors offer their own enticements.

However, it may just be the equipment itself that gives outdoor cooking the greatest appeal. After all, when was the last time a microwave oven inspired a neighborhood cook-off—or even a luke-warm debate? But challenge your neighbor's claim that her gas grill can out-barbecue your old charcoal kettle; debate the flavoring merits of hickory chips over grapevine clippings; or offer advice on how to light a fire in a rock oven; and you're in for some friendly competition—and more than a few great meals!

Cooking Equipment

From hot-dog ace to backyard gourmet, there's an outdoor oven for every outdoor chef. To determine the best one for your needs, consider how much space you have; whether you'll want to move your cooking site from time to time; how many people you'll be feeding and with what kind of food; how much time you have to spend lighting, tending, and cleaning your outdoor oven; and, of course, how much money you're willing to spend.

High-end, wagon-style gas grill

GRILLS

Readily available and easy to operate, a commercial grill makes a great choice for the outdoor chef. You can move your grill wherever you want it—up on the patio one evening, then down to a nice flat portion of the lawn the next afternoon. And with the wide variety of styles and brands available, you're sure to find a grill that will fit your budget and your needs.

Features and Options

Don't think that you have to spend a fortune to get a grill that will produce perfect steaks, veggies, and burgers. Equipped with the right features, even the simplest, least expensive firebox can grill up a feast. For temperature control on charcoal grills, look for air vents, an adjustable grill rack, an adjustable firebox, or a combination of all three. Open grills are perfect for steaks, fish fillets, and other quick-cooking foods, while fattier foods and foods that require more cooking time do best in covered grills. A rotisserie will allow you to cook whole chickens, turkeys, and roasts.

GAS VERSUS CHARCOAL: A HOT DEBATE

The first decision you'll have to make when buying a grill is whether to buy one that's fueled by gas or one that's fueled by charcoal. A devoted charcoal fan is about as likely to admit the advantages of gas grilling as a Texas cattle rancher is to advocate vegetarianism. And charcoal purists do have a point. There's something primordial about cooking over real embers—selecting the right fuel, lighting the fire, tending the coals. There's also something mighty time-consuming about it! Charcoal can take up to three-quarters of an hour to reach cooking temperature; a gas grill can be ready for action in 15 minutes, and cleanup is quicker, too. Charcoal fans claim that their chosen method lends a special flavor to food, but you'll find plenty of tips on page 187 for making gas grills produce tasty fare with flame-kissed flavor.

COMMON GRILL MODELS

Hibachis

Even if your backyard consists of nothing more than a third-story apartment balcony, with this tiny, uncovered charcoal grill, you can still enjoy great grill flavor. Designed for the direct cooking method (see page 186), hibachis have an adjustable grill rack and air vents. If you have limited space and your grilling plans include hamburgers or steaks for just one or two people, the inexpensive hibachi fits the bill.

Kettle Grills

Available in four sizes, several bright colors, and a range of prices, this is

Clockwise from upper left: **wagon grill, traditional kettle grill, hibachi grill**

the most popular of all the charcoal grills. The traditional kettle's round shape and hooded design provide excellent heat distribution, and an opening in its base allows easy ash removal. In most models, the non-adjustable grill rack rests about five inches above the firebox, but air vents offer good temperature control.

A newer and less widely available rectangular version of the kettle has an adjustable grill rack for added versatility; however, the firebox on this model is harder to clean, and spherical kettle purists claim that the rectangular shape doesn't distribute heat as well. Both the round and rectangular versions will accommodate cooking with either the direct or indirect method (see pages 186–187 for descriptions

of these methods), and many models have an optional rotisserie.

Wagon Grills

Available in gas and charcoal models, wagon grills occupy the high end of the portable grill market. An optional hood, rotisseries, extra work space, and an adjustable grill rack and firebox all warrant the added expense. A few more dollars will buy temperature gauges and lighting. In addition, most wagon grills are constructed of sturdy, long-lasting materials that are designed for years of use. With the versatility to cook by both the direct and indirect method, and grilling space to feed a lawn-full of friends, a wagon grill is an excellent choice for the serious backyard chef.

SMOKERS

A good grill can turn out delicious steaks and burgers and even authentic barbecue, but if you love the intense flavor of genuine smoked meats, you'll want a smoker. Readily available at most home stores, commercial smokers come in a wide range of prices and two primary styles. They're easy to use, and although you can't grill with them, they work well for both barbecuing and for hot-smoking cooking (two similar techniques described on page 191).

Like grills, smokers come in charcoal and gas models. The benefits and drawbacks of gas smokers versus charcoal smokers are the same as those of gas grills versus charcoal grills (see pages 166–167).

Bullet Water Smokers

If you're new to smoking and not sure how much space and money you want to invest in the hobby, the compact, inexpensive bullet water smoker is a good choice. The design components are simple: a vertical cooking tower with one or more grill racks at the top, the heat source at the bottom, and a water pan in between. The heat cooks, the smoke flavors, and the steam bastes.

Most bullet water smokers are equipped with thermometers, but they're often installed too high in the units to give accurate readings; thus, you may want to purchase an oven thermometer or a thermometer specially designed for barbecuing, to place on or near the rack (or racks) on which you'll be cooking. Some folks even custom fit their smokers with candy thermometers.

Offset Firebox Smokers

Serious smokers require serious equipment, so if your smoking hobby grows into an obsession, consider purchasing an offset firebox smoker. These pricier smokers typically feature a horizontal cooking chamber set off to the side of a firebox; smoke and heat pass from the firebox, into the cooking chamber, and

Bullet water smoker

out a chimney. You can place a pan of water in the cooking chamber to help keep food moist. Thick steel construction, firebox dampers, and chimney vents allow excellent temperature control, but, as with bullet water smokers, an additional thermometer is still a good idea.

Tips for Using Smokers

A few simple tricks will help you achieve great results with your smoker. First, keep the smoker closed; when you open it, heat and flavorful smoke escape, so keep the lid down unless you're basting the food inside. For added flavor, fill the water pan with beer, marinade, or wine. Finally, to produce a delicious crust on meats, similar to that formed by the barbecue process (see pages 190–194), remove the water pan from the smoker about an hour before cooking is done.

Offset firebox smoker

PERMANENT OUTDOOR OVENS

Before modern grills and smokers became widely available in the 1950s, some families built permanent ovens in their backyards, using stones, bricks, or concrete blocks. These traditional ovens have been making a comeback in recent years, and for good reason! A well-built and carefully situated stone oven can become an inviting centerpiece in your backyard. You'll find dozens of plans for building permanent outdoor ovens on the Internet and at your local library. Keep in mind, though, that a stone, brick, or concrete oven will entail a great deal more expense than a grill or a smoker, both to obtain and to fuel.

COOKING WITH THE SUN

Even if the sun isn't actually hot enough to fry an egg on the sidewalk, you can still use its power to cook tasty meals—with a solar oven! As concerns over energy conservation rise, these portable, easy-to-use cookers are becoming more and more common all over the world.

The idea is simple: Highly reflective panels concentrate the sun's heat in the oven's cooking chamber, resulting in temperatures of up to 400°F (204°C)—hot enough to roast, broil, or steam anything you'd cook in a conventional oven. And because the cooking chamber distributes heat evenly, there's almost no way to burn food. Meats remain moist and flavorful; cakes bake up fluffy and sweet; and pastas will boil to perfection in about the same time it would take to cook them on the stove top.

Solar ovens aren't just for summer use, either. Because they rely on the sun's light, not the ambient temperature, you can cook with one on the coldest winter day. And unlike a grill or a smoker, you won't have to tend the fire or baste the meat; you'll stay cozy and warm inside while the oven and the sun do all the work for you.

OPEN FIRES

There's something about open-fire cooking that can turn the most humble pack of hot dogs into a sumptuous feast. Although we usually associate flame-roasted foods with long hikes and the great outdoors, you don't have to hike ten miles in the pouring rain to savor an authentic camp-side meal. Imagine enjoying the crackling flames and aromatic wood smoke of a real campfire, with the convenience of indoor plumbing just a few steps away. With a commercial portable fire pit or a permanent fire pit, you can enjoy just such an experience in your own backyard!

Commercial Portable Fire Pits

Although these outdoor ovens aren't quite as common as standard grills, you can find them in better-quality mail-order catalogs and at on-line stores. The most popular models look like very large, low-to-the-ground kettle grills (see above), with a round firebox propped up on three legs; in some models, two of the legs have wheels to aid in portability. An optional screen keeps sparks in check on windy days, and an optional hood protects the flames from the occasional rain storm. The hood also helps distribute heat more evenly, both for marshmallow roasting and for hand warming.

Like the campfires you enjoy in the wilderness, commercial portable fire pits burn real logs; just be sure to follow the manufacturer's instructions for lighting, tending, and extinguishing the fire. And although you can place one of these outdoor ovens wherever you like, take some care to avoid windy sites and areas below overhanging branches.

Permanent Fire Pits

If you don't mind clearing out a corner of your yard, you can build a fire pit to rival those at the best summer camps and campgrounds. But before you go searching for a shovel, consult the local fire department regarding your community's open-fire laws. Then read the following instructions carefully.

■ PIT PREPARATION

Choose a wind-sheltered site, with no tree branches looming overhead. Make sure the area has ready access to running water. (As an extra precaution, keep a fire extinguisher—rated for campfire use—nearby.) Dig a narrow trench around the site to prevent buried roots from catching fire—these roots can smolder, sometimes for days, and then suddenly burst into flame many yards away. Clear the entire area within the trench of all vegetation and debris. Ideally, you want a hard-

packed or sandy patch of ground on which to build your fire.

■ FUEL FOR THE FIRE

The best wood for a campfire is, of course, dry. Commercially available manufactured logs are not recommended for cooking purposes, so be sure to use real wood. Gather your tinder and firewood from natural sources, keeping in mind that hardwoods such as oak, beech, and maple create less smoke than softwoods and provide much more heat. (Avoid aspen; it won't burn at all.) Look for dead wood—don't cut branches from living trees; green wood is hard to start and will produce more smoke than fire. If the only available wood is wet, split it with an ax; the interior portions are usually drier, and if a fire is hot enough, it will consume even soaking-wet wood, albeit with a great deal of smoke.

■ LIGHTING THE FIRE

Newspaper makes a great fire-starter. Simply twist individual pages into tight rolls; then tie the rolls into several knots. The knots will catch fire easily, but they'll burn longer than plain sheets, giving tinder more time to catch. Place several newspaper knots in the bottom of your pit and pile thin, dry twigs on top of them. Use a long match to light the newspaper. As soon as the tinder blazes into fire, gradually start adding larger twigs, and then small branches.

Always add fuel to the downwind side of the fire, and remember to let the fire breathe. Never leave your fire untended, and keep your eyes peeled for wandering sparks.

■ THE CAMPFIRE AS COOK STOVE

The classic campfire foods—hot dogs and marshmallows—can be stuck on long sticks or skewers and thrust into the flames. Larger foods require a little more care. For serious cooking, you may want some extra equipment. Hanging arms (from which to suspend pots), spits, Dutch ovens, and spyders (three- or four-legged trivets with rings on which to place pots and pans) will all allow you to use your campfire for more complicated meals. Alternatively, you can let your fire burn down to a bed of hot coals and shove foil-wrapped potatoes, corn, and other tasty foods right into the coals to bake to smoky perfection. Turn to pages 182–183 for more information on cooking with an open fire.

■ PUTTING THE FIRE OUT

Stop adding fuel to the fire about an hour before you plan to put it out. When you're ready to extinguish your campfire, spread out the coals with a stick and sprinkle water over them. Add more water, very slowly, and keep stirring with the stick. The fire isn't out until the coals are cool to the touch, so don't leave until they are!

The Backyard Chef's Must-Have Tools

Peruse any catalog or store that specializes in cooking—outdoor or otherwise—and you're sure to find hundreds of exciting gadgets and shiny trinkets, all proclaiming their indispensability to your cooking endeavors. Enticing as the marketing may be, you won't need exotic or expensive equipment to be a great outdoor chef. The real tools of the trade are simple and familiar, and they're available almost everywhere. As with any tool, buy the best you can afford; more money will usually buy more years of use. And if you find that you just can't live without that chrome-accented vegetable-dehydrator-and-grill-rack-in-one, just make sure it matches your storage shed's decor.

THERMOMETER

Don't even think about cooking meat or poultry without one! The cooking times given in recipes are good approximations of how long a given cut will take to cook, but they're just that—approximations. The only safe way to gauge meat's doneness is to take its temperature. Although a standard meat thermometer is your best all-around bet for most foods, an instant-read thermometer works well for thick cuts of meat and whole poultry.

You'll find temperature guidelines for foods commonly cooked outdoors on page 195.

HEAVY-DUTY OVEN MITTS

Whether you're flipping burgers with a shorter-than-ideal spatula or arranging hot charcoal into a perfect pyramid, long mitts made from flame-retardant material will keep your hands cool and safe.

TONGS

To keep juicy rib eyes succulent, and tender chicken moist, turn them with tongs—not forks. (The sharp tines of forks puncture meat, allowing juices

to escape and the meat to dry out.) Look for tongs with spring-loaded action and handles that are long enough to keep your fingers cool, but short enough to offer good control.

OFFSET SPATULA

Tongs are great for sturdier cuts of meat, but delicate fillets of fish and tender vegetables require more careful handling. An offset spatula will keep your salmon steak in one piece during the turning and transferring process. Your spatula of choice should have a large blade—the longer and broader the better—and a long handle.

GRILLING BASKET

Whether you're smoking a whole 15-pound salmon or grilling a crop of new potatoes and carrots, a hinged, mesh grilling basket will help keep things together and orderly. To turn the food, simply flip the whole basket.

SKEWERS

Look for long skewers with triangular or square tines; morsels of meat and chunks of vegetables may rotate on round tines, which will result in uneven cooking. Wooden skewers are fine; just be sure to soak them in water for at least half an hour before cooking to keep them from charring.

WIRE BRUSH

Although your grill, smoker, or barbecue pit doesn't need to be spick-and-span, giving it a good scrub with a wire brush after every meal will remove large pieces of charred debris that might otherwise give your next meal an off flavor.

BASTING BRUSHES

Keep two on hand: one for basting foods and one used solely for oiling the grill rack. Wash both after every use.

SQUIRT BOTTLE

Flare-ups can char a burger to an inedible cinder in just a few quick seconds. Tame those unruly flames with a blast or two from a water-filled squirt bottle.

DRIP PAN

Strategically placed under rich meats or heavily marinated vegetables, a drip pan will help prevent flare-ups by keeping fatty drippings from falling on hot coals or heating elements.

A FEW HANDY EXTRAS

From wiping up drips and setting down tongs, you'll find dozens of uses for paper towels. Aluminum foil serves multiple purposes, too: Line the bottom of your grill or smoker with it for quick clean-up; fold it around potatoes for roasting; wrap wood chips in it for use in a gas grill or smoker; or use it to cover the potato salad while the burgers finish grilling. Finally, a small table located near your outdoor oven will provide extra work space.

THE BACKYARD CHEF'S MUST-HAVE HERBS

When we cook outdoors, we reach for fresh, whole foods: corn straight from the garden; plump chicken breasts, rather than processed chicken nuggets; trout from the stream, not frozen fish sticks. Foods this fresh and delicious deserve seasonings that are just as sensational. The best herbs for backyard cooking are easy to find, and you can grow many of them yourself. In fact, why not start a container garden or two, planted with some of the culinary herbs listed below? That way, you'll always have fresh herbs right at hand! (See pages 174–175 for more information on growing herbs in containers.)

Pictured in horizontal rows from top left:
Parsley, Tarragon, Chives, Garlic, Sage, Thyme, Rosemary, Basil, Oregano, Marjoram, Dill, Bay

An Herb Garden Plan

Sprinkled on roasted or grilled meats, blended into marinades, or tossed onto coals during the last minutes of cooking, fresh herbs, with their spicy snap and full flavor, will work magic on foods cooked outdoors. Don't bother with expensive herbs from the grocery store, though—growing your own culinary garden couldn't be easier! With the exception of garlic (which must be grown in the ground), most herbs will flourish in pots, so you can grow them in convenient container gardens—right at hand near the grill and the kitchen!

A CHIVES
Allium schoenoprasum

Average, well-drained soil

Full sun to light shade

Onion-like scent; mild onion flavor; use with eggs, chicken, fish, salads, soups, and as a mild substitute for onion

B GREEK OREGANO
Origanum heracleoticum

Rich, well-drained soil

Full sun

Robust, pungent scent; spicy, peppery flavor; use with tomatoes, tomato sauces, and roasted and grilled chicken and meats

C CILANTRO
Coriandrum

Rich, well-drained soil

Full sun to light shade

Warm, spicy aroma; piquant, slightly citrus tang; use in salsas, gumbo, herbal oils, and many Middle Eastern dishes

D FLAT-LEAF PARSLEY
Petroselinum crispum

Rich, well-drained soil

Full sun

Fresh, slightly spicy scent; light, peppery tang; use in soups, stews, savory butters, egg dishes, and as a garnish

E ROSEMARY
Rosmarinus

Well-drained, alkaline soil

Full sun

Aromatic, with camphor and pine overtones; warm, pungent flavor; use with roasted meats, chicken, eggplant, potatoes, and tomatoes

F THYME
Thymus

Average to poor, dry, well-drained, alkaline soil

Full sun

Warm, earthy scent; delicate, piquant flavor; use with grilled vegetables, tomatoes, corn, and in marinades for pork and poultry

G SAGE
Salvia officinalis

Rich, well-drained soil

Full sun

Highly aromatic; hints of rosemary, pine, and mint flavors; use with rich meats and poultry, thread onto kabobs between lamb and onion

H GOLDEN SAGE
Salvia officinalis 'Aurea'

Rich, well-drained soil

Full sun

Same aromas and culinary uses as common sage (above), but the beautifully variegated leaves add visual interest to gardens and meals

I BASIL
Ocimum basilicum

Rich, well-drained soil

Full sun

Warm and aromatic; pungent, fresh flavor; use in salads, soups, grilled and fresh vegetables, tomatoes, fish, and chicken

J TARRAGON
Artemisia dracunculus

Average, well-drained soil

Full sun

Warm, subtle fragrance; licorice flavor; use with tomatoes, salads, herbal vinegars, seafood, and roasted and grilled chicken

K BAY (LAUREL)
Laurus nobilis

Well-drained, lightly composted soil

Full sun to light shade

Intensely aromatic; sweet and spicy flavor; use with stews, tomatoes, and in marinades for beef, lamb, pork and fish

L ELEPHANT GARLIC
Allium ampeloprasum

Rich, well-drained, well-composted soil

Full sun

Pungent aroma; milder garlic flavor than "true" garlic; roast whole cloves, use in marinades, and with all meats, fish, poultry, and vegetables

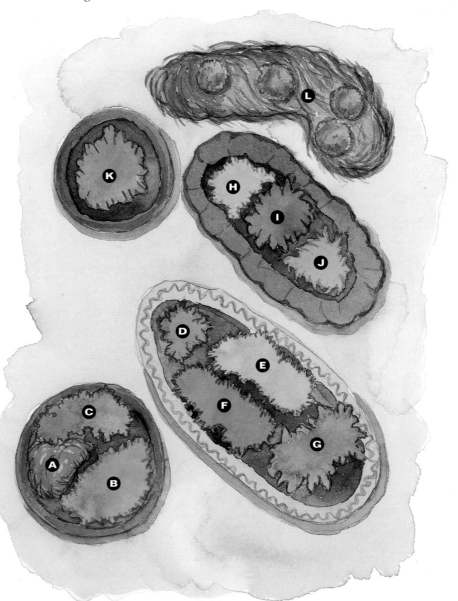

Outdoor Cooking Safety

Cooking outdoors should be fun and relaxing, but don't let your casual attitude extend to grilling and food safety. A few commonsense precautions will ensure a safe and enjoyable meal.

THE GRILL

Before you fire up your grill or other outdoor oven, make sure you've read the manufacturer's operating instructions. Perform all the recommended maintenance and safety checks. Select a site for your grill that's flat, stable, and at least ten feet from your house or any other structure. Never cook in a garage or carport or beneath any other surface that could catch fire, and never grill indoors, where carbon monoxide can build up. Keep the kids and the pets away from the area surrounding your grill, and do not attempt to move a grill that's lit or still hot.

If you're using a gas grill, remember to leave the hood open when lighting it. To get a charcoal fire going, use one of the methods recommended on pages 185–186, and never use any kind of flammable liquid other than charcoal lighter fluid; gasoline, kerosene, and other fuels can create toxic fumes that may contaminate food or even cause an explosion. And no matter how feeble the fire may seem, or how tempted you are to try it just this once, never squirt lighter

fluid onto hot coals. The flame can travel up the stream of fluid and burn you or cause the can to explode. If your fire is struggling, place a handful of new briquettes in a metal can and squirt lighter fluid over them. Then use a pair of long-handled tongs to add these briquettes to the pile in your grill.

Keep a fire extinguisher nearby, and have some baking soda handy in case of grease fires. Use long-handled cooking utensils and flame-retardant oven mitts to protect your hands. Make sure your clothes are close-fitting; loose, billowy clothing presents a fire hazard.

RULES FOR FOOD SAFETY

Cleanliness is imperative when handling any food, especially meats, poultry, and fish. You can reduce your risk of catching a food-borne illness by following these basic rules:

■ Use soap and hot water to thoroughly clean anything that comes in contact with raw meat, poultry, or seafood (including platters, utensils, countertops, and hands).

■ Sanitize cutting boards and other cutting surfaces with a solution of one teaspoon of bleach to one quart of water after each use.

■ Use hot water when laundering dishcloths.

■ Defrost food in the refrigerator—not in cold water or on the countertop.

■ Promptly refrigerate or freeze leftovers; food should never sit out for more than two hours.

■ Always marinate food in the refrigerator, in a plastic bag or a covered dish. Never reuse marinade or baste with marinade that has come in contact with raw meat.

COOKING TEMPERATURES

Thorough cooking kills bacteria, but overcooking can kill taste. So how do you determine when your food is safe to eat? Use a meat thermometer to ensure that your food has reached a sufficient internal temperature. (See the chart on page 195 for general temperature guidelines for various meats and poultry.)

You'll find two primary types of meat thermometers on the market. The traditional, ovenproof varieties are inserted into the food at the beginning of cooking and left in until the food is done. Because they must be inserted to a depth of at least two inches to provide an accurate reading, these thermometers work best for whole poultry and roasts. The newer, digital, instant-read thermometers are best for steaks, burgers, chops, and chicken breasts. They are inserted into food just removed from the grill, and require only one-half inch of penetration to give a quick, accurate reading.

To assure accuracy, a meat thermometer must be inserted into the

deepest area of the food. To safely cook a whole bird, insert the thermometer into the inner-thigh area, near the breast—but be careful not to touch the bone. For steaks and roasts, insert the thermometer into the center of the thickest portion, avoiding fat and gristle. For ground meat and poultry, target the thickest area of the patty or loaf. For burgers, insert the thermometer sideways.

Whichever thermometer you use, remember to wash it well in hot, soapy water after each use (and after you've inserted it into food that is not yet thoroughly cooked). Periodically check its calibration by placing the stem in a container of boiling water; the thermometer should read 212°F (100°C).

Building a Screened Box to Protect Food

Don't share your feast with unwelcome party guests—protect it with this good-looking, easy-to-build project. Simply place the screened box over anything you'd rather not share with hungry insects; the fine-mesh screen will keep even the tiniest bugs well away from your meal. Using prefabricated gallery rail (readily available at hardware stores and home improvement centers) provides handles and decorative detail, and using screen molding as trim eliminates the need for complicated rip cuts.

■ All the finish nails in this project should be countersunk (or set below the wood surface). After driving a nail into the wood, place the nail set on the nail head and tap the nail set with your hammer.

Instructions

1 Cut the walls (A), posts (B), and long and short molding (D and E) to the lengths specified in the "Cutting List." Using a miter box and backsaw, cut the frame pieces (C); their ends should be cut to 45° angles, and their longest edges should be 18⅞". Using a utility knife, cut two 7" x 19¾" pieces and one 18" x 33" piece of window-screen material.

2 Arrange a wall (A) between two posts (B), as shown in figure 1. Fasten the parts together by driving 2½" nails through the outer faces of the posts and into the ends of the wall. Repeat to assemble a second wall panel.

3 Wrap a 7" x 19¾" piece of window screen over each wall panel (see figure 1). Then staple the screens to the top and bottom faces of each wall (A) and to the outer edges of the posts (B). Hammer all the staples to flatten them.

MATERIALS & TOOLS

- Hammer
- Nail set
- Tape measure
- Pencil
- Miter box and backsaw
- Square
- Staple gun and ¼" staples
- Utility knife
- 4d (1½") and 8d (2½") finish nails
- 22" x 60" window-screen material

TIPS

- Gallery rail (see "Cutting List") is available from many home-improvement centers and comes in various lengths. It consists of two narrow boards with decorative spindles between them.
- A miter box is an implement that holds your saw in the correct position when you want to cut a board at an angle.

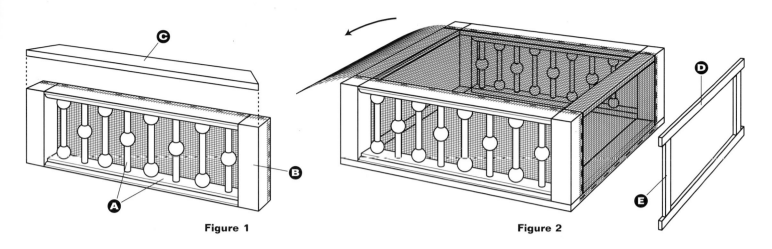

Figure 1

Figure 2

Position a frame piece (C) on the long, top edge of a panel, with its short edge facing the panel's screen-covered side, and its long edge flush with the panel's outer face (see figure 1). Drive 1¼" nails through the face of the frame piece and into the posts beneath. Repeat to attach a frame piece to the other panel.

Position the wall panels on edge, parallel to each other and about 19" apart, with the frame pieces (C) facing up and the screen-covered sides facing each other. Then place two frame pieces across the panels, so their mitered edges meet the mitered edges of the two attached frame pieces. Adjust the panels until the box shape is square, and attach the two frame pieces to the posts (B) with 1¼" finish nails.

Position the box shape with its attached frame pieces (C) face down. Drape the 18" x 33" piece of window screen over the box shape, as shown in figure 2. Staple one end of the screen to the outer edges of the frame piece and the two posts (B) on that side. Then staple the screen along the top faces of the walls (A). Finally, staple the screen to the posts and frame piece on the other side. Make sure you place the staples no more than ⅜" out from the inner edges of each wooden piece, or they'll be visible when the project is finished. Hammer all the staples flat.

Arrange the remaining four frame pieces (C) on top of the box shape to form a frame on top. Attach them to the tops of the posts (B) with 1¼" nails.

Turn the box over so that it is open at the top. Reach inside the box with your staple gun, and staple the screen in the bottom of the box to the two frame pieces (C) along either side.

To disguise the staples on the outside of the box, use 1¼" finish nails to attach the long and short molding pieces (D and E), as shown in the photo and in figure 2. Trim away any exposed screen material with your utility knife.

CUTTING LIST

CODE	DESCRIPTION	QTY.	MATERIAL
A	Walls	2	6" x 16" gallery rail
B	Posts	4	2 x 2 x 6"
C	Frame pieces	8	1 x 2 x 18⅞" (mitered)
D	Long molding	4	18⅞"-long screen molding
E	Short molding	4	5"-long screen molding

Backyard Cooking Techniques

Remember the first time you roasted a hot dog over an open fire? For many of us, that experience kindled a lifelong passion for outdoor cooking. The process was so simple, yet it yielded such tasty results. Even today, with our high-tech equipment, exotic produce, and more experienced palates, the appeal of outdoor cooking remains the same: It's easy to do, and it tastes great.

But just because cooking outdoors is easy doesn't mean that there's only one way to do it, or one type of flavor it can produce. As any food lover can tell you, making crisp, juicy pork chops and preparing tender pulled pork shoulder are entirely different propositions. The first calls for the quick, high-heat searing of grilling; the second requires the low fire and slow cooking of barbecue. Even a potato will taste different depending on whether it's wrapped in foil and tucked under coals; or sliced thin, brushed with olive oil and spices, and placed right on the grill rack.

The keys to truly great outdoor cooking are knowing when to use a given technique, and then mastering it. By the time you finish this chapter, you'll know the when and how of everything from campfire cooking to real backyard barbecuing.

Cooking Over an Open Fire

Before microwaves and indoor ranges, before sophisticated grills and elaborate smokers, our ancestors cooked with nothing more than flame and live coals. And anyone who's ever roasted a hot dog in a campfire will recognize the benefits of returning to our culinary roots on occasion.

COOKING ON A SKEWER

Probably the oldest cooking implements in history, skewers are also among the easiest to find and to use. If your kitchen skewers are at least three feet long, they'll work well for campfire cooking. Keep in mind that any kind of metal skewer will get hot all the way down to the end you're holding, so wear an oven mitt when you use one.

To make wooden skewers, cut a few thin, but sturdy, branches from a nonpoisonous tree; then whittle one end of each stick to a sharp point. Make sure that the sticks are from living trees; deadwood might catch fire. A long-handled, two-pronged fork can also be used for cooking over an open fire and can hold two hot dogs or marshmallows at a time.

If you're cooking one of these two basic campfire food groups—hot dogs

or marshmallows—simply skewer the morsels and hold them over the flames. Most other foods will cook better after the fire has burned down to a bed of hot coals; then hold the skewer a few inches above the embers. Whether you're cooking with flames or coals, slowly turn your skewer throughout the process so the food will cook evenly.

The skewer itself will limit the kind of food you can cook this way. Stick to small chunks of meat and vegetables that will fit easily onto the skewer without bending it; anything larger will cook unevenly.

COOKING IN THE COALS

Larger pieces of meat and whole vegetables should be cooked directly in the coals. Try cooking baking potatoes, corn on the cob, or whole fish this way. Simply place the food on a square of aluminum foil, add butter or oil, and season as desired. Then wrap the foil into a tight package around the food and, using long-handled tongs, bury the package in the hot coals. (Make sure that every surface of the package is surrounded by hot coals.) Cooking times will vary widely because coals burn unevenly; just check the food periodically to make sure it's not burning, and watch out for steam as you unwrap the aluminum foil.

THE SOPHISTICATED CAMPFIRE COOK

To cook more elaborate meals over your campfire, you'll need some additional equipment. A metal grill grate placed over the hot embers will turn your campfire into a simple grill, and will allow you to cook steaks, burgers, and just about anything else you'd prepare on your patio grill. Simply prop the grate on rocks, about four to six inches above the coals. Place a cast-iron skillet on the grill grate, and you'll be able to fry bacon and eggs, sauté vegetables, and even make pancakes. You can also use a spyder (a three- or four-legged rack) or a trammel (an arrangement of linking "arms") to hold or suspend a pan over the embers.

Real campfire cooking enthusiasts will want to try cooking with a Dutch oven. You can make everything from a hearty stew to a batch of biscuits in these sturdy, lidded, cast-iron cooking pots. Simply place the oven on top of a bed of hot coals, and pile more coals on top of and around it, as required by the specific recipe you're following.

(A quick browse on the Internet or at the library will yield hundreds of Dutch-oven recipes.)

THE IMMORTAL S'MORE

It's almost an unwritten law that if you light a campfire, you have to use it to make s'mores—tasty treats of toasted marshmallow, crisp graham crackers, and melted milk chocolate. According to every camp counselor in history, the word *s'more* is actually the sound made by a camper when trying to ask for "some more" around a mouthful of his or her first serving.

Fortunately, making some more couldn't be easier. Start by breaking a graham cracker in half. Place two or three squares of milk chocolate on one half. Toast a couple of marshmallows until they're golden brown and gooey, then place them on top of the chocolate. Arrange the remaining graham cracker

half over the marshmallows, squashing it down to flatten the sandwich slightly. Although waiting will be hard, let the s'more rest for a few seconds while the marshmallows cool down. Although the traditional recipe will yield an undeniably delicious delicacy, you and your family may want to expand upon the basic ingredients. Try adding slices of banana between the marshmallows and the second graham cracker half. Substitute dark or caramel-filled chocolate for milk chocolate. Add a teaspoon of peanut butter. Use flavored marshmallows instead of plain. Who knows? You may invent the next campfire classic. Meantime, take a bite, savor, and start preparing some more.

Classic Dry Rub, Mop, and Sauce Recipes

Dry rubs, mops, and sauces were once solely the domain of barbecue (see pages 190–194), but today's savvy outdoor chefs have found that these flavorful extras can add zest to any kind of outdoor cooking.

	INGREDIENTS	APPLICATIONS	GUIDELINES FOR USE
Rubs	¼ cup coarse salt; ¼ cup black pepper; ¼ cup paprika; 1½ tsp garlic powder	This basic dry rub goes well with beef and pork. Omit the garlic and add ¼ tsp. each of grated lemon peel and sugar for use with poultry.	Brush the meat with a thin layer of oil before applying the rub.
	¼ cup brown sugar; ¼ cup pepper; ¼ cup paprika; 2 tbsp. chili powder; 2 tbsp. salt; 1 tbsp. garlic powder; 1 tsp. onion powder	Excellent as is on beef; adding 1 tbsp. each of nutmeg, allspice, and ground cloves turns it into a perfect rub for pork, too.	Coat the meat with a light layer of oil or prepared brown mustard before applying the dry rub.
Mops	1 quart warm water; ¼ cup salt; 1 tsp. cayenne pepper	This is the most basic mop and can be used on any kind of meat or poultry. Add 1 cup of cider vinegar to create a mop and sauce perfect for pork.	Heat the mop almost to the boiling point; then keep it hot the entire time it's in use.
	2 tbsp. prepared brown mustard; 2 tbsp. lemon juice; ½ cup butter, melted; ⅛ tsp. each garlic powder, onion powder, paprika, salt, and black pepper	Use this as both a marinade and a mop for fish and poultry.	Simmer together all the ingredients for 10 minutes; then allow the mop to cool. Marinate fish or chicken in half the mop for 30 minutes. Use the other half to baste the food while it cooks.
Sauces	1 cup ketchup; 1½ cups water; 2½ cups cider vinegar; 1 tbsp. brown sugar; 1 tsp. salt; 1¼ tsp. cayenne pepper; 1 tbsp. black pepper; commercial hot sauce to taste	Especially good on all types of pork, this sauce also goes well with barbecued chicken.	Combine all the ingredients in a large saucepan and bring the sauce to a boil, stirring constantly. Simmer for 15 minutes; then refrigerate until ready for use.
	2½ tbsp. soy sauce; ¾ cup tomato juice; 2½ tbsp. Worcestershire sauce; ⅓ cup ketchup; ¼ cup cider vinegar; ¼ cup brown sugar; 1 tbsp. lemon juice; ¼ tsp. each cayenne pepper, black pepper, and dry mustard; ⅛ tsp. each garlic powder, onion powder, oregano, allspice, ginger powder, and dried basil	This is a great rib sauce, but don't stop there! Try it on chicken and pulled beef or pork.	Simmer together all the ingredients in a saucepan for 1 hour, stirring occasionally. Refrigerate the sauce for 2 hours; then let it come to room temperature before serving.
	½ cup prepared yellow mustard; ½ cup brown sugar; 2 cups cider vinegar; 1½ tbsp. chili powder; 2 tsp. black pepper; ⅛ tsp. cayenne pepper; 1 tsp. soy sauce; ¼ cup butter, melted	This is a good all-purpose sauce for folks who prefer the flavor of mustard to ketchup.	Simmer together all but the last two ingredients for 10 minutes. Remove from the heat and stir in the soy sauce and butter. Allow the sauce to rest at room temperature for 1 hour before serving.

Backyard Charcoal and Gas Grilling

How many times have you heard someone say, "Hey! Let's pick up some steaks and barbecue them tonight?" If you feel like impressing your friends with your culinary knowledge, you might point out that, technically, they'll be grilling those steaks—not barbecuing them. Although most folks use *barbecue* and *grill* interchangeably, the words actually describe two very different cooking techniques—both of which can be performed on a grill. Barbecuing is all about slow cooking big cuts of meat at low temperatures; you can read more about this American obsession on pages 190–194.

Grilling, on the other hand, involves quickly cooking smaller cuts of food over high heat. The hot fire sears the exterior of foods, trapping juices inside, while the interior cooks to perfection. The result? A delectable, browned crust on the surface and a thoroughly cooked, yet tender and juicy interior. It's an art, but one that anybody with a grill can perfect.

PRE-GRILLING PREPS

Your grill rack doesn't need to be spotless, but it shouldn't have the charred remains of past meals clinging to it, either. Start with a rack that's free from debris and lightly oiled, and get into the habit of scrubbing it off with a wire brush after every use.

Pay some attention to your firebox, too. Keep the fire-box relatively free of ash and debris, which can lend an off taste to food. Check the manufacturer's instructions for other tips and directions. For instance, if you're using a charcoal grill, you may need to line the firebox before adding fuel; a double layer of aluminum foil weighted down with about an inch of fine gravel will work well.

GETTING FIRED UP

If you're grilling with gas, lighting the fire will be a simple matter of turning a knob or two and striking a match or the grill's striker; just be sure to read and follow the manufacturer's instruc-

tions. After you've lit the flame, close the hood and let the grill preheat on high for 10 to 15 minutes.

Firing up a charcoal grill involves a little more work, but for charcoal fans, the work is part of the fun. Start with fuel selection. Today's grillers can choose from common charcoal briquettes, flavored briquettes, self-igniting briquettes, hardwood charcoal, or a combination of any of these. No matter what kind of fuel you choose, you'll need enough to cover the bottom of your grill's firebox.

There are as many ways to light a charcoal fire as there are fuels to feed one. In descending order of desirability, these include: the virtually

seconds is medium: 350°F–375°F (177°C–400°C); three seconds is medium high: about 400°F (204°C); and one to two seconds is high: 425°F–500°F (218°C–260°C).

Adjusting the heat on a gas grill is just a matter of fiddling with the thermostat. Owners of charcoal grills have a few more options for temperature control. Adding more charcoal will step up the heat, and pushing hot coals aside will bring the temperature down. Open air vents help fuel a low fire, and closed vents will check a hot fire. Finally, if your model has an adjustable grill rack or firebox, you can move the cooking surface farther away from or closer to the coals.

THE DIRECT COOKING METHOD

Some foods cook best uncovered and positioned directly over the source of heat; this is known as the direct cooking method, and you'll use it for steaks, chops, and other foods that usually take fewer than 25 minutes to cook. On a gas grill, turn all of the heating elements to high and cook directly over the burners. For charcoal grilling, mound the coals into a pyramid and place the food right over them.

THE INDIRECT COOKING METHOD

Whole vegetables and larger or fattier cuts of meat fare better over lower heat, with the grill's hood closed; this is the indirect cooking method. To cook by the indirect method on a gas

foolproof chimney starter, which is available at most stores that sell grills; kindling—either newspaper twisted into tight knots, or dried twigs from hardwood trees, tucked under the heaped charcoal; solid starters, which are cubes of non-petroleum gel, also placed under a pyramid of charcoal; electric lighters, which are easy to use, but require a source of electricity; and starter fluid, which should always be squirted onto the fuel (in moderation) before striking the match— never add lighter fluid to charcoal that's already burning, even if the flames seem feeble!

Even with one of these methods, getting the fire going is the trickiest part of charcoal grilling, so don't be discouraged if it takes a couple of

tries. Once the charcoal's lit, though, you can sit back and relax for half an hour or so while it burns to readiness, a state indicated by a complete coating of light gray ash.

HOT ENOUGH

Before you toss the steaks (or burgers or kabobs) on the grill rack, you should test the grill's temperature. The universal hand test is the best way to do this. Hold your hand just above the rack and count "one one-thousand, two one-thousand," etc., until you have to pull your hand away. If you can leave your hand in place for seven seconds, the heat is low: 200°F–250°F (93°C–121°C). Six seconds indicates medium-low heat: 300°F–325°F (149°C–163°C); four to five grill, turn off one of the heating elements (the middle one, if your model has three), and cook the food over the unlit burner. On a charcoal grill, push the hot coals into two piles, one on each side of the firebox; then place the food on the grill rack, between the piles. In both gas and charcoal grills, position a drip pan under the food to prevent flare-ups, and keep the hood closed to maintain a more even cooking temperature.

GETTING EVEN TASTIER RESULTS FROM YOUR GRILL

Manufacturers and owners of gas grills will claim that, in a blind taste test, even the most fanatical charcoal lover can't tell the difference between a rib eye that was grilled over propane and one that was grilled over charcoal. And it's true that most of the great flavor of grilled foods comes from the high-heat searing of the process, not a particular kind of fuel. Nevertheless, some discriminating palates will demand even more great grill flavor from gas and charcoal grills alike. Here are some easy ways to do that.

Use Your Grill

Use it a lot! Although it may look impressive, your neighbor's sparkling clean, brand-new outdoor range won't be able to turn out a burger half as good as the ones you cook up on your old workhorse of a grill. Why? Grills

need to be seasoned by using them at least 20 times before they'll really start to impart that distinctive grill flavor.

Wood Chips

Choose from hickory, oak, mesquite, or any other hardwood available in your area. Soak the chips in water for at least 30 minutes before using them. In charcoal grills, sprinkle a few directly onto the coals. For gas grills, wrap a handful in a double layer of aluminum foil, poke some holes in the foil, and place the package on or near the heating elements. (Some gas grills come equipped with a chip box; if your model has one, use it instead.) Keep the grill covered to let some smoke build up inside.

Fresh Herbs and Spices

Whole cloves of garlic, moist sprigs of tarragon, sage, rosemary, oregano, and basil, the peels of citrus fruits, and the soaked clippings of grapevines can all be used in the same manner as wood chips.

Dry Rubs

Once found only in the sacred realm of barbecue, these blends of herbs and spices can do just as much for a grilled pork chop as for a barbecued pork shoulder. Brush the meat with a little oil; then, as the name suggests, rub the spice blend right onto the flesh. You'll find several recipes for great dry rubs on page 184.

Marinades

Turn to pages 188–189 for some classic marinades for all types of meat and vegetables. Set aside some of your marinade before adding meat to it; never baste with marinade in which raw food has soaked.

Great Marinades for Backyard Cooking

Carefully concocted marinades can tenderize the toughest cut of meat, add savor to the most mundane vegetable, and generally liven up any meal.

Start with the recipes in this section and vary the spices to adjust for your family's tastes.

Keep in mind that just because a marinade is recommended for one type of meat, vegetable, or fruit doesn't mean that it won't taste great with another kind of food. For instance, the Mexican Adobo is wonderful with grilled chicken or lamb, and the Provençale Sauce Verte works beautifully with chicken, fish, or fillet of beef. Trust your own palate, soak up the compliments, and have fun!

Just remember to set aside enough of your brew to use as a baste during the cooking process; never baste with marinade in which raw meat has soaked—doing so might carry harmful bacteria from uncooked meat to the finished product.

MARINADES FOR BEEF

Beef has a rich, hearty flavor that teams well with robust spices such as rosemary, black pepper, and garlic. Smaller cuts, such as kabob cubes and most steaks, should marinate for about six hours. Beef brisket, flank steak, whole tenderloin, and other larger or tougher cuts can soak for up to 48 hours.

....

Tuscan: *1 cup extra-virgin olive oil; ¹/₂ cup balsamic vinegar; 6 cloves garlic, crushed; fresh rosemary, chopped; and black pepper*

....

Thai: *4 tbsp. rice wine vinegar and ¹/₃ cup soy sauce whisked with ¹/₃ cup*

peanut butter; fresh lemongrass, chopped; fresh cilantro, chopped; garlic cloves, crushed; and hot red pepper flakes

MARINADES FOR PORK

From sweet cinnamon and nutmeg to hot pepper and mustard, most spices will complement pork's mild, slightly sweet taste. Marinate chops and cutlets for about four hours, and ribs, tenderloin, shoulders, and other large cuts for up to 24 hours.

....

Memphis-Style: *2 medium-sized tomatoes, chopped; ¹/₄ cup hot paprika; 2 tbsp. dark brown sugar; 1 tsp. hot pepper sauce; 4 cloves garlic, chopped;*

celery salt; cayenne pepper; dry mustard; cumin; salt; and black pepper

Jamaican Jerk: *6 hot chilies, chopped (for an extra-spicy marinade, leave the seeds in); 6 scallions, chopped; 1/2 onion, chopped; 2 tsp. fresh ginger, minced; 3 cloves garlic, minced; 1/2 cup white vinegar; 1/4 cup soy sauce; 1/4 cup peanut oil; 2 tbsp. brown sugar; dried thyme; allspice; nutmeg; cinnamon; coarse salt; and white pepper*

MARINADES FOR LAMB

Lamb's distinctive flavor calls for distinctive spices, such as mint and oregano. Marinate chops and cubes for kabobs for six hours. Leg of lamb, shoulder roast, and saddle should soak for up to 48 hours.

Moroccan: *1 cup plain whole-milk yogurt; 1 cup fresh mint leaves, chopped; 1/4 cup lemon juice; whole coriander seeds; cumin; cinnamon; fennel; and mace*

Mexican Adobo: *6 canned chipotle chilies; 5 cloves garlic, minced; 1/2 onion, chopped; 2 tbsp. white vinegar; fresh oregano; cloves; whole allspice; cinnamon; and coarse salt*

MARINADES FOR POULTRY

From chicken and turkey to duck and squab, poultry offers a range of flavors that will meld deliciously with all types of spices and seasonings. Depending on the size of the pieces, marinating times for poultry range from 2 hours to 36 hours.

Provençale Sauce Verte: *1 cup fresh parsley, chopped; 1/2 cup each chervil, basil, and mint, chopped; 3 tbsp. fresh chives, chopped; 4 scallions, minced; 1/2 cup extra-virgin olive oil; thyme; salt; black pepper; and lemon juice*

Tandoori: *1 cup plain yogurt; 3 tbsp. lemon juice; 3 cloves garlic, minced; 2 tbsp. crushed red pepper flakes; ginger powder; coriander; turmeric; and cumin*

MARINADES FOR SEAFOOD

Seafood has delicate, sweet flavors that require fresh, light seasoning with notes of tartness. Just an hour or two of marinating is plenty of time for even the largest steaks or whole fish.

West Indian: *Juice and zest of 4 limes; 4 tsp. fresh ginger, grated; 3 hot chilies, chopped; and coarse salt*

Montauk: *1/2 cup fresh dill, chopped; 1/2 cup white wine; 1/2 cup olive oil; coarse salt; and black pepper*

MARINADES FOR VEGETABLES

The best marinades for vegetables simply enhance their natural flavors and textures, rather than covering or converting them. Quickly douse the vegetables in the marinade right before grilling; then baste them throughout the cooking process. For a quicker cooking time, steam or parboil root vegetables such as potatoes, yams, and beets until they're just tender before finishing them on the grill.

Simple and Delicious: *a quick brush with good-quality walnut oil or extra-virgin olive oil; salt; and black pepper*

Roman: *4 tbsp. lemon juice; 1/4 cup olive oil; fresh basil, chopped; garlic, chopped; fennel seeds, ground; salt; and black pepper*

MARINADES FOR FRUITS

Grilling does wonders for apples, peaches, plums, pears, pineapples, and other fruits. Simply brush the raw sliced fruits with a sweet marinade just before grilling; then baste them frequently.

All-American: *1/2 cup butter, melted; 1/4 cup maple syrup; juice and zest of 1 lemon; ground cinnamon*

Suzette: *Juice and zest of 3 oranges; 1/4 cup brown sugar*

Backyard Barbecuing and Smoking

If you want to start a good fight (or even better, a great cook-off), ask a room filled with people from different states what constitutes real barbecue. The Texans in the crowd might tell you that it's spicy sausage, pulled beef brisket, or even baby goat. The guy from California will draw more than a few blank looks when he rapturously describes something called tri-tip (the triangular bottom sirloin steak that results when the bone is cut from sirloin). The folks from Kansas City and Memphis will agree that barbecue consists of ribs, but they'll disagree about whether to serve them adorned with nothing but the blend of dry spices and herbs in which they were cooked, or smothered in spicy-sweet tomato sauce. After everyone else has had their say, those from the Carolina contingent will shake their heads and carefully explain that there's only one form of barbecue, and that's pork, either pulled or chopped and then doused in red-pepper-and-vinegar sauce.

Obviously, then, there's some dis-agreement about what's fit to barbe-cue. But whether it's beef brisket in Austin, Texas, whole hog in Kinston, North Carolina, or a rack of baby back ribs in Memphis, Tennessee, just about everyone can agree on how bar-becue should be cooked: long and slow, at a temperature somewhere between 190°F (88°C) and 250°F (121°C). If it's done with live coals, all the better. Technically, any kind of meat cooked in this manner can safely be dubbed *barbecue*. And despite some restaurateurs' claims to the con-trary, you can create authentic barbe-cue in your own backyard—provided you have a day or two free to tend the fire and baste the ribs!

BARBECUING OR SMOKING? A SMOLDERING DEBATE

While the line between grilling and barbecuing is hard and fast, the line between barbecuing and smoking is a little hazier. In fact, some people say that the line doesn't even exist—that barbecuing and smoking are exactly the same. But experts in the field of outdoor cooking do make a distinc-tion. Hot smoking for cooking (as opposed to cold smoking for preserva-tion, a technique best left to profes-sionals) takes place at a slightly lower temperature than barbecuing, any-where between 170°F (77°C) and 190°F (88°C). And naturally, smoking

involves a lot of smoke—more than the average grill can produce—so although you can barbecue in a smoker, you can't effectively smoke on a grill. You'll find tips for using commercial smokers on page 168, but be sure to consult the manufac-turer's instruction manual, too.

Except for the heat range and the specialized equipment, though, smok-ing and barbecuing involve almost identical techniques and produce very similar results, the major difference being the more intensely smoky flavor of smoked foods. Thus, the treatment of these two techniques is combined into one section here, with the empha-sis on barbecuing.

The Meat (and the Vegetables, the Bread, the Nuts, the Cheese . . .)

When you think barbecue, think big: pork butt, shoulder, and ribs; whole chickens and large turkey breasts; beef brisket and roast; whole salmon; leg of lamb. The low heat and slow cooking of barbecue work tenderizing magic on what might otherwise be tough cuts of meat. It can also result in out-standing vegetables: Fat Vidalia onions, baking potatoes, corn on the cob, and butternut squash are just a few you might want to try. And as long as you're barbecuing side dishes, try this one: Slice a loaf of French bread, butter both sides of each slice, put the loaf back together, wrap it in aluminum foil, and let it barbecue for about 30 minutes.

When the main course and side dishes are done, folks with smokers can experiment with a couple of other delicacies, too. Right after you've finished cooking the meat and vegetables, place a few cupfuls of raw almonds on the rack, but don't stoke the fire again. Let the almonds smoke in the residual heat for a couple of hours. By the time the almonds are done, the smoker should be cool enough to use for cheese. Wrap a block of gouda, cheddar, Swiss, or any other firm cheese in aluminum foil. Poke a few holes in the package; then place it on the smoker's rack and let the cheese absorb the remaining smoke for an hour or two.

The Pit

Don't be alarmed by the word "pit." Unless you really want to, there's no reason to dig up a corner of your yard to create a traditional in-ground barbecue oven or smoker. You don't need to purchase a large specialty cooker or weld together your own version from a 55-gallon drum, either. You can barbecue quite effectively on a fair-sized kettle or wagon grill, and as soon as you use one for that purpose, you may refer to it ever after as "the pit." The same goes for a commercial smoker. However, if you're having a party and serving barbecue, you may want to consider renting a larger grill or a barbecue cooker; a family-sized grill is great for one or two pork shoulders, but if you're planning to feed the whole neighborhood, you'll need larger equipment.

The Fire

In a charcoal grill, light the fire the same way you would for grilling (see pages 185–186 for more information about different kinds of charcoal and ways to light it). Wait for the charcoal to burn until it's ashy gray all over; then push it into a mound on one side of the grill. Add several generous handfuls of soaked hardwood chips to the charcoal. You'll need to add a few fresh, hot briquettes to the fire about once every hour, so start a second batch of charcoal burning in a chimney starter, in a small pit in the ground, or in a spare grill.

Although purists insist on live coals, a gas grill can produce decent barbecue. Place a pan of water in the bottom of the firebox to help keep the meat moist. (For added flavor, try using beer or a vinegar-and-water mix instead.) Light the grill, but leave one of its heating elements off. Following the directions on page 187, fold several handfuls of soaked hardwood chips in a double layer of aluminum foil and place this package directly on top of one of the lit heating elements. (You'll want to replace the package every few hours, or when you notice that it's no longer producing smoke.) Cover the grill and allow it to preheat for at least 15 minutes.

Use the hand test described on page 186 and the chart on page 195 to determine the correct cooking temperature. If you've installed a commercially available barbecue thermometer on your grill or smoker, be aware that the temperature at cooking height will be about 10°F (6°C) higher than the thermometer reading. When the temperature's right, place the meat on the portion of the grill rack that's not over the heat source; barbecue always cooks by the indirect method.

The Flavor

The very process of slow cooking over low heat with hardwood smoke lends food a special flavor that simply cannot be created in any other way. Add the tang of a secret marinade or the zest of an heirloom sauce or dry rub, and you've got barbecue magic.

Marinades

In grilling, marinades serve primarily as a means of adding extra flavor. In barbecue, they serve an additional purpose—tenderization. Many cuts of meat used for barbecuing can be mighty tough; beef brisket, for example, is almost inedible cooked by any other method. Marinades, with their acidic bases, help break down tough fibers before cooking, and they help keep meat moist and tender when they're used as a mop (or baste) during cooking. Just be sure to set aside some clean marinade for basting. (Never mop with marinade in which you've soaked raw meat; the bacteria in it won't be over the heat long enough to be destroyed.) You'll find some great recipes for marinades, along with the length of time various foods should marinate, on pages 188–189.

Dry Rubs

Rubbed directly into meat before cooking, these blends of herbs and spices can imbue barbecue with a delicious, crusty exterior and a rich, complex flavor. Apply the rub to lightly oiled meat at least one hour before cooking. If you're working with chicken or any other fowl, be sure to get plenty under the skin and inside the body cavity, too.

You'll find several basic recipes for dry rubs on page 184. Use these as a starting point for creating your own secret rub, but exercise some caution when adding sugar or salt to your custom blends; debate rages hot over whether they have a place in dry rubs at all. Some experts insist that salt will suck the moisture and juiciness right out of a rack of ribs, but many prize-winning barbecuers would no more leave out the salt than they would leave out the meat itself. Sugar, too, has its advocates and foes. Foes say it will burn; advocates say the foes aren't watching their meat closely enough. Experiment and let your taste buds tell you what works best for you and your family.

Mops

A mop will keep meat moist and tender as it cooks. The simplest mops are mixtures of salt water or salt water, vinegar, and cayenne pepper. (You'll find some basic recipes on page 184.) Keep the mix warm and brush it onto the meat once every 30 to 45 minutes. If the meat you're cooking lacks an outside layer of fat, the baste should include some oil. As long as a marinade is clean, you can use it as a mop, too, but never use a tomato-based sauce as a mop.

Sauces

Some aficionados argue that good barbecue doesn't need any sauce at all. For other folks, though, a sweet and tangy sauce can turn good barbecue into something approaching perfection. The key to achieving that perfection is simple: Just remember that a tomato-based sauce is neither a marinade nor a baste; its rightful place is on the dinner table, for application to cooked barbecue. It should never be applied to meat before cooking, and the only time it should be used during cooking is in the last 30 minutes before the meat is done. Otherwise, it might burn into an unsavory, unsightly black crust.

There are probably as many barbecue sauces as there are people who barbecue, but we've included a few good basic recipes on page 184. Start with these; then experiment to develop your own family-secret barbecue sauce.

Where There's Smoke, There's Flavor

You've probably heard of barbecuing with hickory or mesquite, but many other woods can spice up a meal, too. Depending on where you live, you may have access to alder, maple, oak, pecan, walnut, and fruit woods such as apple, cherry, or peach. Corncobs, grapevines, soaked herbs and spices,

and even crushed pecan or walnut shells will produce distinctive smoke flavor, too. Just don't use softwoods; evergreens such as pine and spruce contain resins that will form a nasty coating on your food. For suggestions on which woods work with various foods, see the chart on the following page.

PIG PICKINGS

Whether you're politicking, fund-raising, or just plain celebrating, a pig picking is the customary way to do it in the South. At a traditional pig picking, an expert pit-master spends up to two days barbecuing a whole hog over live coals. After many hours of basting, boasting, and, often, beer drinking, the pit-master will announce that the pig is ready for picking. Guests bring their plates up to the pit and pull the meat right off the carcass, preferably with their fingers.

Depending on the geographic location of the feast, creamy cole slaw, molasses-laced baked beans, hush puppies, or crispy French fries may accompany the meltingly tender pork. Add a soft white bun for sandwich making, a glass of iced tea, and a wedge of ripe watermelon, and you've got many folks' idea of barbecue heaven.

Tasty as it may sound, a pig picking is not an undertaking for the beginning barbecuer. If you plan to hold one in your backyard, you may want to consider hiring a professional to conduct the proceedings. Otherwise, you'll need to call your local butcher and order a hog to be slaughtered a couple of days before the roasting is to commence. Then enlist some of your closest friends. You'll need them to help dig the pit (which should be about five feet long, three feet wide, and one foot deep); light the fire; tend the coals; baste the pig; and drink the beer. (Actually, the beer-drinking is optional, although most pit-masters will argue the point.) Keep in mind that barbecuing a 100-pound hog will take all day Saturday and most of Sunday. Eating that much pork will take some time, too, so don't make any other plans for the weekend!

Temperatures, Estimated Times, and Flavoring Tips for Barbecuing Meats

MEAT & SIZE	COOKING TIME & TEMPERATURE	WOODS & FLAVORS	DONENESS GUIDE
Beef brisket roast *6–10 lbs.*	8–12 hours *225°F (107°C)*	Cherry, hickory, mesquite, oak, peach, pecan	Rare: 145°F (63°C); medium: 160°F (71°C); well: 170°F (77°C)
Beef ribs *3 lbs.*	4 hours *200°F–225°F (93°C–107°C)*	Hickory, mesquite	160°F (71°C) pulls easily from bones
Lamb and venison *5–7 lbs.*	5–7 hours *200°F–220°F (93°C–104°C)*	Apple, cherry, grapevine, hickory, oak, peach, pecan	Rare: 145°F (63°C); medium: 160°F (71°C); well: 170°F (77°C)
Pulled pork, whole-leg shoulder *15 lbs.*	8–12 hours *250°F (121°C)*	Apple, cherry, hickory, oak, peach, pecan, walnut	170°F (77°C)
Pork ribs *3 lbs.*	4 hours *200°F–225°F (93°C–107°C)*	Corncobs, hickory	170°F (77°C) pulls easily from bones
Pork roast *5–8 lbs.*	7–8 hours *200–220°F (93°C–104°C)*	Hickory, pecan	170°F (77°C)
Ham, precooked *All sizes*	3–4 hours *200–220°F (93°C–104°C)*	Apple, corncobs, hickory, maple, oak	140°F (60°C)
Ham, uncooked *10 lbs.*	7–12 hours *200–220°F (93°C–104°C)*	Apple, corncobs, hickory, maple, oak	170°F (77°C)
Sausage links *Full grill*	4–5 hours *200°F–250°F (93°C–121°C)*	Hickory, oak, pecan	170°F (77°C) for fresh sausage
Whole chicken *5–7 lbs.*	3–6 hours *220°F–250°F (104°C–121°C)*	Alder, apple, cherry, grapevine, hickory, maple, mesquite, oak, pecan	180°F (82°C) leg moves easily
Whole turkey, unstuffed *12–20 lbs.*	6–8 hours *240°F–250°F (116°C–121°C)*	Alder, apple, cherry, hickory, maple, oak, pecan	180°F (82°C) leg moves easily
Whole duck *5 lbs.*	2½–5 hours *190°F–220°F (96°C–104°C)*	Alder, oak	180°F (82°C) leg moves easily
Whole goose *8–10 lbs.*	7–8 hours *200°F–220°F (93°C–104°C)*	Alder, oak	180°F (82°C) leg moves easily
Whole pheasant *5–6 lbs.*	3½–6 hours *200°F–210°F (93°C–99°C)*	Alder, apple, hickory, oak	160°F (71°C) leg moves easily
Salmon and other fish steaks *Full grill*	2–3 hours *250°F (121°C)*	Alder, apple, cherry, corncobs, grapevine, peach, pecan	Cook until opaque and flakes easily with a fork

Building a Portable Utensil Rack

Even when you cook indoors, there never seems to be enough space for all your cooking utensils. Move the kitchen outdoors, and storage space disappears altogether. With this handy utensil rack, though, you can keep your basting brushes, tongs, and oven mitts right where you need them—next to the grill! The optional frame (shown in the photo above) allows you to place the project in the backyard; if you grill on the back porch or patio, omit the frame and just build the rack portion of the project to fit over your porch railing (see the photo on page 198). Don't worry if you're not an expert woodworker: Designed entirely from standard dimension lumber, this project is within the reach of anyone who can hold a saw and hammer a nail.

MATERIALS & TOOLS

- Measuring tape
- Pencil
- Straightedge
- Handsaw or circular saw
- C-clamps
- Electric drill with $\frac{1}{16}$", $\frac{1}{8}$", $\frac{5}{64}$", and $\frac{13}{32}$" bits
- Stop collar
- Hammer
- 4d (1½") galvanized finish nails
- 2d (1") galvanized finish nails
- Two $\frac{3}{8}$" galvanized eyebolts, each 7½" long
- Two $\frac{3}{8}$" galvanized washers
- Two $\frac{3}{8}$" galvanized wing nuts
- No. 6 x 1¼" decking screws
- No. 2 Phillips-head screwdriver
- Exterior wood glue
- Medium-grit sandpaper
- Exterior paint or finish (optional)
- Paintbrushes (optional)

TIPS

- This project consists of two separate parts: the utensil rack itself and a U-shaped frame for the rack to rest on. Pounding the frame legs into the ground and then setting the rack on top of the frame will allow you to set up the rack anywhere in your yard. (If you'll be doing your cooking on a porch or deck that has a 2 x 4 rail on it, you won't need the U-shaped frame. Fit the utensil rack directly over the rail as shown on page 198.)
- To protect the U-shaped frame from ground moisture, either build it with a weather-resistant lumber such as cedar, redwood, or teak; or use a commercial softwood such as pine, and apply a protective exterior-grade paint or finish.

CUTTING LIST

CODE	DESCRIPTION	QTY.	MATERIAL
A	Rack sides	2	1 x 4 x 30"
B	Pegs	6	3" of $\frac{3}{8}$"-diameter dowel
C	Rack top	1	1 x 6 x 30"
D	Long trim	2	28¾" of $\frac{3}{8}$"-diameter dowel
E	Short trim	2	4⅞" of $\frac{3}{8}$"-diameter dowel
F	Frame legs	2	1 x 4 x 52"
G	Frame top	1	1 x 4 x 28"
H	Frame shelf	1	1 x 4 x 28"

- Use your drill and $\frac{1}{16}$" bit to bore pilot holes (or starter holes) for all the nails in this project, and a $\frac{1}{8}$" bit for all the screws. These predrilled holes will make it much easier to insert the nails and screws.
- A stop collar (see "Materials & Tools") is a drill accessory with which you can set the depth of a drilled hole. If you don't own a stop collar, just make a masking-tape "flag" instead. Wrap a short length of tape around your drill bit to mark the depth to which you want to drill. As the bit sinks into the wood, the flag will warn you to stop drilling by hitting the surface of the wood when the bit has sunk far enough.

Instructions

1 Cut all the lumber to the dimensions specified in the "Cutting List."

2 Referring to the illustration on page 199, mark a point on the face of one rack side (A), 1½" in from one short end and 1¾" in from either long edge. Repeat to mark another hole at the other end of the rack side.

3 Using C-clamps, clamp the two rack sides (A) together, face to face, with their ends and edges even, and the two points you marked in step 2 facing up.

4 Using your drill and a $\frac{13}{32}$" bit, bore a hole all the way through both rack sides, at each of the two marked points. Remove the C-clamps. (When you've finished making the utensil rack, you'll insert eyebolts through these holes in order to secure the rack to the U-shaped frame or to a 2 x 4 porch rail.)

5 To create holes for the dowel pegs (B) on one of the rack sides (A), start by measuring and marking a line down the length of one rack side, 1¾" in from either long edge. (This line will intersect the holes you drilled in step 4.) Then, starting about 5½" in from either end of the board, mark six equidistant points on this line—one hole for each of the dowel pegs.

6 Using a 5/64"-diameter bit and a stop collar or flag, bore a 1/2"-deep hole at each of the six points you marked in step 5. Angle each hole slightly downward toward one long edge of the board, so the dowel pegs (B) that fit into the holes will tilt upward.

7 Place a few drops of wood glue in each of the six holes and on one end of each dowel peg (B); then insert a peg into each hole.

8 Apply glue to the top edges of the two rack sides (A). Then position the rack sides under the rack top (C), as shown in the illustration. The outer faces of the rack sides should be flush with the edges of the rack top, and the short ends of all three boards should be even.

9 To further secure each rack side (A) to the rack top (C), drive seven evenly spaced 4d nails through the upper face of the rack top and down into the glued edge of each rack side. (Inserting these nails will be much easier if you use a drill and a 1/16" bit to create a starter hole for each one.) Allow the glue to dry for six to eight hours before continuing.

10 Using the illustration as a guide, arrange the long trim (D) and short trim (E) to form a rectangle on the upper face of the rack top (C), placing the long trim pieces between the short trim pieces. (These trim pieces will prevent anything that you put on top of the rack from rolling off.)

11 Before nailing the trim pieces (D and E) to the rack top (C), mark points on them for starter holes: two holes on each short trim and four holes on each long trim. (As you mark these hole positions on the long trim pieces, check to make sure that none of the nails you'll drive through the holes will hit any of the nails that are already in the rack top.) Using a drill

and a 1/16" bit, drill a starter hole at each marked point.

12 Glue the trim pieces (D and E) onto the rack top (C), and secure them by driving 2d finish nails through the starter holes.

13 When the glue has dried thoroughly, sand the assembled utensil rack with medium-grit sandpaper to smooth all edges.

14 Unless you've used a weather-resistant wood to make the utensil rack, apply two coats of an exterior-grade paint or finish, allowing the first coat to dry before applying the second.

15 To begin constructing the U-shaped frame portion of this project, you must first cut one end of each frame leg (F) to a point, so the legs can be driven into the ground. Start by clamping the frame legs together, face to face, with their ends and edges even.

16 To mark the angled cutting lines on the clamped frame legs (F), first mark a centerpoint, right at one short end, 1¾" from either long edge. At the same end of the clamped legs, also mark a point on each long edge, 3" from the short end. Then mark two diagonal lines, from the 1¾" centerpoint to each 3" point. Cut along these lines to form pointed ends on the legs, and remove the clamps when you're finished.

17 Glue the frame top (G) between the frame legs (F), as shown in the illustration. The frame top's upper face should be even with the top ends of the frame legs, and its edges should be even with the frame legs' edges.

18 To further secure the frame legs (F) to the frame top (G), first use a drill and ⅛" bit to bore two evenly spaced starter holes through the face of each frame leg and into each end of the frame top. Then drive four 1¼" screws into the holes.

19 Glue the frame shelf (H) between the frame legs (F), with its upper face 20" below the lower face of the frame top (G). Secure the shelf to the legs with screws, just as you secured the frame legs to the frame top in step 18. Allow the glue to dry thoroughly.

20 Using medium-grit sandpaper, sand the U-shaped frame to smooth all rough edges. Unless you've used a weather-resistant wood to construct the frame, apply two coats of exterior-grade paint or finish, allowing the first coat to dry well before applying the second.

21 To set the utensil rack on the U-shaped frame, first drive the frame into the ground by pounding on the upper ends of the frame legs (F). To cushion each leg from your hammer or sledge, place a scrap block of wood over it, and pound on the block rather than on the frame.

22 When the frame is in the ground, set the rack on top of it. Then insert the eyebolts through the holes in the rack sides (A). Place a washer and wing nut over the end of each eye bolt, and tighten the wing nuts until the rack is secure. (The rack may be secured to a 2 x 4 porch rail in the same manner.)

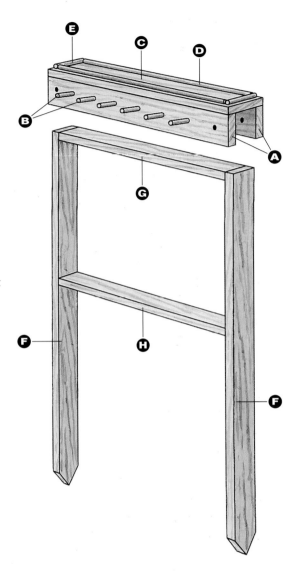

A Vegetable Garden Plan

Every backyard chef knows that few foods respond to grilling, barbecuing, and roasting as well as homegrown vegetables. For one thing, they're fresh; for another, if you've grown them yourself, they're invested with flavors no store-bought veggies could ever match. When considering which veggies are better for roasting and barbecuing, most chefs seem to agree that the meatier varieties are ideal.

A BROCCOLI
Brassica oleracea

Light to moderate shade

A cool season crop, so for early summer harvest, sow seeds just before the last spring frost, or set seedlings out as soon as soil can be worked. Provide afternoon shade, or plant on the east side of tall summer crops such as corn and tomatoes. When plants are 4" tall, thin to 18" to 24" apart.

B CARROTS
Daucus carota

Full sun

Sow seeds thinly in early spring, about ½" deep, in rows 14" apart. Thin seedlings to 2" apart. Carrots prefer cool weather, but some varieties may be grown from early spring till late fall. If your soil isn't loose, select the shorter, stump-rooted varieties.

C CORN
Zea mays

Full sun

Sow seeds when soil has warmed, 2" deep, 4"–5" apart, in rows 24"–36" apart. Planting in several short rows rather than a few long ones will aid in pollination, and setting plants on north side of garden will prevent tall, leafy stalks from shading other plants. Thin seedlings to 12"–18" apart.

D EGGPLANT
Solanum melongena

Full sun

Set seedlings out when soil has warmed, 24"–30" apart, in rows 24"–30" apart; support plants with stakes. As well as planting the classic teardrop-shaped eggplants, try the long, thin Asian varieties, such as the 'Ichiban' cultivar.

E GARLIC
Allium sativum

Full sun

Plant individual cloves in early spring, 1"–2" deep, and 4"–6" apart. Harvest when tops turn yellow in late summer. Elephant garlic *Allium ampeloprasum*—an extra-large member of the leek family—is grown in the same way, but is milder and easier to peel than true garlic.

F ONIONS
Allium cepa

Full sun

Plant *sets* (small seed onions) in early spring, 2"–3" apart, covering each set with ¼" of soil. Rows should be 12"–18" apart. Milder onions, such as 'Vidalias', 'Walla Walla Sweets', and 'Bermudas', are favorites for many outdoor chefs, but more pungent varieties, such as 'Stockton Red', are also delicious roasted.

G CHILI PEPPERS
Capiscum anuum

Full sun

Set seedlings out when soil has warmed, 18"–24" apart. Sweet peppers include bell, banana, and cherry, while hot peppers include 'Red Chili', 'Jalapeno', and 'Anaheim'. Because the root systems of peppers are shallow, they also do well in pots and hanging baskets.

H POTATOES (RUSSET)
Solanum tuberosum

Full sun

Plant seed potatoes or sprouted "eyes" in early spring, 5" deep, 12"–14" apart, in rows 30" apart, at an edge of your garden where they'll have more growing space. Mulch heavily to keep soil cool. Russet potatoes, with their thick skins, are best for roasting.

I SUMMER SQUASH
Cucurbita

Full sun

Sow seeds when soil has warmed, 1" deep and 36" apart, at an edge of the garden where the plants can sprawl. Harvest fruits when 6"–8"

long. Both yellow summer squash and zucchini (*Cucurbita pepo*) are excellent roasted. Compact hybrids such as the 'Raven', 'Yellow Bush Scallop', and 'Peter Pan' varieties will take less space.

J TOMATOES
Lycopersicon esculentum

Full sun

Set seedlings out when soil has warmed, 18"–24" apart, on the garden's north side. Stake plants or mulch them with loose straw. All varieties, from tiny cherries to 2-pound beefsteaks, roast well. Most tomato varieties, due to their shallow root systems, can be grown in pots or hanging baskets.

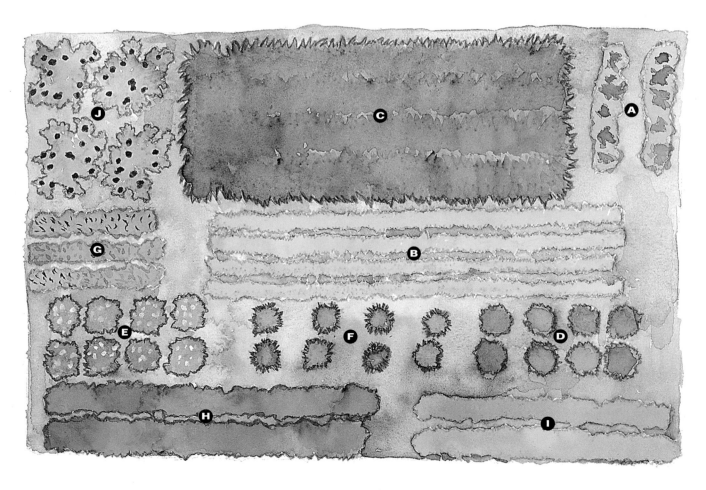

Setting the Scene

Remember the best meal you ever had? Maybe it was an elegant five-course dinner served at a rooftop restaurant. Or perhaps it was Chinese take-out, enjoyed on a foot-bridge that spanned a sleepy river. You may not recall exactly what you ate, but you'll always remember whether you dined by candlelight, or by the flash of fireflies; whether you ate with fine silver, or with simple chopsticks.

Setting the scene—creating the right ambiance—can turn a casual backyard get-together into a special event. It's not hard to do, either. Locating the ideal corner of your lawn for afternoon tea; finding the perfect set of Adirondack chairs or a really great picnic table; setting the table with the family china instead of plastic plates; choosing a wine that goes perfectly with the meal; planning ahead to wrap up all the small details—these all contribute to a memorable atmosphere.

The following chapter will walk you through the basics of setting the scene, from selecting a dining site to planning the perfect potluck. Don't stop with these suggestions, though. Remember that the little touches *you* add will make the greatest impression!

Selecting a Dining Site

It doesn't matter whether your backyard consists of just a modest patio or a sprawling lawn. Large or small, your space awaits transformation as you begin to decide where to site your outdoor gathering. Examine your yard with fresh eyes. Take stock of all its features: Fountains? Swings? Umbrellas? Is that wall wide enough to accommodate a buffet? Will a condiments shelf squeeze between those tree branches? With a bit of creativity and proper planning, you'll have no trouble giving guests a comfortable and inviting space.

ENJOYING THE ELEMENTS

No matter what kind of backyard space you have, you're likely to find that it boasts many features that can enhance an outdoor gathering. A vegetable garden, for example, makes a unique and wonderful setting for a meal, especially one that features the fruits of the harvest.

A grassy stretch of lawn may invite you to spread a few quilts to host a down-to-earth picnic; the informal seating will encourage guests to mix and mingle in new ways. Just be sure to provide alternative seating for those with restricted mobility, and to elevate serving bowls and platters to keep the bugs away. Setting a table near the blankets with food at one end and some seating at the other will address both of these considerations.

Water will add elegance to any outdoor gathering. A nicely lit fountain or waterfall makes an enchanting backdrop for an evening soiree. Fountains and waterfalls will repel the bugs, freshen the air, and fill the lulls in conversation with delightful burbling. Still water, such as the water in a pond, provides light and serenity in the morning or evening. Do avoid serving meals near ponds when the sun is especially bright. The harsh glare of reflected sunlight can be distracting.

PRACTICALITIES

The practicalities of siting your dining experience hinge in part on the type

of event that you're hosting. If it's a romantic dinner for two, the small scale of the event allows for flexibility. You can make an intimate dining nook out of any corner of your backyard. For a substantial crowd, however, take care to provide adequate room for guests to circulate; a tightly packed dining table will keep your guests from being able to feel comfortable and relaxed.

If you set up a dining area on the lawn, make sure the ground is level, or your guests may find that their chairs wobble throughout the meal. Patios and terraces work well here. Decide whether or not you will serve from the dining table, banquet-style, or whether you will designate a separate buffet table. In instances of limited space, it's usually best to set the serving dishes on their own table, separate from the place settings.

Whatever the case, keep the food close to the guests, and protect it from insects by covering it with a screened box (see pages 178–179 for instructions) or with a tent-style draping of mosquito netting. Casual family meals are usually best served in close proximity to the house, as trips for forgotten forks and extra condiments are inevitable.

Finally, weather is a vital component in determining where to seat guests. Always check the forecast before scheduling your outdoor bash, and be prepared to accommodate your party indoors if necessary. Awnings and umbrellas come in handy; both can protect a gathering either during a downpour or on an exceedingly sunny day.

Building a Sun Shade

Nothing feels quite as luxurious on a hot summer afternoon as relaxing in a patch of shade. Unfortunately, growing a stately maple or oak to provide that patch can take more years than you may care to wait. With the instructions provided here, however, you can make one or more portable shade screens and set them up wherever you like—on a deck or patio, or right in the middle of your yard. The open lattice structure will allow you to enjoy summer breezes, too.

MATERIALS & TOOLS

- Pencil
- Tape measure
- Circular saw
- Hammer
- Square
- No. 2 Phillips-head screwdriver
- Two 6" C-clamps
- 3d (1¼") galvanized finish nails
- No. 6 x 1½" decking screws
- Lumber (see "Cutting List")

TIPS

- All the lattice pieces (C, F, G, and H) are attached to the verticals with three finish nails at each joint.
- Remember: A 1 x 2 is actually ¾" thick and 1½" wide; a 2 x 2 is actually 1½" thick and 1½" wide; and a 1 x 4 is actually ¾" thick and 3½" wide.
- If you'd like to make your shade screen a permanent fixture in your yard, just fasten two wooden stakes to each foot (I), and pound the stakes into the ground. Then plant climbing vines at the base of the screen; they'll help provide extra shade.
- If you plan to make two screens (the instructions will show you how), don't forget to double the quantities provided in the "Cutting List."

CUTTING LIST (for one screen)

CODE	DESCRIPTION	QTY.	MATERIAL
A	Spacers	2	1 x 2 x 48"
B	Outer verticals	2	2 x 2 x 84"
C	Lattices	10	1 x 2 x 24"
D	Inner verticals	2	1 x 2 x 81½"
E	Center verticals	2	1 x 2 x 68¾"
F	Lattices	20	1 x 2 x 4½"
G	Lattices	20	1 x 2 x 7"
H	Lattices	3	1 x 2 x 18⅜"
I	Feet	2	1 x 4 x 16"

Instructions

(for two screens)

1 Cut two spacers (A). These won't be functional parts of your shade screens; you'll only use them for measuring the gaps between the lattice pieces as you assemble this project.

2 Cut two outer verticals (B) and place them on a flat work surface, with their outer edges 24" apart.

3 Cut ten 24"-long lattices (C). Place one of these lattices across the outer verticals (B), with one wide face up. Position the ends and upper edge of the lattice flush with the outside edges and top ends of the outer verticals. Fasten the lattice in place with 3d finish nails. (This will be the top of your shade screen.) Set the remaining nine pieces aside.

4 Place one of the spacers (A) under the attached lattice (C), with its wide face up and one long edge against the bottom edge of the lattice. Then position another 24"-long lattice just beneath the spacer, and fasten it to the vertical with 3d finish nails. (The upper edge of this lattice should butt up against the bottom edge of the spacer.) Using the spacer ensures that the gap between the lattices will be the same width as a lattice piece itself.

5 Reposition the spacer (A) beneath the second attached lattice (C) and fasten a third 24"-long lattice beneath it.

6 Before fastening three more 24"-long lattices (C) at the bottom of the two outer verticals (B), measure 9⅝" up from the bottom end of each outer vertical and mark these spots with a pencil.

7 Attach a 24"-long lattice (C) to the outer verticals (B), with its bottom edge at the 9⅝" marks. Using the spacer as before, attach

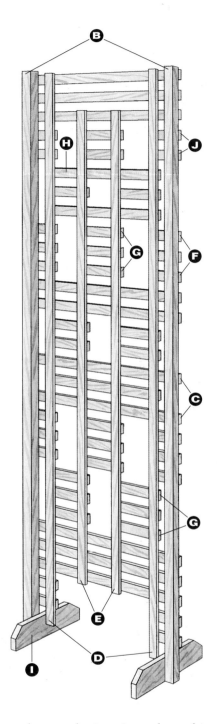

another two lattice pieces above this one. The screen assembly should now have three lattices at its top end and three at its bottom end, and you should have four lattices remaining. Set these four pieces aside.

8 Turn the assembly over so the two outer verticals (B) face up and the attached lattices face down. Cut two inner verticals (D). Position a spacer (A), with its wide face up, against the inner edge of an outer vertical. Then place an inner vertical against the spacer, checking to see that its top end is flush with the top edge of the uppermost lattice piece (C). Fasten the inner vertical to the six attached lattice pieces.

9 Repeat step 8 to attach another inner vertical (D) on the opposite side of the assembly.

10 Cut two center verticals (E). Position one of these verticals on the assembly, with its wide face up and its outer edge 7" from the inner edge of an outer vertical (B). As you can see in the illustration, the bottom end of this center vertical should be flush with the bottom edge of the lattice (C) at the bottom of the assembly.

11 Repeat step 10 to attach the second center vertical (E) to the assembly, with its wide face up and its inner edge 7" from the inner edge of the other outer vertical (B).

12 If you like, repeat steps 1 through 11 to assemble a second shade screen.

13 Position the panels on a flat work surface, edge to edge, with their lattices facing up. Clamp the panels together by tightening two C-clamps over the abutting outer verticals (B), one at the top of the panels and one at the bottom.

14 To make sure the clamped panels are square, fit your square around either top corner, and adjust the panels (they'll give a little, even though each panel has nails in it) until both blades of the square rest firmly against the edges of a lattice (C) and an outer vertical (B). Remove the square and the clamps when you're finished.

15 Cut the remaining lattice pieces (F, G, and H). Next, take a good look at the illustration, which shows their positions on the panel. Then, using a spacer as before and working from the top of each panel to its bottom, lay out all the lattice pieces on each panel. Remove the spacer, and adjust the spacing as necessary. (You may need to trim some lattices to length.) Using finish nails, attach the lattices to the panels.

16 Cut four 16"-long feet (I). At each end of each foot, measure and mark a point 2" down from one long edge. On the same long edge of each foot, measure and mark 2" in

from each end. Then draw a line to connect the two marks at each corner, and cut along the four lines. These cuts will create the two angled edges on the top of each foot.

17 Center a leg (I) on the interior face of an outer vertical (B) and check to see that its bottom edge is flush with the bottom end of the outer vertical. Fasten the leg in place with three 1½" decking screws inserted through the leg and into the outer vertical.

18 Repeat step 17 to fasten a leg (I) to the bottom of each of the three remaining outer verticals (B) on the two panels.

Selecting Outdoor Seating and Tables

The right outdoor furniture will beckon you onto your lawn and tempt you to stay for a glass of iced tea, a quick lunch, or even an elegant dinner. It can turn your porch or backyard into an outdoor room that's just as comfortable and inviting as any room inside. But with so many types, styles, and prices available, choosing the perfect picnic table or the ideal Adirondack chairs can be a daunting task. Don't worry, though. With some knowledge of what's out there, a quick evaluation of your needs, and a few handy shopping tips, you'll soon be enjoying your backyard in comfort and style.

durability being the primary commodities. If comfort is your only concern, you won't need to spend a lot of money; price and relaxation value are not necessarily related. Beauty and durability, however, may cost a little more, depending on what kind of material the furniture is made of. The chart on the following page gives an overview of the most common types of materials and their relative cost, durability, and ease of care.

THE SHOPPING TRIP

Armed with a good idea of your needs and means, a basic knowledge of what's out there, and the pros and cons of various kinds of materials, you're ready to hit the stores. The following tips will ensure shopping success:

■ Dress the part. Wear comfortable clothing in which you'd normally relax. If you usually wear shorts to read the paper and relax, wear shorts!

■ Do the blind seat test: Sit in every chair in the showroom and try out every table. Take note of your impressions and narrow your choices based purely on comfort.

■ Now, notice style, appearance, and features. Will that big, comfy chaise lounge fit in your allotted space? What colors are available? Is

STORABLE OR PERMANENT?

Most outdoor furniture falls into one of two categories—storable or permanent. Anything that can be folded, collapsed, or otherwise compacted or easily moved is, of course, storable. Permanent furniture, as its name suggests, becomes a more or less permanent fixture in your yard; benches and tables made of concrete or exceptionally heavy wood are a few examples.

Deciding which type you need is the first step toward furnishing your garden. If you use your backyard for everything from playing horseshoes to hosting potlucks, or if you have a very small lawn, you'll probably need to move your furnishings around fairly often: Storable furniture will be your best choice. If, on the other hand, you rarely use your backyard for anything but relaxing and dining, or if your lawn is large enough to set aside a section solely for these activities, you should consider permanent furnishings.

GETTING WHAT YOU PAY FOR

Lawn furniture runs the gamut of prices, with comfort, beauty, and inflatable furniture really suitable for your lawn? Weed out the impractical and/or aesthetically offensive pieces.

■ You should now have a group of furniture that's comfortable, attractive, and functional. Take a look at price tags and narrow your choices based on your budget.

■ Evaluate the durability of the remaining pieces. Ideally, you should choose the furniture that's going to last the longest.

■ Write the check and await delivery of your new furniture with iced tea in hand.

Outdoor Furniture Materials

	STYLES	DURABILITY	PRICE	MAINTENANCE
Plastic	Wide range of colors and styles	Fair to excellent: Colors can fade, and most plastics will show scratches.	Inexpensive	Simple with basic cleaners
Metal	Cast aluminum, extruded aluminum, extruded steel, tubular steel, wrought iron, etc.	Good to excellent: Painted metal can rust and chip, but baked-on enamels are very durable.	Medium to expensive	May need sanding and painting if rust develops
Wood	Ranges from rustic to modern, with numerous types of wood available	Fair to excellent: Teak and painted or treated pine are very resistant to weather and physical damage; cedar dents and scratches easily, but resists bugs and weather.	Medium to very expensive	Care varies based on species of wood
Concrete	Various styles, all permanent	Excellent	Expensive	Very little maintenance required, although painted concrete may need to be repainted every few years

Backyard Dining Basics

Whether it's a quick sandwich or an honest-to-goodness sit-down family dinner, dining outdoors just seems more special somehow than eating indoors. It's such an easy pleasure to indulge in, too. Turning your backyard into a dining room involves very little work, but a few tricks and tips will add to your enjoyment.

GETTING IN TOUCH WITH NATURE
When you move your meal outdoors, you put yourself in Mother Nature's hands. Make sure you know what to expect from her and how to cope with all of her offerings! Be sure to consult a weather report. Select a shady site for hot, sunny days. Find a sheltered spot if you're expecting more than a gentle breeze. If rain's a possibility,

consider a covered porch or a market umbrella. For other suggestions on site selection, turn to pages 204–205.

As big and seemingly beyond your control as the weather is, it's often the little things—insects, namely—that can cause the most disruption to your fresh-air repast. Before a swarm of mosquitoes drives you indoors, though, take a few simple steps to keep the bugs at bay. Many pests find sweets irresistible, so leave dessert inside until you're ready to serve it. Clear dirty dishes after each course. For larger parties in very buggy areas, consider renting a mesh tent to protect the food. Pay attention to your choice of centerpiece, too; fragrant flowers such as hyacinth, peony, and jasmine look gorgeous, but they may attract unwelcome flying guests. Citrus fruits contain a bug deterring chemical, and although a bowl of lemons and limes may not contain a high enough concentration of that chemical to stave off every insect in the neighborhood, it will make a pretty centerpiece! And of course, a few citronella candles will offer considerable protection from bugs. Just be sure to set the candles a few feet away from your dining area, as their mild scent can affect the taste of your food.

THE DINING SURFACE

You don't need a table to dine outdoors in style. A quilt or blanket spread over a level spot of lawn can provide the ideal surface for an afternoon picnic. Just be sure to check the ground for dampness before tossing down a family-heirloom quilt.

If you do decide to dine at a table, your choice of table coverings includes paper, plastic, and cloth. Paper coverings can be plain or patterned, or simply yesterday's newspaper—perfect for any kind of shellfish feast. Keep your paper tablecloth from flying up by taping its corners to the table's underside. Plastic coverings also come in a variety of colors and patterns and promise easy cleanup. Check with your local fabric store; plastic coverings are sometimes sold by the yard. A gingham or calico cotton tablecloth is perfect for a more casual evening; linen is lovely for a more elegant meal. If you're using one of your better tablecloths, place a pad or cover underneath to protect it from the rough or stained surface of your outdoor table. Keep any tablecloth from flapping in the wind by tying, clipping, or weighting its corners.

SETTING THE TABLE (OR THE BLANKET) AND THE MOOD

For many people, dining outdoors always means paper plates and plastic cutlery. And there's nothing wrong with the old standards. However, your choice of table setting will, in large part, determine the mood of your meal—and maintaining a formal or romantic atmosphere can be hard to do when your paper plates go up in flames along with the baked Alaska!

Nevertheless, for casual occasions, nothing beats paper for ease of cleanup; just be careful that a breeze doesn't send your table setting into flight. Sturdy plastic dishes offer another good option for informal gatherings. They come in a huge range of colors and styles, and with the non-dispos- able variety you'll save money (and landfill space) in the long run. For those times when you'd like a touch of elegance, though, don't be afraid to bring out the fine china and the silverware! You may be surprised by how much you enjoy dining on "real" dinnerware in the great outdoors.

OTHER EXTRAS

Because the trek from kitchen to outdoor dining room is often more than just a few feet, a sturdy tray will make serving and cleaning up quicker and easier. Keep a trash can or bag handy, too, as well as a separate bag for recyclables. A few damp cloths and easy access to water will come in handy in the event of spills or stickiness. Finally, consider your own comfort; pull out a sun hat for daytime meals, and don't forget a sweater or jacket for evenings.

Preparing a Buffet Table

Whether it's a formal wedding reception or a casual neighborhood potluck, when we gather together, we usually gather around food—the more of it, the better! And when you're feeding a crowd, a buffet table often offers the best way to do it. A well-planned buffet is convenient for guests and host alike, and it complements the party without getting in the way. Although you don't need to be a professional caterer to set up a great buffet table, following a few simple guidelines will yield professional results.

LOCATION, LOCATION, LOCATION

As in marketing, real estate, and just about everything else in life, location is the key to a buffet table's success. Select a site near a door; you'll need to maintain the table throughout the party, so proximity and easy access to the kitchen are important.

You'll also need enough space to accommodate both guests and table without crowding. Allow at least four feet of walkway around the buffet, more if any of your guests have special needs; your friends with wheelchairs, walkers, or canes will notice and appreciate your attention to this detail.

For parties of 30 people or more, make sure that the table is accessible from both sides; this will speed serving, shorten the guests' wait, and improve the traffic flow around the buffet.

CHOOSING THE RIGHT TABLE

When it comes to a buffet table, size matters. So do height, shape, and sturdiness. The table's top should be long enough and wide enough to accommodate all the food you'll be serving, with room left over for utensils, napkins, plates—and an attractive presentation.

For your guests' comfort, choose a table with a top at about hip-height to the average adult. If you expect many children, consider setting up a separate, lower table for them to use.

In general, rectangular tables make the best choice for buffets, although round tables will work for small parties. As long as your picnic table doesn't have attached benches, it will serve admirably. You may also want to consider renting a banquet table—those long folding tables you've seen at catered events. Avoid using card tables, though; they're usually not sturdy enough for the mountains of food you'll be serving!

SETTING UP

For at least part of your party, the buffet table will be the center of attention; make sure it's worthy of that attention by creating a visually pleasing display. Add height and dimension with small boxes, cake stands, bowls—even telephone books. Just make sure the objects you choose are sturdy enough to hold whatever you plan to place on top. Arrange these items on the table, spacing them well apart, and varying elevation and shape. A staircase configuration makes an appetizing display, but experiment to find an arrangement you like.

Keep food placement in mind, too. In general, cold dishes should be placed at the beginning of the table and hot dishes toward the end. The main dish should be the last item in line, before dessert, to ensure that each guest receives an adequate portion. To keep hot foods hot, consider renting or buying chafing dishes; these are metal pans suspended over a heat source (usually a gas or propane flame). Most equipment-rental and restaurant-supply stores carry them. Unless you have something large enough and solid enough to support them, chafing dishes should not be elevated.

Remember to leave room at the beginning of the table for plates, napkins, and silverware. Try rolling individual sets of silverware inside napkins; doing so makes an attractive display, and your guests will have an easier time carrying their forks, knives, and spoons along with their heaping plates.

If there's room on the buffet table, plan to present the drinks at the beginning of the table with the napkins and utensils. Otherwise, set up a separate beverage table nearby, following the same color and elevation schemes.

When you're satisfied with your arrangement, cover it with tablecloths. You'll probably need more than one, so rent or buy several to have on hand.

FINISHING TOUCHES

From an elegant ice sculpture of a swan to a simple vase of homegrown flowers, almost anything goes when you're decorating your buffet table. Before you run out to buy expensive decorations, though, take a look around your house; you'll find all kinds of beautiful and fun knick-knacks. Even the serving dishes you use can (and should) do double duty as embellishment, so pull out those fish-shaped platters and funky handmade bowls!

SERVING IT UP

Put out the food just before your guests begin to arrive. Remember to include appropriate serving utensils for each dish, and make sure all the bowls, plates, and platters are secure and level to prevent spills.

Now, sit back, relax, and have a good time!

Wine and Outdoor Wine Service

48°F (9°C), and red wines are best at about 63°F (17°C). Mix in a sweltering July afternoon, and sustaining these temperatures becomes a bit of a task. If the kitchen is close enough, you may be able to serve the wine from there, but guests generally prefer to have beverages a lot closer at hand. The best solution is to find several large, attractive buckets or carafes and a shady area (which may even be underneath the buffet table if you have no alternative). When serving white wines, fill the buckets with ice and nestle bottles within the cubes. Use cool water, rather than ice, for red wines. Check the buckets every half hour or so; replenish ice as needed and exchange lukewarm water for cool.

Now that your wine is properly cooled or chilled, go ahead and open up a bottle. The basic corkscrew has been unlocking the celebratory spirit for centuries. It may take some practice, and if you've had limited experience, the winged corkscrew offers a good option. This tool relies on rack and pinion mechanics to pry the cork out, rather than on your own grunts and grumbles. Whichever tool you prefer, be sure to have a few out so that guests can help themselves, if appropriate.

Congratulations—you've finally popped open that bottle. Reward

The next time you're in a tizzy over which wines to serve at your dinner party, take comfort in knowing that you share your indecision with five centuries of fretting hosts. Wine snobs have long intimidated the everyday entertainer, and even though we groan when they flaunt their finicky palates, we still panic when they show up at our serving table. Fear not: The truth of the matter is that selecting and serving a great wine requires only a minimum of knowledge and money. Wine is simply too tasty to be left to the upper crust. Incorporate it into your

more casual outdoor functions and shatter the myth that wine should be left as the libation of upscale galas. Provide it at more formal occasions and add a touch of elegance to alfresco dining. Let the following be your guide as you begin to plan how you will choose and serve wine for your outdoor dining occasion.

SERVING UP A TASTE OF AMBIANCE

Maintaining proper temperature presents the primary challenge when serving wine outdoors. Ideally, white wines should be served at around yourself by enjoying a glass. That's right, a glass. Although wine service doesn't have to be fancy, paper and plastic cups can compromise the flavor and enjoyment of wine. Most rental companies can provide glasses for wine service if you don't have enough of your own. Red wines are typically served in bowl-shaped glasses with large mouths; white wines are best in taller glasses with narrower mouths. Keep glasses intact by setting them out on an even surface and by providing adequate, level space for guests to deposit their empty glasses. Remove used glasses as soon as possible to avoid accidental breakage.

If, for whatever reason, glass really isn't an option, use clear plastic cups instead. Some party-supply and rental stores carry plastic wine glasses, with stems and all.

Which Wine to Serve with What

COMMON WINES	FLAVORS AND AROMAS	FOOD PAIRINGS
Cabernet sauvignon *Red*	Black currants, green peppers, chocolate, and spice	Lamb, roast beef, and dishes with garlic
Merlot *Red*	Plums, blueberries, and cherries	Steak, pasta with tomato sauce, and heavy cheeses
Pinot noir *Red*	Cherries, raspberries, and smoke	Lightly sauced dishes, pork, smoked meat, chicken, and smoked cheeses
Zinfandel *Red*	Blackberry jam and black pepper	Roasted pork, pasta, and salmon
Chardonnay *White*	Peas, vanilla, tropical fruits, toast, and nuts (varies by region of production)	Vegetarian dishes, chicken, turkey, and fruit
Sauvignon blanc *White*	Cut grass, herbs, and lemon	Pasta with tomato sauce, white fish, lightly herbed dishes
Riesling *White*	Apricots, citrus, peaches, and flowers	Fruit, cheese, and pork
White zinfandel *Blush*	Strawberries, fruit	Heavily spiced foods, poultry, and Thanksgiving dinner

ALTERNATIVE CHILLING

Just because you're dining outdoors doesn't mean you have to choose between hiding a dingy plastic cooler and sipping lukewarm Chardonnay. If you look around your house, you'll discover all kinds of ingenious ways to keep beverages cool and atmosphere intact.

Something as simple and common as a rope shopping bag can be transformed into an unusual and attractive wine chiller: Just fill the bag with ice, tuck your favorite bottle of wine inside, and suspend the whole package from an accessible tree branch or fence post.

For casual events, try filling an old-fashioned galvanized washtub with crushed ice and bottles of soda, juice, or beer. This folksy cooler will look great under a shady tree or at the foot of a buffet table.

A Salad Garden Plan

No matter how you serve them, homegrown vegetables almost always taste better than their store-bought counterparts. Nowhere is the difference in flavor more evident than in a crisp garden salad. Hand-picked and still warm from the sun, fresh lettuces, crisp carrots, and other salad favorites offer some of summer's most delicious, healthy, and easily attainable treats. And with its lush midsummer green, a salad garden will present a tempting visual feast that will enhance any outdoor meal! All of the following fare best in full sun.

A LETTUCE
Lactuca sativa

Germination: 7–14 days

Sow at a depth of ¼", spacing seedlings 6"–8" apart. Thin to 12" between plants at mid-season, depending on variety. Intersperse with tomatoes, cucumbers, or corn to provide afternoon shade during the heat of summer. May be harvested several times during growing season; chop the head at the base and continue to water. Harvest before the lettuce bolts to prevent bitterness

B RED CABBAGE
Brassica oleracea 'Capitata'

Germination: 7–10 days

Sow at a depth of ¼", spacing seeds 12"–18" apart. Provide with a steady to moderate supply of water and add manure or compost to topsoil every week after heads begin to form. Will continue to produce small heads after first harvest if outer leaves are left growing on plant

C CELERY
Apium graveolens

Germination: 12–21 days

Sow seeds at depth of 1/16" directly into the ground in warm regions. In colder regions, sow indoors or under glass 12 weeks before last frost is expected. Allow 14" between plants. Requires rich soil and steady water supply; may need mulch with compost, leaves, or manure to attain prime soil conditions

D CUCUMBERS
Cucumis sativus

Germination: 7–10 days

Sow seeds at depth of 1", 3–4 weeks before last frost, allowing 6' between vine varieties and 2' between bush plants. Requires rich soil and frequent watering

E CHIVES
Allium schoenprasum

Germination: 10 days

Sow seeds at a depth of 3", spacing them 8"–10" apart. Keep soil moist. Allow to mature (20–30 days, or 12" high), but not to flower. Leave bulbs in the ground over winter to regenerate the following year

F RADISHES
Raphanus sativus

Germination: 3–4 days

Sow seeds at a depth of 3", spacing them 1"–2" apart in sandy, light soil. Plant alongside carrots, beets, and lettuce. Water moderately

G CARROTS
Daucus carota

Germination: 14–21 days

Sow seeds ½" deep, in rows 14" apart in soil that is light, loose, rich, and moist

H BEETS
Beta vulgaris

Germination: varies

Sow seeds ½" deep, 2"–4" apart in light, loose, rich soil. Water moderately

Planning the Perfect Potluck

THE NATURE OF THE FEAST

By its very definition, a potluck hints at something of a lottery—with all the associated pitfalls and rewards. We've all heard about the winter potluck where everyone thought chili would be a great idea; or the summer version, where the menu ran to eleven varieties of salad, but no further. Fortunately, with forethought, planning, and a little common sense, you and your guests can avoid the vagaries of random choice.

THE NATURE OF THE FEAST
The first task on your list is to decide the nature of your potluck. Will there be ten guests or fifty? For brunch, lunch, or dinner? Will you have a theme?

As a rule, unless you live on a farm and measure your backyard in acres, smaller is better. Keeping your guest list paired down to reasonable size will ensure room to mix and mingle. It will also increase the likelihood that everyone will have a chance to sample each dish. Providing adequate seating and table space is easier at smaller gatherings, too. And perhaps most important of all, your job as potluck coordinator and menu planner will be much more manageable.

Themes can provide a friendly challenge to guests' imaginations and instant conversation topics once the potluck gets underway. A "Night with the Stars" motif might produce cauliflower comets with asparagus tails, or pâté squares with "Marilyn" or "Marlon" etched beneath tiny handprints. A "Bounty of the Garden" theme will allow people to show off their gardening skills. Italian and Greek themes work well because these cuisines evolved around the Mediterranean passion for mixing food and conversation over extended periods of time.

MAKING A LIST AND CHECKING IT TWICE

Call or send invitations at least a week in advance; this will give everyone plenty of time to decide what to bring, and then get back to you about it. Urge your guests to steer away from dishes that require last-minute preparation; kitchen space can get very tight if too many cooks need sink and counter space at the same time. Ask them to avoid egg-based dishes, too, including anything with mayonnaise; eggs outside of their shells do not handle exposure very well.

Keep track of who's bringing what, and if you see much duplication, ask one or two people to try something different. Have a few suggestions in mind. Some folks like to be told exactly what kind of food to bring; others may appreciate specific recipes.

And even in these enlightened times, a bachelor or bachelorette might be grateful for the opportunity to supply paper plates or plastic cutlery.

Regardless of what each person decides upon, ask them to jot down the recipe and bring it, too; folks with

food allergies or other dietary restrictions will be able to check a dish's contents for forbidden ingredients. Everyone else will come away with a few new favorites to try at home.

PREPARING FOR THE EVENT

Start making room in your refrigerator a few days in advance; some dishes will need to stay cold right up until the time they're served. You may be able to store items you don't need for the potluck in a neighbor's fridge—but only if the neighbor's been invited! Buy plenty of ice, too, to keep cold

dishes cold once they've been set out. At the other end of the Fahrenheit scale, not everyone has a chafing dish (a metal pan suspended over a heat source), so plenty of microwave-safe containers are a must.

Make sure you have enough table space for the number of dishes you expect. (See pages 214–215 for tips on setting up a buffet table.) Rent or borrow extra tables if you need them.

Stock up on plastic wrap and aluminum foil for leftovers that don't have lids or that are being shared once the potluck's over. (See pages 222–223 for ideas on setting up a take-it-home station.) Raid your utensil drawers for extra serving spoons; if you don't have enough, beg, borrow, or buy extras—otherwise, guests may find spaghetti sauce tainting the coleslaw. Make sure you have several garbage bins on hand, too. Place them in obvious (but inconspicuous) places and equip them with tight-fitting lids to discourage bees and other bugs.

Finally, sit back, relax, and wait for the fun to begin!

Setting Up a Take-It-Home Station

At the end of a potluck, you and each of your guests will probably be faced with a week's worth of a single kind of leftover. Spare your guests from potato-salad, coleslaw, or apple-pie overload—and help speed your own cleanup tasks—by setting up a take-it-home station where diners can wrap up servings of their favorite dishes. Set out plenty of aluminum foil, plastic plates and cups, and roomy paper bags that guests can carry it all home in. As an extra touch, top off each take-it-home bag with a simple party favor, such as a handful of butter mints tied up in tulle. In just a few simple steps, you and all your guests can wrap up tomorrow's lunch.

MATERIALS & TOOLS

- Scissors
- Tulle
- Butter mints
- Colorful ribbons
- Bowl for the party favors
- Sturdy table
- Tablecloth
- Aluminum foil
- Serving utensils
- Container for serving utensils
- Sturdy disposable plates, cups, and bowls (about two of each per guest)
- Large paper or plastic bags, one for each guest
- Container for bags

TIPS

- Place the station as near the end of the potluck serving line as possible and leave space around at least three sides for easy circulation.
- Plastic plates such as those shown in the photo to the left help keep different foods separate from one another.
- Sheets of tinfoil make excellent covers for plates and cups, but you may also want to add sealable plastic bags, plastic food wrap, and transparent tape to your take-it-home station.
- If your potluck has a theme, consider decorating the large paper or plastic bags to match the theme.
- Make sure to use a washable tablecloth at your take-it-home station; spills are inevitable!

Instructions

1 Start by making the party favors. Cut the tulle into 4" x 4" squares, one or two for each guest. Place a small handful of butter mints at the center of each tulle square. Then, one square at a time, gather the tulle around the candy, and use a length of colorful ribbon to tie up the package. Place the party favors in an attractive bowl.

2 Cut squares of aluminum foil that are large enough to completely cover the plates you'll be setting out at your station. You may want to cut separate squares for the cups and bowls. Your guests will also use these tinfoil sheets to wrap up foods such as cookies, so plan to have about six squares on hand for each person.

3 Before your guests begin to arrive, place the table near the end of the potluck serving line. Cover it with the tablecloth. You may want to place a trash can nearby.

4 Set the plates, cups, paper towels, squares of aluminum foil, party favors, and two containers (for the paper bags and serving utensils) on the table. Roll up the paper bags and place them in one of the containers; place the serving utensils in the other. Arrange all these items in an attractive manner, and add a bouquet of fresh flowers if you like.

5 Be sure to tell everyone at the potluck about the station so they'll be able to take advantage of it!

Three Great Backyard Meals

Nobody needs an excuse to barbecue ribs or grill steaks, but some occasions cry out for the flavor and ambiance of meals cooked and enjoyed outdoors. Dinner for two begs for twilight, china, and simple, light fare. A late Sunday lunch goes best with plenty of sunshine, cool breezes, and traditional flavors. And these days, a sit-down family dinner is an event in itself; the meal you serve needs to be tempting enough to lure everyone to the picnic table!

If you're planning a romantic evening, the last thing you want to do is spend hours cooking and preparing a meal; that's why the Twilight Dinner for Two menu in this chapter features a quickly grilled entree, simple side dishes, and the easiest of desserts.

Sunday mornings, on the other hand, are lovely, lazy times. A tender smoked ham takes time, but very little care. While it cooks, you can read the Sunday paper, or bake a sweet coffee cake.

Get the whole gang involved with a family dinner—and not just with eating it! None of the recipes in this menu is hard to master, so everyone can pitch in and enjoy the results.

A Casual Family Dinner

WARM MOROCCAN RED AND SWEET POTATO SALAD ■ GREEN BEANS WITH CAPERS
BARBECUED LEMON-PAPRIKA CHICKEN WITH SWEET DRIED FIG RELISH ■ SLICED BEEFSTEAK TOMATOES
GRILLED BAGUETTE ■ SUMMERTIME STRAWBERRY-RHUBARB PIE

These days, it seems to take a special event to coerce the whole family into sitting down and eating a meal together. Fortunately, a barbecued dinner served outdoors often qualifies as just such an occurrence, in and of itself. Add a really spectacular, yet easy-to-make menu, and you'll soon rediscover the simple pleasure of an honest-to-goodness, sit-down family dinner.

International flavors transform the familiar barbecued-chicken-and-potato-salad menu into a new taste adventure that the whole family will enjoy.

WARM MOROCCAN RED AND SWEET POTATO SALAD
(Serves 6)

This savory potato salad is a little more elegant than the standard picnic version, but it's just as simple to prepare.

- 10 small red potatoes
- 2 sweet potatoes, peeled and cut into 1" pieces
- 2 tablespoons of grainy mustard
- ⅓ cup of white wine vinegar
- 2 tablespoons of high-quality olive oil
- ⅓ cup of plain yogurt
- 1 bunch of scallions, chopped
- 1 red bell pepper, finely minced
- ½ teaspoon of ground cumin
- ¾–1 cup of fresh mint, chopped
- ½ cup of fresh parsley, chopped
- Salt and pepper to taste

Boil the red potatoes and sweet potatoes until they're just tender. While the potatoes are cooking, whisk together the mustard, vinegar, olive oil, and yogurt in a large bowl. Add the scallions, red pepper, cumin, mint, and parsley. Cut the cooked red potatoes into 1" pieces (or, if they're very small, leave them whole), and add them and the sweet potatoes, warm, to the mixture in the bowl. Toss well and let the potato salad sit for at least 30 minutes before serving, warm or cold.

GREEN BEANS WITH CAPERS
(Serves 6)

Capers and tarragon add a Mediterranean touch to fresh green beans.

- 1 pound of green beans, trimmed
- 1 cup of high-quality olive oil
- ¼ cup of lemon juice
- 2 tablespoons of grainy mustard
- 2 tablespoons of fresh tarragon, chopped
- ¼ cup of fresh parsley, chopped
- 4 teaspoons of capers, drained and slightly crushed with a fork
- Salt and pepper to taste

Steam or boil the green beans until cooked to your taste (about 5 minutes for "al dente" beans, or 12 minutes for more tender beans). Place the beans in a colander and run them under very cold water for 1 minute. In a larger bowl, mix together all the remaining ingredients except the salt and pepper. Add the cooked beans, toss well, and let them sit for at least 30 minutes before serving. Add salt and pepper to taste.

BARBECUED LEMON-PAPRIKA CHICKEN
(Serves 6)

The cool zest of lemon and the hot spices in this recipe transform ordinary barbecued chicken into an exotic treat.

- 1 cup of high-quality olive oil
- ⅔ cup of fresh lemon juice
- 4 teaspoons of hot pepper sauce (adjust the amount to your taste)
- 2 tablespoons of hot paprika
- 2 tablespoons of ground coriander
- 10 cloves of garlic, peeled
- 10 shallots, chopped
- 1 cup of fresh parsley, chopped
- 2" of fresh ginger, peeled and sliced
- 1 teaspoon of coarse salt
- 1 teaspoon of freshly ground black pepper
- 2 small whole chickens, approximately 3 pounds each
- 2 small onions
- 2 lemons

The night before the meal, puree the first 11 ingredients in a blender to create a marinade. Remove and discard excess fat from the cavities of the chickens; then rinse and dry the birds inside and out. Cut the whole onions and lemons in half, insert 2 onion halves and 2 lemon halves into the cavity of each chicken; then truss the birds. Coat the chickens with one-third of the marinade, reserving one-third for basting and one-third to serve with the meal. Cover and refrigerate the chickens and marinate overnight.

About 3 hours before you'd like to serve dinner, prepare the grill for indirect cooking (see pages 186–187) at medium-low temperature. (Use the hand test described on page 186 to determine the correct temperature.) The heat must remain low throughout the cooking process, or the meat will burn and dry out. Place a drip pan in the center of the grill, under the grate, to catch the fat and prevent flare-ups. Remove the chickens from the marinade; discard the used marinade. Place the chickens on the grill, breast side up, and cover. After 30 minutes, carefully turn the birds onto their sides, and cover again. Cook for another 30 minutes; then turn and cover the chickens again. If you're using a charcoal grill, you'll probably need to add 10 to 12 fresh, hot briquettes to the fire at this point. Baste the chickens with one-third of the remaining marinade. Allow the remaining one-third of the marinade to come to room temperature. Cover the chickens again and continue cooking at a low heat, basting as desired, until a meat thermometer inserted in the thigh muscle registers 180°F (82°C).

When the chickens are cooked, wrap them in aluminum foil and let them rest for 10 minutes before carving. Serve the chickens, carved, with the remaining one-third of the room-temperature marinade and a bowl of Sweet Dried Fig Relish.

SWEET DRIED FIG RELISH
(Yields 1¼ pounds of relish)

Prepare this relish at least two days in advance to allow the flavors to fully develop and blend. It's delicious served with any roasted or barbecued meat and will keep for up to two weeks in the refrigerator.

  1 pound of dried figs, cut into
  quarters
  ½ cup of cider vinegar
  3 large lemons
  ½ cup of brown sugar
  ½ cup of honey
  1 cinnamon stick
  2 bay leaves

  1 teaspoon of paprika
  2 teaspoons of coarse salt

Soak the figs in the cider vinegar overnight. The following day, drain off the vinegar and reserve it. Peel and juice the lemons. Julienne the lemon peel and place it, the lemon juice, and the vinegar in a heavy pot with all the remaining ingredients, except the figs, and bring to a boil; cook at a boil for 3 minutes before adding the figs. Cook over medium heat for 20 minutes, stirring occasionally. Remove from the heat. After the mixture cools, remove and discard the cinnamon stick and bay leaf. Pour the relish into an airtight container and refrigerate for at least 2 days.

SLICED BEEFSTEAK TOMATOES
(Serves 6)

What could be better than a freshly picked beefsteak tomato, on its own or with just a pinch of salt? Prepare this dish only if you can find fruits at their ripest, firmest peak of perfection.

  4 large, ripe beefsteak tomatoes
  Salt (optional)
  Sprigs of fresh basil for garnish

Cut the tomatoes into ¼-inch slices, sprinkle them with salt, garnish with fresh basil, and serve them raw; or, if the slices are good and firm, grill them over high heat for 1 minute on each side before salting, garnishing, and serving.

GRILLED BAGUETTE

(Serves 6)

Bread grills very quickly, so this dish should be prepared at the very last moment, after everyone is already seated at the table.

    1 high-quality baguette or
    other crusty loaf
    1 stick (½ cup) of unsalted butter,
    at room temperature

Cut bread on the diagonal into 1"-thick slices. Lightly butter both sides of each slice; then grill over high heat for 1 to 2 minutes on each side, being careful not to burn the bread. Serve immediately.

SUMMERTIME STRAWBERRY-RHUBARB PIE

(Yields one 9" pie)

The tartness of rhubarb and the tang of fresh ginger perfectly balance the sweetness of red strawberries in this summertime classic. Homemade pie pastry is a special, flaky treat, but feel free to use a commercial frozen crust to cut down on preparation time.

PASTRY

    2 cups of unbleached
    all-purpose flour
    ½ teaspoon of ground cinnamon
    4 tablespoons of sugar
    1 teaspoon of salt
    2 sticks (1 cup) of unsalted butter
    5–6 tablespoons of ice water
    1 egg white

FILLING

    1 pint of strawberries, rinsed,
    hulled, and cut in half
    2 stalks of rhubarb, leaves removed
    and discarded, stalks peeled and
    cut into ¾" slices
    ¾ cup of sugar
    ¼ cup of instant tapioca
    2 tablespoons of unsalted butter,
    cut into small pieces
    ½ teaspoon of ground cinnamon
    Zest and juice of 1 lemon
    1 tablespoon of fresh, grated ginger
    (or 1 teaspoon of powdered ginger)
    ½ teaspoon of vanilla extract
    Ice cream and strawberries for
    garnish (optional)

To make the pastry, start by sifting together the flour, cinnamon, 2 tablespoons of the sugar, and the salt. Cut the chilled butter into 1-tablespoon bits and add to the flour. With a pastry cutter (or 2 knives), work the mixture together until it resembles coarse meal. Add the cold water, 1 tablespoon at a time, using your fingers to incorporate the moisture quickly without overworking the pastry.

When the pastry is just smooth and holds together, divide it into 2 balls, wrap each in wax paper or plastic wrap, and chill for at least 1 hour. After the pastry has rested, remove 1 ball from the refrigerator and, on a floured surface, roll it into a rough circle that is ⅛" thick. Carefully place this circle of dough into a 9" pie dish, and press gently into place. Roll the second ball into a slightly smaller circle. Chill both layers of dough for at least 30 minutes.

To prepare the pie, start by pre-heating the oven to 350°F (177°C). Combine all the pie-filling ingredients in a bowl and let the mixture rest for 30 minutes. Using a slotted spoon, place the mixture into the bottom shell of the pie crust. Brush one-half of the egg white around the edges of pie shell; then place remaining pastry on top and pinch edges together. Trim excess pastry, and cut slits in the pie's top to allow steam to escape.

Bake for 30 minutes; then remove the pie from the oven and brush the top with the remaining egg white. Sprinkle the remaining 2 tablespoons of sugar over the top. Bake for another 10 minutes. Cool for at least 1 hour. Serve with ice cream and fresh strawberries.

Cool Summer Salads

SALAD	INGREDIENTS	DRESSING	PREPARATION
Spicy Black Bean Salad	1 can (16 ounces) black beans, rinsed; 1½ tbsp. salt; ¼ cup red onion, chopped; 1 green onion, minced; 1 minced hot green chili, seeds removed; ¼ cup celery, chopped; 1 medium tomato, chopped	¼ cup olive oil; 2 tbsp. fresh lemon juice; 2 tbsp. fresh lime juice; ⅓ cup cilantro, chopped	Toss together all of the salad ingredients. Mix the dressing ingredients, pour over the salad, and toss well. Chill for at least 2 hours before serving.
Pasta and Herb Salad	12 ounces dry, medium-sized shell pasta; 10 Roma tomatoes, chopped; 1 cup steamed arugula; 3½ tbsp. fresh basil, chopped; 2½ tbsp. fresh parsley, chopped; 1 tbsp. fresh dill, chopped; 1 tbsp. fresh thyme, chopped	⅓ cup white wine vinegar; ½ cup high-quality olive oil; 2 cloves garlic, minced; ¼ tbsp. sugar; salt and pepper to taste	Cook pasta until just tender, about 6 minutes; drain and rinse under cold water. Toss together with remaining salad ingredients. Whisk together the dressing ingredients and pour over salad. Toss well. Serve warm or cold.
Minty Fruit Salad	1 large orange; 1 large pink grapefruit; 1 green apple, cored and diced; 1½ cups diced honeydew melon; 1½ cups fresh pineapple, diced; ½ cup seedless grapes, halved; 8 strawberries, hulled and diced	3 tbsp. fresh lime juice; 1 tbsp. honey; ½ tbsp. fresh mint, minced	Whisk together the dressing ingredients in a large bowl. Peel the orange and grapefruit; remove white membranes, section, and cut each section into 2–3 pieces. Place all the fruit in the bowl with the dressing, toss to mix, and chill for 1 hour before serving.
Crisp and Creamy Salad	10–15 red radishes, trimmed and sliced thinly; ¼ cup chives, minced; ¼ cup fresh dill, chopped; 2 small, crisp cucumbers, diced; ¼ cup mild yellow onion, diced	1½ cups plain yogurt; ½ cup sour cream; 1 tbsp. fresh lemon juice; salt and pepper to taste	Place all the salad ingredients in a large bowl. Whisk together the dressing ingredients and pour over the salad. Toss to mix well and chill for at least 1 hour before serving.

Making Frozen Treats

With the wide availability of inexpensive, easy-to-use electric ice-cream makers, there's simply no reason not to indulge in homemade ice cream, gelato, and sorbet.

ICE CREAM

Even today, with dozens of brands and hundreds of flavors on the market, you still won't find anything in your supermarket's freezer that can match the flavor and texture of real, homemade ice cream.

CLASSIC VANILLA ICE CREAM
(Makes a generous quart)

4 cups (1 quart) of half-and-half
10 egg yolks, or 4 whole eggs, slightly beaten
1¼ cups of granulated sugar
1 split vanilla bean, or 1½ tablespoons of pure vanilla extract

Combine the half-and-half, egg yolks or eggs, and sugar in a large saucepan. Heat this mixture over low heat, stirring constantly, for 15 to 20 minutes, or until it thickens slightly and will coat a metal spoon.

Remove from the heat and stir in the vanilla bean or vanilla extract. Following the manufacturer's instructions, freeze the mixture in an ice-cream maker. Transfer the ice cream to a plastic container and place it in the freezer to ripen for at least 3 hours before serving.

CHOCOLATE FUDGE ICE CREAM
(Makes about 1½ quarts)

5 ounces of unsweetened chocolate, melted
14 ounces (1 can) of sweetened condensed milk (*not* evaporated milk)
2 teaspoons of vanilla extract
2 cups (1 pint) of half-and-half
2 cups (1 pint) of whipping cream
½ cup of chopped nuts (optional)

In a large mixing bowl, beat together the chocolate, sweetened condensed milk, and vanilla extract until well blended. Stir in the half-and-half, whipping cream, and nuts (if desired) and mix well. Following the manufacturer's instructions, freeze the mixture in an ice-cream maker. For soft ice cream, serve immediately. For harder ice cream, transfer to a plastic container and place in the freezer for 2 to 3 hours before serving.

GELATO

Outside of Italy, the word gelato *has come to describe a densely textured, more powerfully flavored form of ice cream, and that's exactly what these two recipes will produce. Technically, though, gelato is any kind of frozen concoction served in an Italian ice-cream shop.*

COFFEE GELATO
(Makes a generous pint)

- ⅔ cup of granulated sugar
- 4 egg yolks
- 1 cup of milk, at room temperature
- ⅛ teaspoon of salt
- 4 teaspoons of instant coffee
- 1 cup of heavy cream, chilled

Beat together the sugar and egg yolks until they're pale yellow and very thick. Slowly add the milk, blending gently to avoid foaming. Stir in the salt. Place this custard in the top of a double boiler, over 1" of boiling water. Keeping the water at a boil, cook the custard for about 8 minutes, stirring constantly, or until it thickens and

will coat a metal spoon. Remove the top of the double boiler and place it in a large bowl of cold water for 2 minutes, stirring constantly. Transfer the custard to a large mixing bowl and add the instant coffee, stirring until the coffee crystals have dissolved completely. Cover and refrigerate until well chilled. Whip the heavy cream

until it holds soft peaks. Slowly fold the whipped cream into the chilled custard. Following the manufacturer's instructions, freeze the gelato in an ice-cream maker. Transfer to a plastic container and allow to ripen for 3 hours before serving.

CHOCOLATE GELATO
(Makes a generous pint)

- 1 cup of sugar
- 2 cups of milk
- 1 cup of cocoa powder, sifted
- 3½ ounces of bittersweet chocolate, chopped
- 4 egg yolks

Place ¼ cup of the sugar in a heavy saucepan and cook, undisturbed, over medium heat until it begins to melt. As the sugar begins to melt, gently stir it with a fork until it dissolves completely and turns to golden-brown caramel. Remove the saucepan from the heat and dip it into a bowl of cold water.

The caramel will harden. Allow it to cool for 5 minutes; then return the saucepan to medium heat and add the milk. Whisk until the caramel melts again. Add the cocoa and continue to whisk until well blended. Turn the heat to very low to keep the mixture warm.

Melt the chocolate in the top half of a double boiler over 1" of simmering water. Remove the melted chocolate from the heat. In a separate bowl, beat together the egg yolks and the remaining ¾ cup of sugar until the combination is thick and pale yellow. Slowly add the chocolate and caramel mixture in streams, whisking to blend. Pour the custard into a heavy saucepan and cook over medium-low heat until it reaches a temperature of 140°F (60°C); use a candy thermometer to test the temperature. Cook the custard for 4 more minutes, stirring constantly and keeping it from reaching a boil. Remove from the heat and allow to cool completely. Then freeze the custard in an ice-cream maker, following the manufacturer's instructions. Transfer the gelato to a plastic container and place in the freezer to ripen for 2 to 3 hours before serving.

SORBET

Light, refreshing, and totally fat-free, sorbet may very well be the perfect summer dessert.

LEMON SORBET
(Makes about 1 pint)

1 cup of water
1 cup of sugar
¾ cup of lemon juice
2½ tablespoons of lemon zest

Combine the sugar and water in a medium saucepan and warm over medium heat until the sugar dissolves completely. Bring the sugar syrup to a boil and simmer for 2 minutes. Remove from the heat and allow to cool. Add the lemon juice and lemon zest to the cooled sugar syrup, mix well, and place in the refrigerator to chill for at least an hour. Freeze the sorbet in an ice-cream maker, following the manufacturer's instructions. Transfer the sorbet to a plastic container and place in the freezer to ripen for 2 hours before serving.

RASPBERRY-CHIANTI SORBET
(Makes a generous pint)

¾ pound of fresh, ripe raspberries
1½ cups of sugar
2 tablespoons of fresh lemon juice
¼ cup of Chianti or other dry red wine
¼ cup of light corn syrup
1 cup of ice water

Stir together the raspberries, sugar, and lemon juice in a large mixing bowl. Cover and chill in the refrigerator for at least 1 hour. Add the Chianti, corn syrup, and water to the chilled raspberry mixture and stir well. Freeze in an ice-cream maker, following the manufacturer's instructions. Transfer the sorbet to a plastic container and allow it to ripen in the freezer for 2 to 3 hours before serving.

A Twilight Dinner for Two

CHILLED CUCUMBER SOUP ■ GRILLED SALMON FILLETS ■ GRILL-ROASTED CORN ROUNDS WITH BASIL-GARLIC BUTTER
STEAMED ASPARAGUS WITH MUSTARD-DILL SAUCE ■ FRESH BERRIES WITH HAND-WHIPPED CREAM

Imagine an elegant outdoor dining room where you can watch as the sun sets and the stars emerge—where you can enjoy a delicious meal, a glass of wine, and your companion's company, uninterrupted by waiters or other diners. If this sounds too expensive or too far away for you to ever enjoy, think again! Candlelight, a beautifully set table, and, of course, the right menu, can transform your backyard into a romantic twilight cafe to rival any in Paris or Rome. This elegant menu is simple to prepare and will leave you with plenty of time to enjoy the evening.

CHILLED CUCUMBER SOUP
(Makes four ½-cup servings)

Cool and refreshing, this tempting soup is the perfect way to start a summer meal.

- ¼ cup of water
- ¾ teaspoon of unflavored gelatin
- 1 large cucumber, peeled and chopped coarsely
- 1 green onion, chopped coarsely
- ⅓ cup of plain yogurt
- ⅛ teaspoon of wasabi powder or dry mustard
- ½ teaspoon of sugar
- ⅛ teaspoon of salt
- Freshly ground black pepper to taste
- ¾ cup of buttermilk
- 1½ tablespoons of sour cream
- 1½ tablespoons of cottage cheese
- ½ teaspoon of fresh dill, chopped finely

In a small saucepan, bring the water to a boil and add the gelatin. Stir until the gelatin has dissolved completely. Allow the water to cool slightly; then add it to a food processor or blender with the cucumber, onion, yogurt, wasabi powder, sugar, salt, and pepper. Process until the mixture is very smooth; then add it to a mixing bowl with the remaining ingredients. Stir until the soup is well blended, adjust the seasonings to taste, and refrigerate for at least 1 hour before serving.

GRILLED SALMON FILLETS
(Serves 2)

Delicious served hot or chilled, this lightly seasoned salmon grills to perfection in just minutes.

- ½ teaspoon of coarse salt
- 1 teaspoon of brown sugar
- ¼ teaspoon of freshly ground black pepper
- 2 center-cut salmon fillets with skin, each approximately ½ pound
- 2 teaspoons of olive oil

Light the grill and prepare it for the direct cooking method (see page 186). Mix together the salt, sugar, and pepper; rub this mixture evenly onto both sides of each salmon fillet. Drizzle about ½ teaspoon of olive oil on each side of the fillets; then rub to coat evenly. You can refrigerate the salmon for up to 1 hour while the grill heats up. When the grill is very hot, add the salmon and cook each side for about 3 minutes; the center should remain a slightly darker shade of pink than the rest of the fillet. Serve immediately or chill in the refrigerator.

GRILL-ROASTED CORN ROUNDS WITH BASIL-GARLIC BUTTER

Sliced into manageable "cobbettes" and slathered with savory herb butter, this unbeatable finger food offers a fun interlude in a meal of otherwise seriously romantic fare.

CORN ROUNDS
(Serves 2)

- 2 medium ears of fresh sweet corn, husks on
- 1½ tablespoons of Basil-Garlic Butter (see page 236)

Light the grill and prepare it for the direct cooking method (see page 186). Soak the corn cobs, husks on, in cold

water for at least 10 minutes. Place the corn, husks and all, on the hot grill and cook for 15 to 20 minutes, or until the husks are charred all around, turning as needed. Shuck the corn and remove the silk, wearing heavy cooking mitts to protect your hands. Cut the cobs into 2"-thick rounds and place the rounds in a plastic bag with the basil-garlic butter. Shake until the butter has melted and completely coats the corn. Serve hot.

BASIL-GARLIC BUTTER
(Makes a generous cup)

Heavenly on roasted corn, this mouth-watering butter also pairs nicely with grilled fish and crusty French bread.

- 2 sticks (1 cup)
  of unsalted butter, softened
- 4 cloves of garlic, minced finely
- ½ cup of fresh basil, minced finely
- 1 tablespoon of Chardonnay or
  other white wine
- 2 tablespoons of
  Parmesan cheese, grated
- Cayenne pepper to taste
- Salt to taste

Blend together all of the ingredients in a medium mixing bowl. Serve immediately in an attractive crock, or roll the butter into a log (use waxed paper to do this) and store it in the refrigerator or freezer.

STEAMED ASPARAGUS WITH MUSTARD-DILL SAUCE
(Serves 2)

The subtle zest of mustard enhances the elegance of fresh, young asparagus—exquisite in its own right.

- 12–14 fresh asparagus spears
- Mustard-Dill Sauce

Steam the asparagus on the stove top for 2 to 4 minutes; the spears should be crisp-tender, firm, and bright green. Top with mustard-dill sauce.

MUSTARD-DILL SAUCE
(Makes about 1 cup)

In addition to adding zest to asparagus, broccoli, brussel sprouts, and other green vegetables, this simple sauce is the perfect mate for grilled fish and chicken.

- ½ cup of evaporated milk
- Zest of 1 lemon
- Juice of 1 lemon
- ⅓ cup of mayonnaise
- 2 teaspoons of prepared
  yellow mustard
- 1 tablespoon of fresh dill, chopped
  finely, or ¼ teaspoon of dried dill
- 1 teaspoon of sugar
- ⅛ teaspoon of salt
- ⅛ teaspoon of freshly ground
  black pepper

In a medium bowl, add together the evaporated milk, the lemon zest, and the lemon juice. Stir until the milk thickens slightly; then add the remaining ingredients and stir well. Refrigerate for at least 1 hour before serving.

FRESH BERRIES WITH HAND-WHIPPED CREAM
(Serves 2)

Nothing tastes as fresh and good as ripe berries in season, topped with freshly whipped cream.

- ¼ cup of heavy whipping cream
- ½ teaspoon of sugar
- ⅛ teaspoon of vanilla extract
- 1 cup of fresh berries

Place the cream, sugar, and vanilla in a small bowl, and whisk together until the cream thickens, stopping before it holds peaks. Divide the berries into attractive bowls and pour the cream over them. Serve immediately.

The Romance of Outdoor Dining

Take any backyard, add a cozy table, the setting sun, soft candlelight, and an orchestra of crickets, and you have the perfect backdrop for a romantic evening. Whether your dinner companion is a date or your spouse, outdoor scenery is relaxing; fresh air makes any meal taste better; and candlelight, of course, is always flattering. While it's true that romance walks hand in hand with spontaneity, the path it treads must first be paved with preparation. Scrambling to pull burning rolls from the oven while the kitchen fills with smoke is no way to set the mood for the evening.

PLANNING

Make sure you have everything that you'll need on hand. Nothing is less conducive to romance than having to search for matches when a candle blows out, so place a small table next to your dining area and set all those "extras" on it: a corkscrew, extra napkins, an ice bucket, a dish towel for spills, new candles—and the matches.

Select a menu that will allow you to enjoy your food—and the moment—without having to dash back indoors to check on the soufflé or stir the risotto. And consider making the cooking itself a shared part of the evening's activities. Chop, chat, blend, and mix *together*. The evening's success will depend on the genuine pleasure the two of you derive from spending time together—not on the quality of the salad dressing.

DINING IN PEACE

If you can hear your telephone ringing when you're sitting outdoors, turn it off before the evening begins.

Keep the lighting low, both to set the mood and to keep bugs at bay. The odors given off by most chemical insect repellents will detract from your enjoyment of the food, but slapping wildly at a mosquito will definitely break the mood. Try hanging sprigs of lavender, lemon balm, rosemary, basil, or geranium around the perimeters of your dining area. They're all helpful for repelling insects.

Beverages, Hot and Cold

During the summer, smoldering charcoal and the promise of a perfectly grilled burger may draw us outdoors, but it's the glass of iced tea that invites us to sit and stay a while. And in the cooler months, a steaming mug of hot chocolate or fragrant mulled cider can take the chill off an evening of pumpkin carving. Drinks may not be the main attraction at an outdoor meal, but they certainly can be among the more enjoyable sideshows!

SUMMER CLASSICS

Whether your summer beverage of choice is as simple as a pitcher of ice water with sliced lime, or as elaborate as a crystal bowl full of fizzy punch, just make sure it's cool, refreshing, and plentiful. For lazy family weekends, nothing beats freshly squeezed lemonade and sun-brewed iced tea. Lemon slices and a few sprigs of just-clipped mint make a festive, traditional garnish for both concoctions, while peeled slices of fresh ginger will lend them a spicy, exotic snap. For larger gatherings, add punch, chilled beer, wine, or even cocktails to the drink repertoire.

Tuck pitchers and bottles into trays or buckets of crushed ice to keep their contents well chilled. Set out a separate tub of ice and a plastic scoop so that guests may add ice to their drinks as they like. Make extra iced tea, lemonade, or punch and freeze it into ice cubes; these cubes will keep your beverage cool without watering it down. Frozen fruits, such as pineapple, watermelon, and cantaloupe make fun and tasty ice-cube substitutes, too.

COCKTAILS

Imagine a luau without piña coladas or a Cinco de Mayo bash that was missing margaritas. Some parties simply require mixed drinks! If you're planning such a gathering, allow for about three cocktails per guest. Stock up on tonic water, club soda, and sweet and sour mixers. Or, you may want to keep matters simple by offering just two or three kinds of cocktails.

Be sure to provide alternative, non-alcoholic beverages for designated drivers and others who choose not to drink alcohol.

If you're expecting more than 15 guests, consider asking a friend to help "tend bar," or hire a professional bartender for really large or elaborate get-togethers.

COLD-WEATHER FAVORITES

Hot drinks can make an outdoor evening that might otherwise be on the chilly side seem warm and cozy. Frothy homemade cocoa will please kids and adults alike. A robust cup of coffee is the perfect way to end a meal, especially when it's paired with dessert. To turn java into classic Irish coffee, just add a shot of whiskey and a dollop of whipped cream. And hot apple cider and mulled wine are both wonderfully festive and easy to make.

Keeping hot beverages hot in cold weather can be a little more

challenging than keeping cold drinks cold in hot weather. But don't let that stop you or your guests from enjoying them! Coffee, cocoa, and other drinks will stay hot in an insulated carafe or thermos. Pour your mulled wine or spiced apple cider into a large kettle and place it right on the grill, over low heat. Nothing will take the steam out of hot cocoa as quickly as an icy cold mug, so leave the mugs inside where it's warm until the last minute.

BEVERAGE EXTRAS

When you serve drinks outdoors, remember all the little extras. Cocktails napkins are always useful,

whether you're serving cocktails or not. Provide cream, sugar, and spoons or stirring sticks for coffee service; offer cinnamon, nutmeg, and cocoa powder for a special touch. Serve tea—hot or cold—with wedges of lemon, sugar, and teaspoons. Consider offering sugar cubes instead of granulated sugar; they're easier and less messy to serve.

At a potluck or buffet, you can place coffee, tea, and water at the end of the table, or at the beginning, with the napkins and utensils. If there's not room on the table, or if you're serving cocktails, place drinks and their accompaniments on a separate table, nearby.

A Fruit and Berry Garden Plan

While it's certainly no secret that fresh fruit is one of the most tempting foods we have, it's a less well-known fact that it's easy to grow sweet, splendid fruit in your own backyard. When growing fruit, the frequency of rainfall and the type of soil are less important than site selection and winter temperatures. Most fruit plants need six or more hours of full sunlight each day. Extremely low winter temperatures can injure or kill fruit plants altogether, so consult with your local Cooperative Extension Service to determine which varieties are right for your backyard.

A APPLES
Malus

Full sun

Plant young trees 18'–20' apart in early spring. Apples do best in rich, well-drained loam. 'Golden Delicious' apples grow well in most parts of the country; gardeners in the Southeast should try the 'Summer Champion', while the 'McIntosh' will thrive in most parts of the Midwest.

B BLACKBERRIES
Rubus

Full sun to partial shade

Plant blackberries in rich, well-drained soil. Training bushes to a trellis will ensure easy access to the berries when they ripen. 'Darrow' demonstrates the most resistance to cold; 'Hall' is adapted to the East and Northeast. The 'Olallie' grows well in California and the Pacific Northwest.

C CHERRIES
Prunus

Full sun

Plant young cherry trees 15'–18' apart in well-drained soil in early spring. Most species will do well in the northern two-thirds of the country, as long as winter temperatures don't dip below -20°F (-29°C). Cherries do not do as well in the hot, humid South.

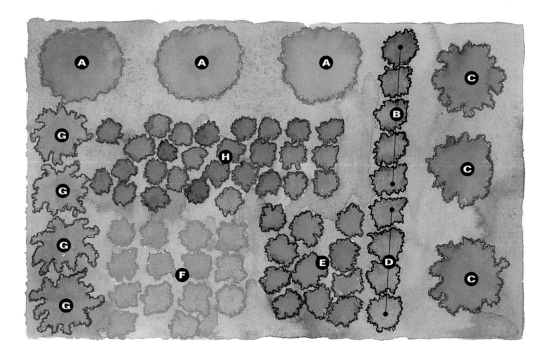

D BLUEBERRIES
Vaccinium

Full sun to partial shade

Plant blueberry bushes 5'–8' apart in acidic, well-drained, peaty or sandy soil. The Highbush is native to the eastern part of the country, although it will do well in most temperate climates. The Rabbiteye is best adapted to the Southeast, and the Lowbush grows well in the Northeast.

E WATERMELON
Citrullus lanatus

Full sun

Sow seeds in small mounds of sandy soil, spacing the mounds about 6' apart and planting 3 to 5 seeds in each one. As the plants grow, thin each mound to the two strongest vines. Place baby watermelons on straw. The 'Yellow Doll' cultivar is well adapted to the Northwest, while the 'Charleston Gray No. 133' does well in the

South. The 'Sweet Meat', the 'Moon and Stars', and the 'Tendersweet Orange Flesh' cultivars are good bets for gardeners in the Northeast.

F CANTALOUPE
Cucumis melo

Full sun

Set out after the last frost of the season in well-drained, sandy, slightly alkaline soil. Place growing melons on straw, and water frequently. The 'Iroquois', 'Earligold', and 'Alaska' cultivars are good choices for cooler climes. Try the 'Ambrosia', 'Gold Star', and 'Tennessee' varieties in more moderate areas of the country.

G PEACHES
Prunus persica

Full sun

Plant peach trees in a sunny, wind-protected portion of the garden, spacing them 12'–15' apart. The 'Redhaven', 'Jerseyqueen', and 'Harrow Beauty' varieties grow well in the

Northeast. The 'Texstar' and 'LaSeliana' are well adapted to the Southeast. Western gardeners should try the 'Flavorcrest', 'Suncrest', and 'O'Henry' varieties.

H STRAWBERRIES
Fragaria

Full sun

Set plants 12"–18" apart in early or mid-spring in slightly acidic, well-drained, normal or sandy soil, or in loam. The 'Catskill', 'Guardian', and 'Sparkle' varieties are well adapted to chilly northern climates. The 'Hood' and the 'Brighton' will do well in the West. The 'Tennessee Beauty' and the 'Surecrop' will thrive in the Southeast and Midwest.

A Sunday Lunch

CANTALOUPE, STRAWBERRY, AND KIWI SALAD ■ GLOBE ARTICHOKES WITH TARRAGON HOLLANDAISE SAUCE
HOME-SMOKED SPICY GINGER HAM ■ GRILLED PINEAPPLE RINGS ■ SOUR CREAM AND PECAN COFFEE CAKE ■ CLASSIC LEMONADE

Long Sunday afternoons beg for savory lunches to linger over and enjoy. But why crowd into a packed restaurant to share late Sunday lunch with dozens of strangers when you can prepare a feast in your own backyard? You'll cook the food just the way you like it, admire your garden as you cook, and best of all, you won't even have to change out of your robe and slippers! This menu provides plenty of flavor to stimulate Sunday-afternoon palates, and plenty of food—both light and hearty—to satisfy lunch-time appetites.

CANTALOUPE, STRAWBERRY, AND KIWI SALAD
(Serves 6)

This delectable side dish will add a splash of color to your table, as well as refreshingly cool flavors.

2 ripe, medium-sized cantaloupes, cut into 1" chunks
1 cup of fresh strawberries, hulled and cut into halves
4 kiwis, peeled and sliced
¼ cup of grated coconut (unsweetened)
4 tablespoons of honey
Sparkling white wine and fresh mint for garnish

Combine all the salad ingredients in a large bowl. Add a splash of sparkling white wine and a sprig of mint to each guest's bowl just before serving.

GLOBE ARTICHOKES WITH TARRAGON HOLLANDAISE SAUCE
(Serves 6)

Whole artichokes make elegant, easy-to-prepare appetizers. Team them with Tarragon Hollandaise Sauce for a truly tempting opener.

6 medium-sized artichokes
¾ cup of butter
3 tablespoons of water
3 egg yolks
Salt and white pepper, to taste
Juice of ½ lemon
¼ cup of fresh tarragon, very finely chopped
Lemon slices and sprigs of fresh tarragon for garnish

Steam or boil the artichokes until you can easily pull off their outer leaves.

Make the tarragon hollandaise sauce while the artichokes cook. Start by melting the butter. Skim the froth from the surface and let the butter cool to tepid. In a small saucepan, whisk together the water and egg yolks with a little salt and pepper for 30 seconds. Transfer the mixture to the top of a double boiler over 1" of simmering water. Continue to whisk until the mixture has thickened to a creamy consistency.

Remove the sauce from the heat and whisk in the tepid butter, a few drops at a time. (Adding the butter too fast may cause it to curdle.) When the sauce begins to thicken, the butter may be added more quickly, but don't add the milky sediment from the bottom of the butter. When the butter has been incorporated, whisk in the lemon juice and chopped tarragon. This sauce may be kept warm for up to 2 hours in a water bath, but re-heating will cause it to curdle.

Remove the cooked artichokes from the heat and serve each one with a small bowl of tarragon hollandaise sauce. Garnish with lemon slices and sprigs of fresh tarragon.

HOME-SMOKED SPICY GINGER HAM
(Serves 10–12)

Rise and shine! This hearty main course takes several hours to cook, so pour that mug of coffee and start the smoker!

12- to 14-pound cooked, ready-to-eat Boston butt or shoulder ham

RUB

½ cup of brown sugar

¼ cup of Dijon mustard

2 tablespoons of ground black pepper

2 tablespoons of paprika

2 teaspoons of ground ginger

1 tablespoon of salt

½ teaspoon of cayenne pepper

GINGER GLAZE

1 cup of ginger preserves

¼ cup of pineapple juice or orange juice

1 teaspoon of ground ginger

½ teaspoon of dry mustard

¼ teaspoon of ground cloves

The night before you plan to smoke the ham, combine the rub ingredients. Evenly apply the rub to the ham.

Tightly cover the ham in plastic wrap and refrigerate.

A water-smoker or an offset firebox smoker (see page 168 for descriptions of these common smokers) will produce equally successful results. Remove the ham from the refrigerator and allow it to come to room temperature (45 minutes to an hour). Heat the smoker to a temperature of 180°F to 240°F (82°C to 116°C). Place the ham in the smoker. Because the ham is pre-cooked, you're smoking it to add flavor, not to cook it. Let the ham smoke for 4½ to 5 hours, or until it reaches the desired level of smoky flavor. While the ham is smoking, combine all of the ingredients for the ginger

glaze; baste the ham with the glaze twice during the last hour of cooking.

Tightly wrap the ham in aluminum foil, and let it rest for 15 minutes before carving. Serve with a small bowl of sweet mustard and grilled pineapple rings.

GRILLED PINEAPPLE RINGS
(Serves 6–8)

Lime juice adds just a touch of tartness to this sweetly satisfying grilled treat.

1 ripe fresh pineapple (look for a golden color and an inner leaf that can be easily pulled out)

1 stick (½ cup) of unsalted butter, melted

¾ cup of brown sugar

Zest and juice of 2 limes

Pinch of ground cloves

Preheat the grill to high (use the hand test on page 186 to determine temperature) and oil the grate just before grilling.

Cut the top off the pineapple and remove the rind and any spots in the flesh. Slice the pineapple into 1"-thick rounds.

Combine the melted butter and lime juice in a bowl. In a separate bowl, combine the sugar, lime zest, and ground cloves. Dip each slice of pineapple in the butter and lime-juice mixture before dipping it in the sugar mixture. Shake off any excess sugar before placing the rounds on the grill.

Grill the pineapple rounds for about 5 minutes on each side, or until they're sizzling and browned. Serve on a separate dish, or arranged around the ham on a platter.

SOUR CREAM AND PECAN COFFEE CAKE
(Yields one 10" bundt cake)

What would an outdoor feast be without a sinfully delicious grand finale?

2 sticks (1 cup) of unsalted butter
2¾ cups of sugar
2 eggs, lightly beaten
2 cups of unbleached all-purpose flour
1 tablespoon of baking powder
Pinch of salt
2 cups of sour cream
1 teaspoon of vanilla extract
Zest of 1 orange
2 cups of chopped pecans
1 tablespoon of ground cinnamon
¼ teaspoon of ground allspice

Preheat the oven to 350°F (177°C). Grease and lightly flour a 10" bundt pan.

In a large bowl, cream together the butter and 2 cups of the sugar. Add the eggs and mix well. Then stir in the sour cream, orange zest, and vanilla. In a separate bowl, sift together the flour, baking powder, and salt. Fold the flour mixture into the sour-cream batter until it's just incorporated.

In another bowl, mix the remaining ¾ cup of sugar with the pecans, cinnamon, and allspice.

Pour half of the batter into the bundt pan. Sprinkle half of the pecan and sugar mixture on top; then pour the remaining batter in and top it with the rest of the pecan and sugar topping.

Bake the cake on the middle rack of the oven for about 60 minutes, or until a cake tester inserted in the center comes out clean. Cool for 30 minutes before serving.

CLASSIC LEMONADE
(Makes 1 gallon)

The perfect thirst quencher, freshly squeezed lemonade is a snap to make.

8–10 large lemons
1 cup of super-fine sugar
Just under 1 gallon of cold water
Ice
Lemon slices for garnish

Wash the lemons well and allow them to come to room temperature. Cut the lemons in half and juice them. Pick out the seeds before pouring the lemon juice into a gallon-sized container (glass is best). Add the sugar and stir well. Add the lemon rinds and let the mixture sit for an hour before adding the water. Stir well. Remove and discard the lemon rinds. Serve the lemonade in tall glasses with ice and slices of lemon.

Variation: To add an exotic, spicy snap to your lemonade, boil the water with 3" of sliced and peeled ginger. Chill the water in the refrigerator for at least an hour; then remove and discard the ginger and add the water to the lemon-juice and sugar mixture.

Parties & Celebrations

Whatever the occasion—a barbecue bash with all your friends, a child's birthday party, or an elegant soiree, your yard can be the perfect place to host a memorable event.

By definition, a real barbecue bash—complete with dripping watermelon slices and mounds of pulled pork—almost has to be held outdoors. A lush stretch of lawn and a few shady trees or garden umbrellas will help provide the ideal backdrop for an afternoon of barbecuing, gabbing—and watermelon-seed-spitting contests.

The backyard always holds a little more magic for kids than for adults. Add a piñata stuffed with gifts, a fun game or two, and a classic birthday cake—and that bit of magic will turn into a lot of fun!

As the sun begins to set, strings of tiny white lights, flickering candles, and glowing luminaries can transform your yard into an enchanting outdoor drawing room for more sophisticated entertainment. Your guests will love the novelty of mixing and mingling while the stars sparkle overhead.

So forget about renting a restaurant for your big event or spending hours cleaning your home. Instead, throw your back door open, and step outside!

The Hard-Core Barbecue Bash

To many, the word *barbecue* connotes any gathering at which the cooking takes place outdoors—an event that can happen in any backyard at any time, and at which food can be cooked in any way. Venture below the Mason-Dixon line, however, and into parts of Texas, and you'll find that the word is uttered with deep reverence, a sense of history, and a specific meaning.

Claim that you're hosting a barbecue in those parts, and you'd better mean business: smoke-cooked meat over an open fire, a big hungry crowd to devour it, and plenty of celebration

and thanksgiving. Such an event does require a bit more care and planning than the average backyard barbecue, but the tradition wouldn't have survived as long as it has if the effort weren't worth it. Weddings, graduations, landmark birthdays and anniversaries, family reunions, and other special occasions merit a true bash, and a hard-core barbecue is the best bash of all.

PIGGING OUT

Technically, anything can be barbecued. However, the Caribbeans who pioneered this cooking technique

discovered that an astonishing transformation takes place when pork is barbecued. The meat achieves a smoky succulence that's out of this world. Even if you're someone who usually bypasses the bacon at breakfast or groans at the thought of a holiday honey-baked ham, you'll want to give barbecued pork a try. You're not likely to find a whole hog in your local supermarket, so contact a caterer who specializes in barbecue events to obtain your pork. Chicken is also an option, and many vegetables barbecue well, too.

Once you decide on your main course, choose an assortment of complementary side dishes, and do offer coleslaw, so guests will get their greens. Corn on the cob and watermelon are both barbecue basics. Breads such as rolls or cornbread's southern cousin, hush puppies, make excellent sauce soppers. Down-home desserts such as cobblers, pies, and brownies will satisfy everyone's sweet tooth. Finally, serve an ice-cold beverage to counter the steaming-hot meat. Iced tea, lemonade, and cold beer are prime beverage choices.

When it's time to serve the meal, don't be ashamed to use heavy paper plates and plastic flatware. At traditional barbecues, so much work goes into cooking that these steps are taken to minimize cleanup. Stay stocked on napkins, and have a couple of large trash barrels available so that guests can clean up as easily as hosts. If you have leftovers, pack some of them up for guests to take home (see pages 222–223).

RAISING A RUCKUS

Back when the farmer raised the pig before cooking it, he made sure that plenty of folks were on hand to enjoy the fruits of his labor. If they weren't, the pig would go to waste (pork is one of the more difficult meats to preserve). The barbecue, therefore, was a true feast—a time for socially acceptable gluttony. To further infuse your bash with the spirit of plenty and of carefree celebration, gather together the biggest crowd you can and make sure there's plenty of entertainment. Music, dancing, and storytelling are all excellent components of a barbecue bash.

PACKING PORTABLE MEALS

The last thing you want on a picnic is to unwrap your delicious sandwich only to find that the spread in it has indeed spread—all over your moist butterscotch brownies. To enjoy the perfect picnic, first you have to *pack* it!

Start by preparing the food. (If you don't have a well-insulated cooler, avoid perishable dishes such as egg salad.) Then make a list of all the non-food items you'll need. With so many other details on your mind, it's all too easy to forget the essential corkscrew as you focus on remembering the wine. If you're planning a really special picnic, don't be afraid to use your good china and silverware! For easy cleanup, however, disposable cups, cutlery, napkins, and plates are best. (Fortunately, improvements in paper-plate technology have eliminated that eating-off-a-soggy-piece-of-typing-paper sensation you've probably experienced in the past; paper plates are now quite sturdy.)

Wrap food such as sandwiches and cookies in heavy-duty aluminum foil so they'll stay fresh. Place the wrapped packages in lidded plastic containers so they won't be crushed in your cooler or hamper. When you pack food and other items in your hamper or cooler, start with the ones you'll need last, setting them in the bottom, and finish by placing the ones you'll need first on the top. To conserve space, stack flat items, separating the layers with waxed paper, aluminum foil, or several layers of paper towels. If you're taking the china, make sure that it's well padded or secured safely against bumps and jostling.

Finally, pack a little extra. Fresh air tends to improve appetites, and you'll never regret having one more butterscotch brownie on hand!

Birthday Parties for Children

Remember when you were younger and much closer to the ground? Back then, everything seemed more exciting: The backyard was rich with buried treasure, exotic insect life, and nooks just waiting to become forts; your pets possessed Lassie-like intelligence; and an invitation to a party filled you with such anticipation that you thought you'd burst before the big day arrived. Recreate that excitement for your child—and for yourself—by holding a backyard birthday party.

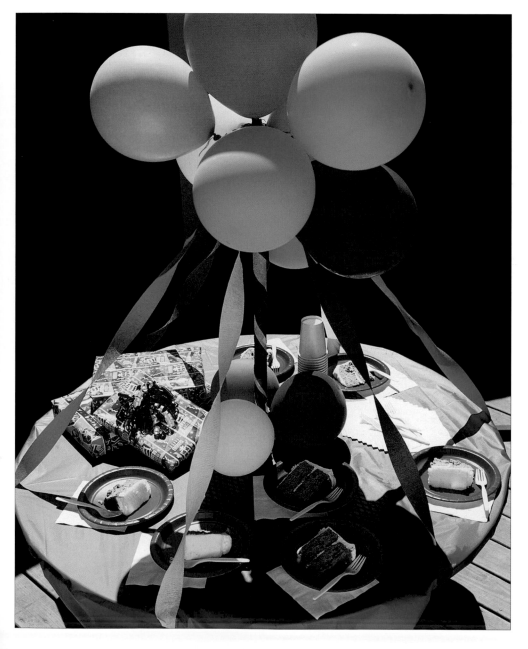

PLANNING

Any parent who's ever held a successful party for kids will tell you that planning is the best way to guarantee a great time—for the children and for yourself. Preparing before the big event will let you enjoy the actual party and will allow for the spontaneity and flexibility that are always required when children are involved.

Start planning the party at least two weeks in advance. Choose a date and time; then compose a guest list. If you're wondering how many kids to invite, use the "child's age plus one" rule of thumb. For instance, if the birthday boy or girl is turning six, a party of seven is a good, manageable size. (Don't feel bound by this rule, though. If there are nine girls in your daughter's kindergarten class, consider inviting them all; leaving three girls out may result in hurt feelings.)

Your child's age can also help you determine how long the party should last. An hour will be more than enough time for toddlers and just enough for four- to five-year-olds. Older children will want slightly longer parties, but remember: To an eight-year-old, three hours can seem like a very long time.

Send your invitations by mail, at least one week in advance; dates and times are often forgotten when they're relayed over the phone. Make sure the invitations include the date, starting and ending times, directions to your home, your telephone number, and the theme of the party (if there is one). Ask parents to RSVP right away, so you'll know how many children to expect. Also ask them to let you know if their children have any dietary restrictions.

DECORATIONS

As with parties for adults, the decorations you choose will set the mood for your child's birthday party. Don't worry about spending a lot of money on fancy decorations, though. A bright paper tablecloth and matching paper plates, cups, and napkins will give your porch or backyard a festive look. Paper decorations and plastic tableware will make cleanup easier, too. Streamers and balloons will add the finishing touch. (Helium balloons are especially fun; check the yellow pages of your local telephone book under "balloons" for suppliers in your area.)

If you'd like to follow a theme, ask your child what he or she would like; there may be a popular cartoon character that all the kids love, or a particular color that's "in" (or "out") at school. If your child is old enough, ask him or her to help put up the decorations, too; hanging streamers and decorating with balloons will add to your child's anticipation. (Just remember that young children should not be allowed to blow up balloons themselves; balloons can pose a choking hazard.)

FUN AND GAMES

Plan several age-appropriate outdoor games before the party starts. The children may not have time to play them all, but nothing creates chaos faster than a group of bored children. Turn to pages 276–277 for ideas on games to play. Be sure to consult your child, too; he or she will know exactly what the guests will and won't enjoy playing. If an activity or game requires equipment, check to see that you have enough and get it set up and organized ahead of time.

Children love backyard treasure hunts. For very young children, don't "hide" the treasures at all. Instead, select brightly-colored prizes and set them out in clearly visible places just before the search begins. Have parents help you place these items, so that every child is sure to find one—with a little adult guidance. Older children will enjoy the challenge of well-hidden treasures. Give each child a personal treasure map that leads to a special gift.

If your party is planned for one of the hottest days of summer, let the children play under a sprinkler. (Just be sure the invitations request bathing suits or a change of clothes.) Remember the old game called "hot potato"? Substitute a large, soaking-wet sponge for the potato, and you'll witness a good bit of happy shrieking. The game's only goal is to keep the sponge moving from child to child. In general,

you'll find that minimizing competition in games will result in fewer disappointed children.

REFRESHMENTS

Menu planning for children's parties is easy. There's the main course (the birthday cake) and the appetizers (healthier fare that you'll serve before the cake is presented). Most of your young guests will probably either bolt their food or be too excited to eat, anyway, so don't waste time preparing fancy dishes. Avoid caffeine-laden drinks (the children won't need any extra stimulation). And leave cookies and candies off the menu; the cake should satisfy every sweet tooth.

OTHER HELPFUL TIPS

Backyard children's parties do require careful monitoring to ensure your young guests' safety. In addition to great memories and a party favor or two, the children may collect a few bumps, scrapes, or insect bites. Be prepared with kid-friendly insect repellent, sunscreen, and a fully-equipped first-aid kit. And when parents are unable to attend, first find out where you can contact them if an emergency should arise. Then persuade adult friends or neighborhood baby-sitters to take their places. If parents are able to attend, ask that they each bring a blanket or a folding chair; that way, everyone will have a comfortable place to sit.

Making a Humpty-Dumpty Piñata

Who doesn't love a piñata? Especially when it's everyone's favorite fragile character: Humpty Dumpty! For a perfect finale to a child's birthday party, first make this paper mache Humpty and fill him with treats. Then suspend him from a tree branch. Each child gets one chance to break Humpty open by hitting him with a broomstick—while wearing a blindfold. (Make sure that the other children stay a safe distance from the swinging broomstick.) When the treats finally come pouring out, you'll see kids scrambling to clean the yard in ways you've never seen before!

MATERIALS & TOOLS

- Pen
- Scissors
- Plastic tarp or drop cloth
- 30"-diameter balloon
- Newspapers
- Plastic tray or bucket
- White craft glue
- Water
- Spray varnish
- Craft knife
- White spray paint
- 8½" x 11" sheets of felt (one each of white, red, and purple; two each of black and pink)
- Red construction paper, 6" x 30"
- Stapler
- 12"-long pipe cleaner (black)
- Bandanna
- Gold poster board
- Black marker
- Batting
- Black electrician's tape
- Contact cement (strong bond glue)
- Cowboy hat (available at many toy stores)
- Strong nylon cord, 20' long
- Awl
- Clear packing tape
- Broomstick
- Treats for filling (see "Tips")

TIPS

- Don't be alarmed by the number of steps involved in making a piñata. Each step is quite simple, and this project is very easy to make!
- Start this project at least one week in advance. Paper mache can dry very slowly, especially when the weather is rainy or humid, and the coats of varnish and paint that you apply will also take time to dry.

- Fill the piñata with lightweight treats, such as popcorn-caramel balls covered with plastic wrap and tied with colorful ribbons; or with an assortment of festive noisemakers and other lightweight party favors. For heavier gifts, just use a smaller balloon and reduce the sizes of the facial features, arms, hands, and boots.

- Although patterns are provided for the piñata's facial features, hands and boots, feel free to create your own designs. Humpty Dumpty's face can bear all manner of expressions, from hilariously silly to downright determined! Instead of completing step 1, and when you get to step 11, use white chalk or crayon to draw your own designs on the felt; then cut them out.

Instructions

1 Photocopy the patterns shown to the right, enlarging each one to the dimensions provided. You'll need one copy each of figure 1 (the eyelash); figure 2 (the eyelid); figure 3 (the eye); figure 4 (the iris); figure 5 (the cheek); figure 6 (the moustache); figure 7 (the lips); figure 8 (the mouth); figure 9 (the hand); and figure 10 (the boot). Cut out the paper patterns and label each one.

2 Cover a smooth, flat work surface with a plastic tarp or drop cloth. Brush away any debris; even tiny pieces of gravel or wood may pop the balloon. Then blow up the balloon and place it on the covered work surface.

3 Tear the newspapers into wide strips. You'll need plenty of them, so don't skimp here!

4 In the plastic bucket or tray, mix two parts white craft glue with one part water. Because this project is so large, you'll probably need to replenish your supply of glue solution as you go. Just mix up more glue and water when the solution gets low.

5 Begin covering the balloon by dipping one strip of newspaper into the glue solution, lifting it out and running your fingers down each side to skim off the excess liquid. Position the strip on the balloon vertically. Continue applying vertical strips, working around the balloon until the entire surface is covered with a single layer of strips.

6 Apply another layer of dipped newspaper strips, but this time position them horizontally. (It's best to alternate the directions of the layers, so you can tell how many layers have been applied.)

7 Apply two more layers of dipped newspaper strips, alternating their directions as before. Then set the piñata in a well-ventilated area to dry. (Depending on the weather conditions and ventilation, this may take three days. Be patient!) Rotate the

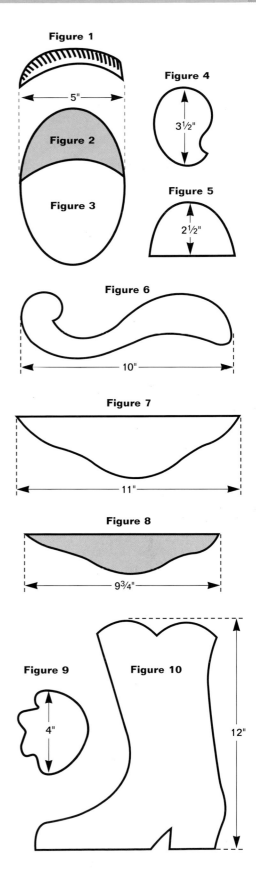

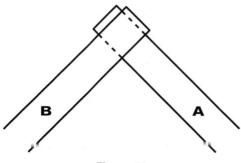

Figure 11

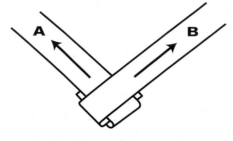

Figure 12

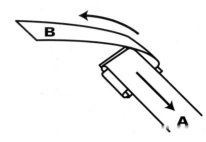

Figure 13

balloon occasionally to allow the entire surface to dry thoroughly.

8 When the piñata form is dry, you must seal its surface with spray varnish. Varnish vapors can be dangerous to inhale, so either work outdoors or make sure your indoor work area is well ventilated. Start by covering your work surface with newspapers. Set the piñata form on the covered surface, and apply two coats of spray varnish, allowing the first coat to dry before applying the second. There's no need to apply varnish to the very bottom of the form, as this will become the top of the finished piñata and will be covered by a hat.

9 When the second coat of varnish has dried, rotate the piñata so the unvarnished portion is at the top. In order to make sure that your gifts will fit inside the finished piñata, first measure the largest one. Then, using a craft knife, make three cuts in the form's back to make an upside-down, U-shaped flap (or "door") that is slightly larger than the gift you mea-

sured. (The balloon will pop as you do this.) Pry the flap open and down to reveal the balloon inside. Pull out the popped balloon and discard it.

10 Apply three coats of white spray paint to the piñata form, allowing each coat to dry completely before applying the next. It's best to apply several thin coats of paint rather than one or two thick coats, especially when working with a paper base.

11 Using the paper patterns that you cut in step 1—and the project photo as a color guide—cut out the facial features and the hands from the sheets of felt. Cut one mouth and one set of lips; two hands; two cheeks; two of every portion of the eye; and two moustache halves.

12 Each arm is folded from two strips of red construction paper. Begin by cutting four 1½" x 30" strips. Then position two strips (A and B) as shown in figure 11, with their ends overlapping to form a 90° angle. Staple the ends together.

13 Referring to figure 12, fold strip A up and over strip B. Then fold strip B over strip A. Fold strip A back down over strip B, and fold strip B back down over strip A (see figure 13). Continue this folding process (A over B, and B over A) until you reach the ends of the strips. Staple the strips together at the last fold, and cut away any excess paper. Repeat step 12 and this step to make another arm. Then staple a felt hand to one end of each.

14 Apply white craft glue to the back of each of the felt facial features, and press the features gently onto the piñata. Attach the arms in the same fashion. Then, using the photo as a guide, bend the black pipe cleaner to form a nose shape, and use white craft glue to attach it to the piñata.

15 Fold the bandanna as desired and use contact cement to secure it around Humpty Dumpty's "neck." (The bandanna won't reach all the way around the balloon—simply glue its ends down.) Allow the glued felt pieces and bandanna to dry completely before handling the piñata.

16 Using the boot template, trace two boots onto the gold poster board. Turn the template over and trace another two boots. Cut the four boot pieces out, and use the black marker to decorate the outer face of each one with western designs, such as curlicues and simple diamonds.

17 Place one boot shape on top of another, and staple the shapes together at the bottom. Also staple the sides of the boot, leaving about one-third of each side unstapled. (Don't staple the top closed!) Repeat to staple the other two boot shapes together.

18 Fold a piece of the black electrician's tape along the length of each boot bottom and the vertical edge of the toe. Then stuff each boot with a moderate amount of batting (enough to expand the boot without bursting its stapled and taped seams).

19 Fold down the top flaps of each boot. Position a boot so the inner face of each boot flap is pressed against the piñata. Using a pen, mark the boot position lightly onto the piñata. Repeat with the second boot. Then apply contact cement to the boot flaps and to the marked positions on the piñata. Allow the

cement to set up for 10 minutes or more; then press each boot onto the piñata body and allow the glue to dry.

20 If the cowboy hat includes a cord, remove and discard it. If the hat is cordless, use an awl to punch two holes through the brim, one on each side of the hat's crown and as close to the crown as possible. Set the hat on top of the piñata, and insert the awl through the holes in the hat in order to punch two holes through the piñata.

21 Cut a 7' length of nylon cord and thread one end down through each hole in the hat, so the cord ends emerge from the hat's bottom. Carefully thread a few inches of each cord end down through a hole in the piñata. Then reach inside the piñata by inserting your hand through the opening you cut in step 9, pull the cord ends out, and tie them together.

22 Position the cowboy hat on top of the piñata and mark its position lightly with a pen. Apply contact cement to this area and to the underside of the hat brim. Allow the cement to set up for at least 10 minutes. Then press the hat down onto the piñata, and pull the cord up so that the knotted ends pull back inside the piñata.

23 Tie the remaining length of nylon cord to the looped cord extending from the hat.

24 Fill the piñata with individually wrapped goodies (see "Tips"). Close the door flap, secure it with clear packing tape, and suspend the piñata from a tree branch.

Soirees

oiree (that's "swah-ray"): Don't let this French word intimidate you. It's derived from the Latin word *sero*, which means "late hour" and refers to a party or reception that takes place after the sun has set. By definition, however, soirees are very different from after-dark family cook-outs or campfire gatherings. A soiree is an elegant affair. Your guests will arrive in formal attire, the dishes you serve will rival those of a master chef, and not one plastic fork or spoon will appear on the buffet table. You certainly won't need to commission an ice sculpture or order five pounds of caviar, but you will need to spend some time setting the perfect scene and selecting a menu that will make your guests feel as if they're indulging in an evening of luxury.

BEFORE THE PARTY

Set the mood for your soiree well in advance by sending elegant invitations to everyone on the guest list. A gorgeous invitation that arrives by mail will signal that this outdoor party is *not* a casual barbecue! Reiterate the message by suggesting evening wear, but be sure to emphasize that guests will be spending the evening outside, under the stars; suggest an extra wrap to guard against nighttime chill.

Two or three days before the party, take a critical look at your backyard and porch. Mow the grass and, if they need it, trim the shrubs. You may want to rent a pressure washer to spray your porch clean of dirt and stains. The cover of night will hide most other flaws, so don't worry about spending too much time on cleanup and maintenance.

AMBIANCE

Why sequester guests indoors when the night itself offers a naturally elegant ambiance? A clear sky, a scattering of stars, and the glowing moon practically whisper "sophistication."

If your lawn and garden tend to be damp at night, keep evening-gown hems, trouser cuffs, and leather shoes dry by making your deck, patio, or porch the center of entertainment. Provide seating for your guests, but not too much. (Did you know that when people at parties are all encouraged to sit, they tend to stay in one place rather than mingle?)

To set the mood for a memorable soiree, harness the mystery of the dark, rather than fighting it. Start by turning off all bright lights in your garden and home, except the lighting along any paths or walkways. Then set out lanterns, candles, torches, or luminaries instead. The subtle flickering of their flames and the shadows they cast will provide plenty of light. What's more, the light they don't cast will tease your guests' other senses, including the senses of hearing, taste, and smell.

Prepare to soothe your guests with soft background music. (The key words here are *soft* and *background*.) Classical music and light jazz are often best. Live music is ideal, but if you're unable to hire a professional musician or persuade a willing friend to play, just select a few CDs, turn the volume to low, and place the speakers in open windows. If the night air doesn't already bear a hint of your garden, arrange lightly scented flowers in vases. For a special touch, place fresh floral corsages and boutonnieres on a small side table by the front door, and encourage each arriving guest to wear one.

THE MENU AND SERVICE

A soiree calls for an exquisite menu, but the food you serve doesn't have to be outrageously expensive, and you don't have to serve a great deal of it. Consider preparing a selection of appetizers rather than a full meal, and let the guests nibble throughout the evening. Unless you have help, select dishes that can be prepared in advance and that can be served chilled (or

heated quickly) just before serving.

Boiled shrimp presented on glistening beds of ice; thin, sliced rounds of French bread served with an assortment of patés and other spreads; cold soups; cheeses; and light salads will all be savored. The truth is that while some foods don't belong on a soiree menu (save the hamburgers for tomorrow), how you present each dish is probably more important than the food itself. A huge bowl of potato salad, with a wooden spoon stuck into its center, belongs at a backyard potluck. Small mounds of potato salad, each garnished with slivers of red and green bell peppers and served on an individual bed of lettuce, belong at a soiree. No matter what you serve, use your best china, your finest cutlery, and your linen napkins and tablecloths.

IMBIBING IN STYLE

Chilled white wines, rosés, and champagnes; and red wines served at room temperature are often the beverages of choice for sophisticated gatherings. A wise host or hostess, however, will also offer a selection of nonalcoholic bever-

ages, including bottled water and clear sodas. (When it's served in a crystal wine glass, even fruit juice will acquire a certain panache!)

If you can afford to hire a bartender, by all means do. You'll not only have more time to spend with your guests if someone else is mixing the drinks, you'll also have some help keeping an eye on your guests' consumption of alcohol. Remember: If alcohol has encouraged anyone to have *too* good a time, make sure that he or she gets a lift home from someone who can drive safely.

Lighting for Parties

The light that falls on your yard at night will have a subtle but sure effect on the spirit of any evening gathering, whether it's the soft haze offered by candles and votives, the warm glow of lanterns, or the bright shine of torches or electric lighting. The choices that face any homeowner when it comes to permanent garden lighting take time to make, but setting up temporary lighting—tailored to a particular event—is really quite easy.

NATURAL LIGHTING

Lighting a yard with flames—from simple candles, votives, and luminaries to lanterns and torches or flares—is the classic choice for temporary outdoor illumination. Unlike most forms of electric lighting, flame lights have the advantage of flexibility: They're easy to position and rearrange to suit your needs. And if you're wondering whether a few lanterns or candles will provide enough light, in most cases the

answer is "yes." A healthy collection of lanterns, candles, and torches will cast ample light for any evening gathering.

Flame lights can also serve as a form of insect control. A few drops of citronella oil on top of a candle or in the oil that fuels many lanterns will help keep mosquitoes at bay. Just be sure not to place citronella-scented candles or lanterns too close to your dining area, as the scent may interfere with the flavors of the foods.

Flame lights come in many shapes, sizes, and styles. Hurricane lanterns, with their bowl-like bases and bulb-shaped globes, are famous for their ability to stay lit in even the strongest of winds. Barn lanterns are also wind-proof, and can be safely suspended. Flares—usually mounted on bamboo posts—can be set directly in the ground and will burn for up to two hours. Candles are popular, but unless they're placed inside protective containers, they tend to go out whenever the breeze picks up, and can be a fire hazard when they're forgotten. To safely enjoy candlelight outdoors, make simple luminaries. For the classic version, spread an inch or two of sand in the bottom of a paper bag, and set a candle down in the sand. Line a path, walkway, or staircase with these modest lights for a surprisingly elegant look. Although the sand will hold the candle firmly in place and the bag will protect the flame from breezes, you should always keep a close eye on paper-bag luminaries. You can make more permanent, stable, and colorful luminaries from painted glass canning jars. (Turn to pages 260 and 261 for complete instructions.)

ELECTRIC LIGHTING

Permanent electric lighting, which must be installed by an electrician, is a must for most yards, especially along paths, walkways, steps, and the entrances to the house. If your backyard party plans include after-dark volleyball games or dances on your lawn, make sure that these outdoor lights are turned on; it's all too easy to twist an ankle on uneven turf when you can't see the ground beneath your feet. For less energetic party activities, however, there's no need to flood your entire yard with light. Do make sure that high-traffic areas are well lit, but turn off any harsh electric lights that aren't necessary, and bring out the natural lighting instead.

To supplement the light offered by lanterns and candles, you might also want to arrange a few strands of electric lights—similar to the lights used to decorate Christmas trees. These widely available lights often come with bulb covers in amusing shapes—from chili peppers and animals to flowers. Choose the icon that best complements the theme of your gathering!

Low-voltage outdoor lighting kits that any homeowner can install are also widely available at home-improvement centers. While these lights are usually considered to be permanent once they're installed, there's no reason why you shouldn't take the time to purchase and install one for a special party. The easiest ones to set up are mounted on posts that can be driven into the ground wherever you like.

Making Painted Glass-Jar Lanterns

Have you ever wondered what to do with all those old glass jars you have lying around the house? Here's the perfect answer: Make them into fun, festive lanterns! The instructions that follow will walk you through the process of making the colorful lanterns shown in the photo, but don't stop there. Craft stores all over the country stock a huge variety of easy-to-use glass paints in every imaginable hue and shade, so no matter what your party's theme, you can create fabulous lighting, custom-designed for the occasion.

MATERIALS & TOOLS
(for four painted-glass jar lanterns)

- 4 clear glass jars
- Warm, soapy water
- Isopropyl alcohol
- Glass-paint surface conditioner (if necessary for the brand of paint you choose)
- 1 sheet of acetate (clear plastic available at art-supply and craft stores)
- Craft knife
- Permanent black marker with a fine point
- Starter kit of water-based, air-dry glass paints, in the colors of your choice
- Paintbrushes
- Kitchen or craft sponge
- Glass-paint finishing sealant (if necessary for the brand of paint you choose)
- 4 cups of sand, plain or colored
- 4 candlesticks, about ½" in diameter and short enough to fit easily into the canning jars

Instructions

1 Remove and discard any labels or stickers that may be on your glass jars. Wash the jars in warm, soapy water and rinse them thoroughly. Allow the jars to dry completely; then wipe them with isopropyl alcohol and let them air dry. Some glass-paint manufacturers also recommend "conditioning" the glass with their surface conditioner. (Most such conditioners are primarily isopropyl alcohol mixtures.) If your paint requires a conditioner, apply it and allow it to dry according to the manufacturer's instructions.

2 The jars shown in the photo were decorated using homemade stencils. To make stencils, choose a pattern you like and trace or draw it onto the sheet of acetate. Cut out the pattern with a craft knife.

3 Position the stencil against a jar, and use the fine-point, permanent black marker to draw the image onto the glass.

4 Repeat step 3 until you have the desired number of images on each jar. If your jars have embossed images on them, you may also want to outline them with the marker. Allow the black ink to dry completely before moving on to the next step.

5 Using a paintbrush and following the paint manufacturer's instructions, fill in the stenciled images with the paint colors of your choice. If your jars have embossed images, you may want to paint those, too. Allow the paint to dry.

6 Add additional details to the designs, such as the black dots on the ladybugs' wings on the jar to the left in the photo. Let the paint dry completely.

7 Use a sponge to paint the remaining surfaces, switching to a fine paintbrush to apply color around the stenciled images. Allow the paint to dry.

8 If your paint requires finishing sealant, apply it, following the manufacturer's instructions. Allow the sealant to dry completely.

9 Place about a cup of sand in the bottom of each jar. (The amount of sand you use will vary, depending on the size of your jars; you'll need enough to hold your candlesticks upright.)

10 Place a candlestick in each jar, firmly burying one end in the sand. Light each candle and enjoy your new lanterns!

Before & After the Meal

Whether you're trying to keep lively young-sters busy while you grill their hot dogs, or entertain adults after dinner, your backyard offers dozens of ways to have a good time. A friendly horseshoe match or a badminton game can be played in even a small yard, and both games are easy to set up. If your lawn is well tended and large, turn it into a course for croquet or for the popular Italian lawn-bowling game known as bocce. For more sedentary guests, move a table or two —and a few board games—out to the yard.

Teach children some of your own favorite childhood games. A handful of jacks and a rubber ball can still work wonders. Mix up a batch of bubble solution, give everyone bubble-blowing wands, and start a bubble-blowing contest. Or start a game of tag, Red Rover, or farmer-in-the-dell.

When the sun starts to set, snuff the candles and lanterns, lie back on a blanket, and settle in for an evening of stargazing. Or build a campfire and gather 'round. There's nothing quite like the smell of wood smoke to stimulate conversation, fond memories, or perhaps even a ghost story or two.

Evening Activities

If you haven't spent much time in your backyard or on your patio after sunset, try spending some time there tonight. Step outside for just a minute or two and notice the differences between your daytime yard and the yard you experience at night.

It's quieter, for one thing: There are fewer cars and no lawns being mown. If it's summertime, you'll probably hear a symphony of wildlife. In the winter, especially if snow has coated the ground, you may come as close to blissful silence as possible in today's suburban landscape. Your yard will also be cooler at night—a welcome change in the summer, and a brisk reminder of the season during winter. The air probably smells fresher, too. And you won't have to remember to slather on the sunscreen. Overall, your backyard is a great place to be in the evening.

EVENING ENTERTAINMENT

Light a few candles, sip drinks with your guests, and just enjoy the night's special ambiance; or try any number of activities that take advantage of the dark side of day. Encourage your guests to take in the evening sky by equipping your patio with comfortable chairs, a telescope, and binoculars: Stargazing is a natural for evening parties. For more informal gatherings, try a backyard campfire. You'll find all kinds of inspiring information about both stargazing and campfires in the following pages, but don't stop there!

Plan a moonlit theatrical production or a game of shadow charades. For the play, create a makeshift stage and light it with torches—just as stages were lit in Shakespeare's day. Have a core group of "actors" put on the play, or ask each guest to take a role; either way, hand out highlighted scripts and small flashlights to each participant at the beginning of the party.

For shadow charades, set up a plain, white backdrop and have guests take turns casting shadow animals, monsters, or entire scenes on it. The other revelers must guess what the shadow-caster is trying to portray. If your party falls on the night of a full moon, you may not need additional lighting to create good shadows; otherwise, be sure to have a few candles, a torch, or a spotlight on hand.

Under the cover of dark, even the most self-conscious guests may be willing to join in a sing-along. If you or any of your friends play the guitar or another portable musical instrument, bring it out, play a few notes, and start singing old favorites that everyone knows.

EVENING ACTIVITIES
FOR THE FAMILY

If your children enjoy the backyard during the day, imagine how much more exciting it can be for them at night. Hold an overnight camping adventure—for the whole family, or for the younger members only—without ever leaving home. Your kids will love the change of pace, and you'll love having an inexpensive way to keep them entertained. All you'll need is a tent (and not even that, if the weather's right), sleeping bags, and sleeping pads. A campfire, a bag of marshmallows, and some long sticks for toasting will round out this backyard camping experience.

Or use your backyard as a living science lab. Show your children how flora and fauna change from day to

night, starting with something as simple as catching fireflies. Take a trip to the library or spend some time on the Internet doing research about the nocturnal wildlife in your area; then go on a nighttime nature walk. Just remember to give visitors such as raccoons and possums a wide berth; wildlife can be unpredictable.

If it's an especially dark night, play a game of "What's That?" Tuck common household or backyard items into a bag and take turns trying to figure out what each one is—using only your sense of touch. Or have a "blind" drawing contest, in which everyone sketches a few pictures by starlight;

compare the results the next morning over breakfast.

Dark nights also add an extra element to the simple game of hide-and-seek. And what could be more fun than a moonlight treasure hunt? Just make a treasure map of your backyard with glow-in-the-dark ink, or use a regular pencil or pen and provide each treasure-hunter with a flashlight. And speaking of flashlights, you'd be surprised by how long kids can keep themselves entertained by making scary faces with flashlights under their chins. Keep a few extra batteries on hand to make sure the fun doesn't come to an untimely end.

BACKYARD CAMPFIRES

Whether you're roasting hot dogs with your family, holding a backyard slumber party, or winding down after a cookout, a campfire can provide the perfect cozy ending for an outdoor gathering. Most of us have fond memories of evenings passed in the glow of a campfire, and there's no better inspiration for great conversation, a sing-along, or hours of storytelling. So prepare the pit, find some kindling and logs, and settle in for a great time! (You'll find plenty of information for starting, tending, and cooking over campfires on pages 170–171 and 182–183.)

When the guests know one another, campfire gatherings often take on a life of their own. Someone will say "Remember when . . . ?" and before you know it, the last ember will be dying, but the conversation will still be going strong. If you're entertaining new friends or children, however, a little planning will guarantee that the evening is a memorable one.

Getting Comfortable

If you want the real campfire experience—the one you remember from summer camp or your last trek into the woods—wear old clothing and just plop yourself directly on the ground in front of the fire. For guests who may not be hankering for quite this authentic an experience, stack some old quilts, blankets, or tarps at a safe distance from the flames. (Let

people unfold and place these as they like, but do keep an eye out for any that get too close to the fire.) The young at heart but not so young in the joints will appreciate lawn chairs, too; if you don't have many, ask guests to bring their own.

If evenings in your area tend to get chilly, remind everyone to bring an

extra layer of clothing. Keep an insect repellent on hand—make sure it's effective against ticks as well as mosquitoes. And don't forget to prepare a few campfire snacks. Even people who have just finished dinner may be hungry again when offered the chance to toast marshmallows over an open fire.

Storytelling

Everyone loves a good story, especially when it's told outside in the dark. Tall tales, folklore, and Native American stories are all classic campfire fare. If you don't have any family favorites, go to the library beforehand; you'll find plenty of stories there. Ask your guests to contribute a few tales, too. If you're an actor at heart, by all means rehearse before the party starts. A few appropriate props and special-effect sounds will keep your audience captivated!

For more spontaneous (and often, more hilarious) tale telling, try a chain story. Simply set the scene by starting the story, bring your listeners to an exciting point, and then let the person next to you take it from there. Assure everyone that the story doesn't necessarily have to make sense.

Music

No campfire is complete without music—a round or two of "Kumbaya," or "This Land Is Your Land," a harmonica solo, or a few guitar melodies —so invite guests to bring along any portable instruments they might play. Try singing traditional camp songs, folk songs, or even tunes that were popular while you were in high school. Everyone will have their special favorites; encourage guests to take turns choosing theirs. Ask the kids for suggestions, too; they'll probably surprise you with their repertoire.

Children will also love participating in a modern version of an ancient rite—the drumming circle. The kids won't even need real drums. Any nonbreakable household items that make sounds when they're struck—from pots and pans to plastic trash cans—can serve as percussion instruments. Add a few plastic containers filled with dried beans or macaroni, and you'll have homemade maracas. Choose one child to get the rhythm started and let everyone join in. It's a wonderfully upbeat way to end the evening.

GHOST STORIES

The sun has set, and the flames are casting flickering shadows over you and your companions. Tree leaves whisper and hiss in the breeze. A chill runs down your spine. It's time for ghost stories.

Do a little ghoulish research before your campfire gathering. Your hometown might have its very own spooky legend or resident ghost. If so, find out all about it; the best ghost stories are the ones that strike closest to home!

Be sure to begin your tale by insisting that the story you're about to share is true. Then proceed by lowering your voice slightly and drawing your listeners in close. As you get to the frightening parts, pretend to be dis-

tracted by noises coming from the bushes, or ask if anyone else suddenly feels cold; a lull in the storytelling will make your listeners clamor for you to continue.

When they settle back down, go on. Add a little more drama as you approach the end of the story and use any props you have on hand. The ending should scare the wits out of everyone—or leave them eerily hanging. Either way, end your tale by saying, "I swear it's true!" If your guests guffaw, just shrug. Then place a flashlight under your chin, pause, turn it on, and contort your face into an expression of sheer horror.

Laugh, enjoy, and pass the s'mores!

The second factor that makes it more difficult to spot stars is the presence of surrounding light—be it from streetlights, tall buildings, or even the moon. Pure darkness can be a pipe dream in our predominantly suburban landscape, but do your best to find a viewing site that's as dark as possible. The less glow on the ground, the more glow you'll see in the sky.

A little ground glow isn't such a bad thing, however, when it comes to finding the major constellations. The shapes of most constellations are built around a "skeleton" that consists of a few very bright stars. You'll find that it's actually easier to pick out the bright stars of the constellations (Virgo, Scorpius, and others) when ground glow eliminates the distraction of smaller, surrounding stars.

STARGAZING 101

Night after night, an amazing show is going on above our heads, but most of us rarely stop to look up and notice it. It's a star-studded display you and your guests can take in for free. We're talking, of course, about the night sky. Stargazing is the perfect way to end an evening outdoors. Just spread a blanket on the lawn, unfold a few chairs, and invite your guests to join history's oldest game of connect the dots.

Seeing Stars

There's no need to worry about fancy equipment; a telescope or pair of binoculars can add to the fun, but on a clear night, you may be able to see many as 2,000 stars with the naked eye alone. After all, finding constellations (groups of stars that form patterns in the sky) is a low-tech party game that's been around for thousands of years.

A couple of factors will affect your potential to see what the night sky has to offer. The first is night vision. The human eye generally takes about 30 minutes to become fully accustomed to the dark. If you set up your food and beverages outside, you can avoid having to run back into your brightly lit house.

Mapping It Out

Start with a cloudless and moonless night, perhaps a blanket to lie back on, and a face tilted skyward. In North America, 30 of the 88 constellations are waiting to catch your eye, depending on the time of year. A star map or chart (browse through the astronomy section of your local library) will help you in your search. Photocopy a few maps for your guests, too, and study up before heading out. That way, you'll know which constellations will be visible during that particular time of year. Flashlights will come in handy for reading the maps (if you cover the ends of the flashlights with red cellophane, their light won't spoil your night vision).

To an untrained eye, the best place to start an evening of stargazing is with a search for the constellation known as Ursa Major (or the Great Bear)—one of the constellations that can be seen year-round. What makes Ursa Major so friendly is that it's composed, in part, of a group of stars most of us learned to spot as children: the Big Dipper. The Big Dipper's handle forms the bear's tail, with the cup or bowl marking the high point of the bear's rump. The two stars that form the front of the dipper's bowl point to the North Star (Polaris)—one of the brightest lights in the sky and the only one that seems to remain stationary throughout the year.

Scorpius, a constellation made up of stars in the shape of a scorpion, appears in the summer sky. To find it, face south and look for a bright red star. This is Antares (a red giant that's hundreds of times wider than the sun). Antares is close to the scorpion's head and claws; some visualize it as the creature's heart. It is followed in the other direction by the stars that form the scorpion's tail and stinger.

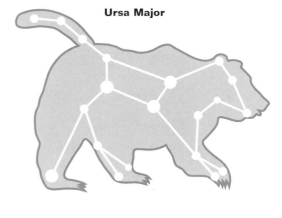

Ursa Major

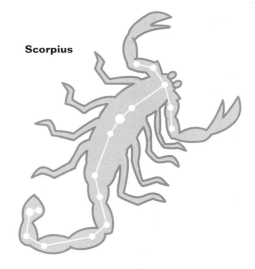

Scorpius

Daytime Activities

Having a backyard is a little like owning your very own private park. Take another look at your lawn. Try to see it as something other than a stretch of grass that you have to mow every week, or a convenient spot for the grill. In addition to being a great substitute for your indoor kitchen, that expanse of green makes the perfect playing field for all kinds of games, both informal and structured. Whether you've invited a few friends over for the afternoon, or you're simply enjoying a day with your family, your backyard can offer hours of fun.

IMPROMPTU PLAY

You don't need to be at the beach to spike a volleyball or to start up an informal game of touch football. And as your dog is well aware, the backyard is also a great place to toss around the frisbee. Try starting or ending a party with a casual match of badminton; the equipment is inexpensive and the object of the game—to hit the shuttle to the ground on your opponent's side of the net—is easy to grasp and, depending on your opponent, easy to accomplish. Read more about this game on page 275.

Encourage impromptu play by having the equipment available and, if necessary, assembled. (A volleyball or badminton net will only take a few

minutes to put up.) Simply place a football or a frisbee in an accessible area, and before long, your guests will be tossing, catching, and laughing until the sun goes down.

If you're interested in a more structured activity, set up a game of horseshoes, croquet, or bocce (Italian lawn bowling). Information and instructions for playing each of these outdoor classics follows.

HORSESHOES

The supply of equine footwear may have dwindled since the invention of the automobile, but folks still enjoy tossing horseshoes at stakes in backyards across the country. Believed to have first been played by Roman soldiers, the game of horseshoes has been an American tradition since Colonial times. It's a perfect activity for the casual backyard gathering since it requires little equipment and can be enjoyed by first-time players. Exact rules of play have always varied from one backyard court to the next, but here you'll find useful information to rouse up a good game of horseshoes among friends.

Setting Up the Court

You'll first need to turn a patch of backyard into a pitching court. This game is tough on your lawn, so choose a plot of grass you don't mind subjecting to wear and tear. An official court is 6 feet wide and 46 feet long with a 3-foot by 4-foot clay, sand, or gravel pit at each end, but you can adjust these dimensions to suit your yard or the skill of the players.

In official games, 15-inch high, 1-inch diameter stakes are set in the center of each pit, 40 feet apart. This distance can be adjusted, too; however, do make sure the stakes are not set completely straight, but rather tilted toward each other slightly. Pack sand around each stake to ensure anchorage, and place a wooden stop around the pit to keep the sand in place. Arrange gravel around the stop to protect the grass in the immediate vicinity from bouncing horseshoes. Now, measure out a foul line 3 feet in front of each stake.

Aside from the stakes, the only equipment you'll need for a casual game of horseshoes is—well, horseshoes. Lack of uniformity renders real horseshoes inappropriate for the game, so go with the specially manufactured sets, which are slightly bigger and heavier than the real thing.

Ready . . . Set . . . Pitch!

The object of the game is to toss the shoe in an underhand pitch (from behind the foul line) so that it comes to rest encircling the stake (a "ringer"). The game is divided into innings; each player pitches two shoes per inning. You may play with either a predetermined number of innings (15 to 25) or a predetermined number of points (40 to 50). During the game, the pitcher's feet must remain behind the foul line until the horseshoe is released. Both players remain at the same end of the court until each has pitched his turn.

Taunting or making catcalls while a pitch is in progress is technically against the rules (though, admittedly, in a casual game it can add a bit of spice).

There are several methods of scoring a game of horseshoes, the most common being the cancellation method. With this approach, only one player scores in an inning, because only the closest shoe scores.

A shoe only scores if it comes to rest six inches or less from the stake. The shoe closest to the stake scores one point. Ringers each score three points, but if both opponents throw ringers, the throws cancel each other out. At the end of an inning, only the difference between scores is recorded. If scores are the same, no points are earned.

The Basics

An official backyard croquet course is 100 feet long and 50 feet wide. At the height of the game's popularity, elaborate private courts were constructed, complete with sand pits and water hazards; but a grassy area as small as 10 feet by 20 feet will do, even one that curves around the corner of your house. If you've got a backyard, you can find a way to play croquet.

The typical backyard croquet set, available from most sporting goods stores, consists of six mallets, six balls (red, yellow, orange, blue, black, and green), nine wickets (the hoops through which the balls are driven), and two pegs that are set up at the ends of the course. These affordable and durable sets can last a lifetime and almost always come with a set of playing rules.

To Play

The official rules for backyard croquet are lengthy, but the game itself is really just a race among balls—a race run by using mallets to strike the balls through an obstacle course made up of wickets. Although the rules call for laying out the nine wickets in a double-diamond pattern (as shown in the illustration to the right), many backyard players set up the wickets any way they like. Circular or slalom patterns add a dash of novelty to the game!

Players are entitled to one stroke

CROQUET

The game of croquet was immortalized by Lewis Caroll, when his heroine, Alice, played in Wonderland, using flamingos as mallets, hedgehogs as balls, and soldiers as wickets. But you don't have to fall down a rabbit hole to play this wonderful game. Your own backyard can serve as the perfect croquet court.

History

Some say croquet had its origins in fourteenth-century France, in a peasant game of ball and hoops called Pall Mall. Others point to eighteenth-century Ireland, where the game was played in its more modern form.

Croquet was introduced to England during the mid-nineteenth century, and by the turn of that century was popular throughout the United States. Croquet has always had a certain panache. It was a favorite of New York's literary set (members of the famous Algonquin Round Table played it) and of Hollywood's glitterati (Samuel Goldwyn and Darryl Zanuck were devotees).

Several varieties of croquet are played today, from the British six-wicket tournament game—played in white flannels—to the traditional backyard (or lawn) nine-wicket croquet—playable in shorts and T-shirts.

per turn and earn extra strokes by passing the ball through a wicket or striking another ball. Fine players can actually make it through a set of wickets in only one turn by using special shots such as the drive, the stop shot, the roll, the take off, and the jump shot.

The game includes a couple of signature shots. When your ball hits an opponent's ball, the shot is called a "roquet"—and you get two bonus shots as a reward. The first bonus shot, called the "croquet," can be played in one of two ways. You may place your ball next to the opponent's and strike your ball to make both balls move. During this shot, you may

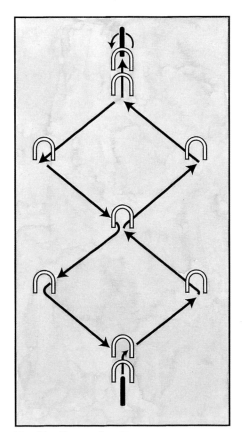

Double-diamond pattern

hold your ball still by placing your foot on top if it. When you strike it, the force of the shot moves the ball next to it. The croquet shot may also be taken at a mallet-head's distance from the opponent's ball.

The second bonus shot is called the "continuation" stroke. You make this shot from wherever your ball has come to a halt after the croquet shot. A complete set of rules will come with your croquet set; the plays described here are just the basics.

The most important thing to remember about croquet is that the game is an occasion for fun. Young or old, amateur or expert—almost anyone can enjoy this easy-to-learn game, so the next time you're planning a garden party, consider the very social and civilized game of croquet. Its rich history and associations make it the perfect centerpiece for a theme party. How about a Hollywood Heyday party, a Victorian affair, a celebration of Irish, French, or English heritage, or an Alice-in-Wonderland party? Long considered the traditional game for garden parties, croquet is actually an ideal game for almost any backyard event.

BOCCE

Add a little European-style fun to your outdoor gathering with a game of bocce (Italian lawn bowling). Although bocce has only recently gained popularity in this country, it's one of the most widely played

games in the world—and for good reasons: The rules and strategies are simple, the equipment is inexpensive, the court is simply a stretch of level ground, and people of all ages and abilities can play. These qualities also make bocce the ideal way to get everyone up and having fun at your backyard party!

Bocce is a team game, with room for up to eight players. The rules and the terminology of the sport vary from place to place, but the main ingredient is a small target ball, called a pallina, that's tossed onto the court. Players from two opposing teams attempt to throw or roll bocce balls as close to the pallina as possible. Players may also roll or toss their bocce balls to knock opposing bocce balls away from the pallina, or to push the pallina closer to their own balls.

To Play

To get started, you'll need a bocce set: one pallina and eight larger bocce balls (four each of two different colors or patterns). A tape measure comes in handy to settle close calls; aside from that, all you need is a flat, level surface. If you're playing on grass, you might want to mow an area extra short to demarcate the playing area and to allow for unimpeded rolling. (A driveway of hard-packed dirt, sand-dusted asphalt, or gravel will also work.) Official bocce courts are 76 feet long and 10 feet wide, but any similarly shaped space, in a size your lawn will accommodate, will do.

Begin play by choosing two teams, each consisting of one, two, or four players. If each team has only a single player, each person gets four bocce balls; if there are two players per team, each gets two balls, and in four-member teams, every player gets one ball.

Start the game with a coin toss. The team that wins the toss picks a player to pitch the pallina from a throw (or pitch) line at one end of the court. The pallina should land about 30 feet from the pitch line. The same player then tries (from behind the pitch line) to throw or roll a bocce ball as close to the pallina as possible. It's good strategy to try and place the first bocce ball in front of the pallina —a ball that's placed beyond the pallina can only be pushed farther away by other throws.

Now the opposing team is up. One of its players tries to place a bocce ball closer to the pallina, with a more accurate (or lucky) throw, by knocking the other team's bocce ball out of the way or even by hitting the pallina itself. If the player succeeds, the starting team is up again and must try to get one of its bocce balls even closer to the pallina to "better the point."

If the player on the second team doesn't place the ball closer to the pallina than the first ball thrown by the starting team, then the next player on the second team takes a turn. If no balls thrown by the second team better the first ball thrown, then the starting team is up again. The starting team needs only to place its remaining balls closer to the pallina than the second team's closest ball.

Scoring

Scoring takes place at the end of each round (or "frame"), and only one team (the one with the ball closest to the pallina) scores points during any given frame. This team earns one point for each ball that is closer to the pallina than the closest ball of the opposing team. If a ball is touching the pallina, it's worth two points. If both teams' closest balls are equidistant from the pallina, no one scores a point for that frame.

The scoring team of the first frame begins the next frame by tossing the pallina and then rolling or tossing its first bocce ball. Successive frames are played until one team reaches a set point total. For informal, backyard games, 12 points would work well; choose a lower final total if you want the game to be shorter.

Your Technique

You'll use three types of throws in bocce: the puntata—a roll; the volo— a high underhand throw similar to a softball pitch, with a backspin that keeps the ball from rolling once it hits the ground; and the raffa—a strong, close-to-the-ground throw used to knock an opponent ball away from the pallina. For the volo and raffa, take a few running steps, and don't forget the follow-through (you may cross the throw line once you've let go of the ball).

In more advanced games, the type of throw and the opposition ball that you're attempting to best are called before each play, but in your own yard, forget the formalities. Just break out the bocce and have a ball!

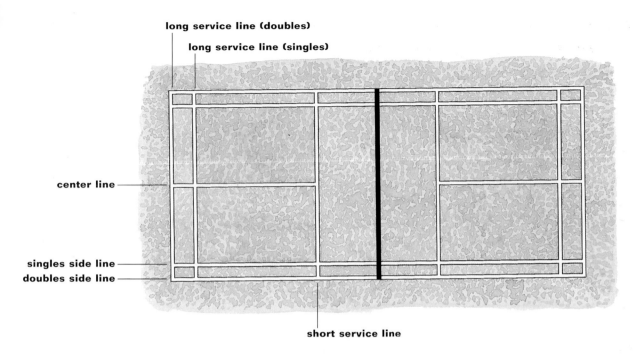

long service line (doubles)

long service line (singles)

center line

singles side line

doubles side line

short service line

BADMINTON

English royalty played it in the nineteenth century. Hollywood's biggest stars—including James Cagney and Bette Davis—picked it up in this century. In 1992, it even joined the ranks of "serious" play by becoming a sanctioned Olympic sport. But don't let badminton's pedigree intimidate you! Its simple rules and inexpensive equipment make it an ideal game to enjoy in your backyard.

The Court

In official play, the badminton court is 17 feet by 44 feet for a singles match and 20 feet by 44 feet for a doubles match. A 30-inch-deep, 5-foot-high net divides the court in half. Long service lines and short service lines demarcate the service court (the playable portion of the court). The short service line is

located 6½ feet back from the net. In doubles play, the long service line is 19½ feet back from the net; in singles play, it's 22 feet from the net. But since you're not competing for Olympic gold, adjust the court size and service lines to fit your backyard.

To Play

Start your match of badminton by tossing a coin. The winner of the toss can choose to serve first or select the end of the court he or she wants to play. On a sunny summer day, having first choice of court ends can be a key tactical advantage! However, players are supposed to switch court ends between the first two games in a three-game match, and again, halfway through the third game.

The object of the game is to hit the shuttlecock—a small, rounded piece of rubber or cork crowned with feath-

ers—over the net and inside the opposite court so that it cannot be returned. The server should call the score before serving. Then he or she puts the shuttlecock into play with an underhand serve, hitting it into the service court diagonally opposite. The opponent has to return the shuttlecock before it hits the ground. If the opponent does not successfully return the shuttlecock over the net (or hits it out of bounds), the server wins one point and serves again. If the opponent *does* send the shuttlecock back over the net and it hits the ground before the server can hit it (or the server hits it out of bounds), then no points are scored and the opponent serves. Most games go to 15 points, but if the game is tied at 14–all, you may keep playing to 18.

Kids' Play

While you and the other adults are sipping wine, talking politics, and stoking coals, what are your kids up to? Although they're probably content to hang out in front of the TV as the kebabs grill, introducing them to some games will encourage them to get out into the fresh air and sunshine. (It might even let them work out enough of that kid energy to allow them to actually sit at the picnic table when mealtime comes.) Outdoor games are also the perfect opportunity for the grown-ups to practice a skill they sometimes can use a little help with — remembering how to play!

ORGANIZED GAMES

The two most popular children's games worldwide—tag and hide-and-seek—were not games at all originally, but rather ways for hunters to practice stalking prey. And although most youngsters today need only ambush the refrigerator for sustenance, the concept of tag remains fundamental to children's games.

Variations abound: In freeze tag, the one person who's "It" chases after all the other players in an attempt to tag them. The tagged players must freeze in whatever wild pose they were in when "It" touched them, until a player who's still free "thaws" them. If "It" freezes everyone, he or she wins.

Almost everyone enjoys playing hide-and-seek, but if your kids are looking for an alternative, have them try sardines. In this game, "It" hides and players must rely on their own tracking skills to find him or her. When a player finds "It," he or she must squeeze into the same hiding place. The last player left becomes "It" for the next round.

Team sports are a great way for kids to learn cooperation. Aside from football, soccer, baseball, and basketball, there remains a host of team sports that you won't find in a local organized league. Preserve the tradition of capture the flag, for example, by introducing it to neighborhood kids at your next barbecue. In capture the flag, players divide into two teams and sanction a playing field about 30 feet by 30 feet, dividing it down the middle with a boundary line. Each player begins by placing a "flag"—a handkerchief, scarf, or scrap of fabric—at the far end of his or her side of the playing field. At the starting signal, each team rushes to the opposing side of the field to try to capture the other team's flags. If a player is tagged by an opponent before obtaining a flag, he or she is sequestered to the far end of the opponent's side of the field. The player may be freed if tagged by a teammate.

Newcombe is another good team sport for kids. The game is played just like volleyball, except players try to catch the ball rather than return it with a hit.

GAMES FOR YOUNGER KIDS

Often the younger children's needs are ignored at social gatherings. Scolded and told to get out from "underfoot," they quickly become anxious for activity and attention. Games offer younger kids a way to expend energy without being destructive or mischievous.

Red Rover is a high-energy game that allows younger kids to engage in cooperation without the complexities of most team sports. Players divide into two even lines facing one another, usually 30 to 50 feet apart. Each line joins hands and chooses a captain. One captain orders, "Red Rover, Red Rover, send _____ right over". The chosen player races toward the opposing line with the intention of bursting though the linked hands. Successful chargers take a captive back to their home team; those that fail must join the opposing team. The team boasting the most players at the end of the predetermined time frame wins.

Aside from being generally exuberant, younger kids are also known for having the most liberated imaginations of us all, and can often entertain themselves quite easily. If you anticipate hosting too few children to organize for a formal game, prompt their creativity by putting a trunk of dress-up clothes outside. Or make jump ropes available (in several sizes) so that kids can jump together or alone. Then listen as they chant their nonsensical jumping rhymes in lilting, singsong voices.

Children from age six on up will also love mastering jacks. The smallest patch of asphalt or concrete—your driveway or the pad in front of your back door—will provide the perfect court for this fun game of speed and coordination. Players take turns throwing a small rubber ball into the air, picking up the correct number of jacks, and letting the ball bounce once before catching it—all with one hand.

If all else fails, bring out a bubble-blowing kit. Even the adults will want to join in a bubble-blowing contest!

Building a Game Table

Bring your game of dominoes, bridge, or poker out into the open with this attractive game table. The tabletop is just the right size for up to four players, and plastic cups built right into the corners will hold extra game pieces or glasses of iced tea. The table is built entirely from standard dimension lumber, and most of the pieces can be cut to length with a handsaw. The 6 x 6 base, however, is so thick that you'll need to cut it with a circular saw or—if you're a woodworker with a fully-equipped workshop—a stationary power saw.

MATERIALS & TOOLS

- Pencil
- Tape measure
- Straightedge
- Square
- Drill and No. 8 countersink drill bit
- No. 2 Phillips-head screwdriver
- Jigsaw
- Circular saw
- 4 PVC drain grates, 3" in diameter
- No. 8 decking screws: 1", 1⅝", 2", and 3½"
- Sandpaper
- Exterior-grade sealer or paint (optional)

TIPS

- The cups at each corner of the table are 3" PVC drain grates. Most home-improvement centers and hardware stores carry these, but if you can't find 3"-diameter grates, just use the next largest size available.
- To cut the 6 x 6 base (B) to length (see step 1), first use a circular saw to cut halfway through one of its faces. Then turn it over and finish the cut through the opposite face.
- Drilling pilot holes (starter holes) for each screw will make inserting the screws easier and may prevent the wood from splitting. Use a No. 8 countersink bit to bore all the pilot holes for this project. (The countersink creates a cavity into which the head of the screw can be recessed so that it will rest just below the surface of the wood.)
- Remember:
  A 6 x 6 is 5½" thick and 5½" wide.
  A 2 x 8 is 1½" thick and 7½" wide.
  A 2 x 2 is 1½" thick and 1½" wide.
  A 2 x 4 is 1½" thick and 3½" wide.
  ⅝ x 6 decking is 1" thick and 5½" wide.

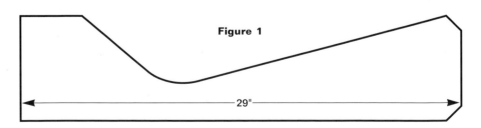

Figure 1

29"

CUTTING LIST

CODE	DESCRIPTION	QTY.	MATERIAL
A	Leg pieces	4	2 x 8 x 29"
B	Base	1	6 x 6 x 29"
C	Leg braces	8	2 x 2 x 7"
D	Short frame pieces	2	2 x 4 x 27"
E	Long frame pieces	2	2 x 4 x 30"
F	Tabletop slats	6	⁵⁄₄ x 6 x 34¼" decking

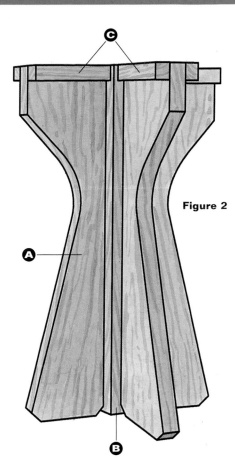

Figure 2

Instructions

1 Cut all the pieces to the dimensions specified in the "Cutting List."

2 Photocopy figure 1, enlarging it to the length shown. (You may have to make a photocopy at the original size first, cut it into three pieces, enlarge each piece by an equal percentage, and then tape the enlarged sheets together.) This finished photocopy will serve as a cutting template.

3 Trace the template onto each leg piece (A). Then use a jigsaw to cut out the legs.

4 Center the straight edge of one leg (A) over one face of the base (B), as shown in figure 2. Attach the two pieces by driving a 3½" screw into the edge of the leg, at the leg's narrowest point, and into the base. Countersink the screw about ½" into the leg's curved edge. Repeat to attach the remaining legs to the other faces of the base.

5 As you can see in figure 2, at the top of the base assembly, a leg brace (C) is attached to each face of each leg (A). (You'll attach the tabletop to the base assembly by inserting screws through these leg braces.) Position a leg brace against a leg as shown; its top edge should be flush with the top end of the base (B) and the top end of the leg, and its inner end should fit snugly against the base. To attach the leg brace to the leg, insert a 2" screw about 1" in from each end of the leg brace, and centered across the brace's width. Countersink each screw about ½". Repeat to attach the remaining leg braces and set the completed base assembly aside.

6 Place the short frame pieces (D) between the long frame pieces (E), as shown in figure 3 on page 280, to form the square tabletop frame. Attach the frame pieces with two 3½" screws at each joint. (Insert these screws through the faces of the long frame pieces and into the ends of the adjacent short frame pieces.)

7 On a large, flat work surface, lay out the tabletop slats (F) side by side, with their best-looking faces down. Leave ¼" spaces between their edges and make sure their ends are even. The distance between the outer edges of the two outermost tabletop slats should be about 34¼".

8 Using figure 3 as a guide, place the frame that you built in step 6 on top of the tabletop slats (F), centering the frame so that the outside face of each frame piece (D or E) is about 2⅛" from the edge or ends of the tabletop slats. Use a square to check that the frame is placed squarely on the tabletop slats.

9 Attach the frame to the tabletop slats (F) by driving two 1⅝" screws, at an angle, through the inside face of a frame piece and into each tabletop slat.

10 Flip the tabletop over, so the frame rests on the work surface. Mark the corners of the tabletop for the PVC drain grates, as shown in figure 4. Use one of your PVC drain grates to trace the circle at each corner.

11 Use a jigsaw to cut each corner as shown in figure 4. Start by cutting the straight, diagonal line; then cut out the half-circle shape.

12 Turn the tabletop back over, so the frame faces up. Place the base assembly—brace end down—on the tabletop, and center it inside the frame.

13 Attach the base assembly to the tabletop by driving two, evenly spaced 2" screws through each leg brace (C) and into the tabletop slat (F) beneath.

14 Turn the table right side up and sand it smooth.

15 Apply two or three coats of an exterior-grade sealer or paint to the table, if desired, allowing each

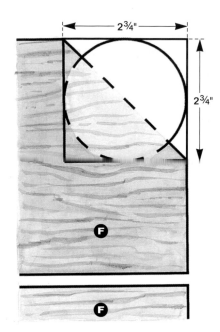

Figure 4

coat to dry completely before applying the next.

16 Fit a drain grate into one cut corner of the tabletop; its top edge should be flush with the top face of the tabletop slat (F). To attach the drain grate, drive two 1" screws through its inner, curved surface and into the edge of the tabletop slat. Repeat to attach the remaining drain grates.

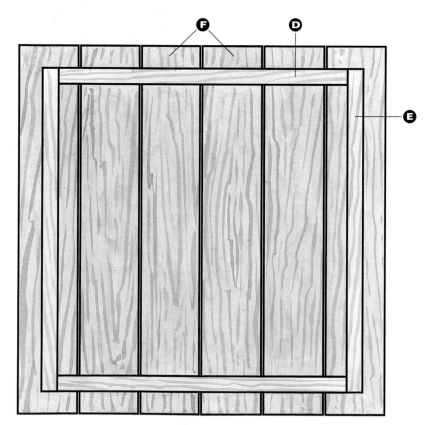

Figure 3

Hardiness-Zone Map

A plant's winter hardiness is critical in deciding whether it is suitable for your garden. The map below divides the United States and Canada into 11 climatic zones based on average minimum temperatures, as compiled by the U.S. Department of Agriculture. Find your zone and check the zone information in the garden plans to help you choose the plants most likely to flourish in your climate.

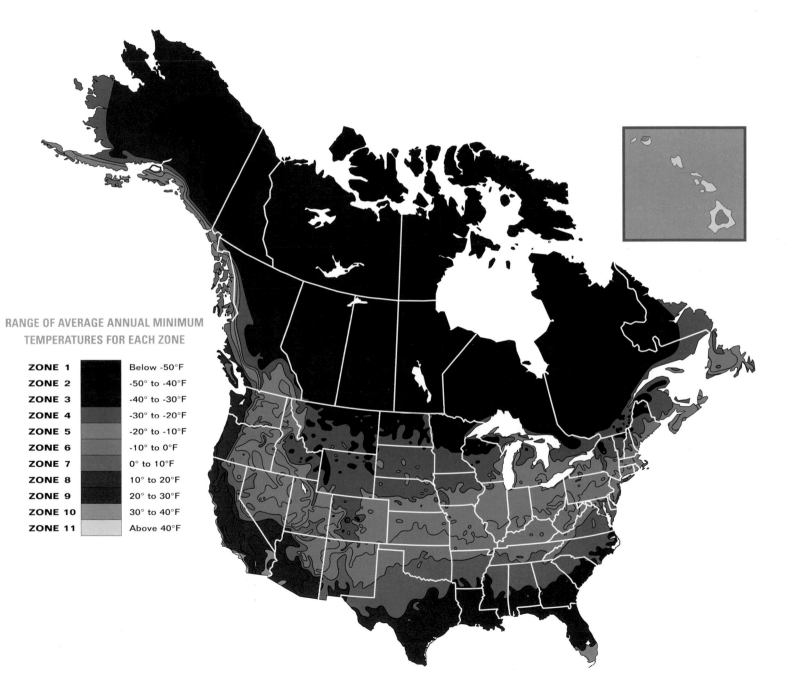

RANGE OF AVERAGE ANNUAL MINIMUM TEMPERATURES FOR EACH ZONE

ZONE 1		Below -50°F
ZONE 2		-50° to -40°F
ZONE 3		-40° to -30°F
ZONE 4		-30° to -20°F
ZONE 5		-20° to -10°F
ZONE 6		-10° to 0°F
ZONE 7		0° to 10°F
ZONE 8		10° to 20°F
ZONE 9		20° to 30°F
ZONE 10		30° to 40°F
ZONE 11		Above 40°F

Bibliography

Adams, George. *Birdscaping Your Garden.* Emmaus, Pa.: Rodale Press, 1994.

Anthenat, Kathy S. *American Tree Houses and Play Houses.* Crozet, Va.: Betterway Publications, 1991.

Appleton, Bonnie Lee, and Alfred F. Scheidler. *Rodale's Successful Organic Gardening: Trees, Shrubs, and Vines.* Emmaus, Pa.: Rodale Press, 1993.

Asimov, Isaac, with revisions and updating by Francis Reddy. *A Stargazer's Guide.* Milwaukee, Wis.: Gareth Stevens, 1995.

Ausubel, Kenny. *Seeds of Change: The Living Treasure.* San Francisco: HarperSanFrancisco, 1994.

Ball, Jeff, and Liz Ball. *Yardening.* New York: Macmillan Publishing Company, 1991.

Barash, Cathy Wilkinson. *Evening Gardens: Planning & Planting a Landscape to Dazzle the Senses after Sundown.* Shelburne, Vt.: Chapters Publishing, 1993.

Barash, Cathy Wilkinson, and Jim Wilson. *The Cultivated Gardener.* New York: Simon and Schuster, 1996.

Beaton, Clare. *The Complete Book of Children's Parties.* New York: Kingfisher Books, 1992.

Belsinger, Susan and Carolyn Dille. *Herbs in the Kitchen.* Loveland, Colo.: Interweave Press, 1992.

Bender, Steve and Felder Rushing. *Passalong Plants.* Chapel Hill, N.C.: The University of North Carolina Press, 1993.

The Big Book of Flower Gardening. Alexandria, Va.: Time-Life Books, 1996.

Blomgren, Paige G. *Making Paths and Walkways: Creative Ideas and Simple Techniques.* Asheville, N.C.: Lark Books, 1999.

Blose, Norma, and Dawn Cusick. *Herb Drying Handbook.* New York: Sterling Publishing, 1993.

Bonanno, Joseph T. *The Firehouse Grilling Cookbook.* New York: Broadway Books, 1998.

Bradley, Fern Marshall, ed. *Gardening with Perennials.* Emmaus, Pa.: Rodale Press, 1996.

Broido, Bing. *Spalding Book of Rules.* Indianapolis, Ind.: Masters Press, 1997.

Cathey, H. Marc, with Linda Bellamy. *Heat-Zone Gardening: How to Choose Plants That Thrive in Your Region's Warmest Weather.* Alexandria, Va.: Time-Life Books, 1998.

Cave, Janet, ed. *Perennials.* Alexandria, Va.: Time-Life Books, 1995.

Coleman, Eliot. *The New Organic Grower's Four-Season Harvest: How to Harvest Fresh Organic Vegetables from Your Home.* White River Junction, Vt.: Chelsea Green Publishing Company, 1992.

Cook, Ferris. *The Garden Trellis: Designs to Build and Vines to Cultivate.* New York: Artisan, 1996.

Cox, Jeff. *Decorating Your Garden.* New York: Abbeville Press, 1999.

Creasy, Rosalind. *Cooking from the Garden.* San Francisco: Sierra Club Books, 1988.

Dannenmaier, Molly. *A Child's Garden: Enchanting Outdoor Spaces for Children and Parents.* New York: Simon & Schuster, 1998.

Davis, Rich and Shifra Stein. *The All-American Barbecue Book.* New York: Vintage Books, 1988.

Erler, Catriona Tudor. *Garden Rooms: Creating and Decorating Garden Spaces.* Alexandria, Va.: Time-Life Books, 1999.

Evans, Michele. *Sensational Salads.* New York: Signet, 1989.

Evans, Hazel. *The Patio Garden.* New York: Viking and Penguin Books, 1986.

Garland, Sarah. *The Complete Book of Herbs and Spices.* Pleasantville, N.Y.: Reader's Digest, 1993.

Hemphill, John, and Rosemary Hemphill. *What Herb Is That? How to Grow and Use the Culinary Herbs.* Mechanicsburg, Pa.: Stackpole Books, 1997.

Heriteau, Jacqueline. *Ortho's Complete Guide to Vegetables.* Des Moines, Iowa: Ortho Books, 1997.

Hutson, Lucinda. *The Herb Garden Cookbook.* Austin, Tex.: Texas Monthly Press, 1987.

Idone, Christopher. *Christopher Idone's Salad Days.* New York: Random House, 1989.

Kafka, Barbara. *Roasting.* New York: William Morrow, 1995.

Lacy, Allen. *The Inviting Garden: Gardening for the Senses, Mind, and Spirit.* New York: Henry Holt and Company, 1998.

LaLiberte, Katherine and Ben Watson. *Gardener's Supply Company Passport to Gardening: A Sourcebook for the 21st-Century Gardener.* White River Junction, Vt.: Chelsea Green Publishing Company, 1997.

Loewer, Peter. *The Evening Garden.* New York: Macmillan Publishing Company, 1993.

McConnell, Shelli, ed. *Grill It Right!* Des Moines, Iowa: Better Homes and Gardens Books®, 1993.

Michalak, Patricia S. *Controlling Pests and Diseases*. Emmaus, Pa.: Rodale Press, 1994.

Nash, Helen. *Low-Maintenance Water Gardens*. New York: Sterling Publishing, 1996.

The New International Bartender's Guide. New York: Random House, 1984.

Norman, Jill. *The Classic Herb Cookbook*. London: Dorling Kindersley, 1997.

Paterson, Allen. *Herbs in the Garden*. London: J. M. Dent and Sons, 1985.

Pavord, Anna. *The New Kitchen Garden*. London: Dorling Kindersley, 1996.

Reed, David. *The Art and Craft of Stonescaping*. Asheville, N.C.: Lark Books, 1998.

Rey, H.A. *Find the Constellations*. Boston: Houghton Mifflin, 1988.

Rodale's No-Fail Flower Gardens. Emmaus, Pa.: Rodale Press, 1994.

Schremp, Gerry, ed. *Outdoor Cooking*. Alexandria, Va.: Time-Life Books, 1984.

Schwartz, Leonard. *Salads: 150 Classic and Innovative Recipes for Every Course and Every Meal*. New York: HarpersCollins, 1992.

Sinnes, A. Cort. *The Grilling Book*. New York: Simon and Schuster, 1985.

Sombke, Laurence. *Beautiful Easy Flower Gardens*. Emmaus, Pa.: Rodale Press, 1995.

Sombke, Laurence. *Beautiful Easy Herbs: How to Get the Most from Herbs—In Your Garden and in Your Home*. Emmaus, Pa.: Rodale Press, 1997.

Stott, Carole. *Night Sky*. London: Dorling Kindersley, 1993.

Swenson, Allan A. *The Gardener's Book of Berries*. New York: Lyons and Burford, 1994.

Taylor, Patricia, A. *Step-by-Step Shade Gardens*. Des Moines, Iowa: Better Homes and Gardens® Books, 1995.

Thompson, C. E. *Glow in the Dark Constellations: A Field Guide for Young Stargazers*. New York: Grosset and Dunlap, 1989.

Thorne, John with Matt Lewis Thorne. *Serious Pig: An American Cook in Search of His Roots*. New York: North Point Press, 1996.

Time-Life How-To Garden Designs: Simple Steps to Beautiful Flower Gardens. Alexandria, Va.: Time-Life Books, 1997.

Tlusty, Lois, ed. *Betty Crocker's Buffets*. Minneapolis, Minn.: General Mills, 1984.

Tufts, Craig, and Peter Loewer. *Gardening for Wildlife*. Emmaus, Pa.: Rodale Press, 1995.

Voltz, Jeanne. *Barbecued Ribs, Smoked Butts, and Other Great Feeds*. New York: Alfred A. Knopf, 1990.

von Trapp, Sara Jane. *Landscaping from the Ground Up*. Newton, Conn.: The Tauton Press, 1997.

White, Linda. *Cooking on a Stick: Campfire Recipes for Kids*. Salt Lake City: Gibbs-Smith, 1996.

Worth, Sylvia, ed. *Rules of the Game*. New York: St. Martin's Press, 1990.

Yard & Garden Projects: Easy, Step-by-Step Plans and Designs for Beautiful Outdoor Spaces. Alexandria, Va.: Time-Life Books, 1998.

Metric Conversions

Length

Inches	CM		
⅛	0.3	19	48.3
¼	0.6	20	50.8
⅜	1.0	21	53.3
½	1.3	22	55.9
⅝	1.6	23	58.4
¾	1.9	24	61.0
⅞	2.2	25	63.5
1	2.5	26	66.0
1¼	3.2	27	68.6
1½	3.8	28	71.1
1¾	4.4	29	73.7
2	5.1	30	76.2
2½	6.4	31	78.7
3	7.6	32	81.3
3½	8.9	33	83.8
4	10.2	34	86.4
4½	11.4	35	88.9
5	12.7	36	91.4
6	15.2	37	94.0
7	17.8	38	96.5
8	20.3	39	99.1
9	22.9	40	101.6
10	25.4	41	104.1
11	27.9	42	106.7
12	30.5	43	109.2
13	33.0	44	111.8
14	35.6	45	114.3
15	38.1	46	116.8
16	40.6	47	119.4
17	43.2	48	121.9
18	45.7	49	124.5
		50	127.0

Volume

1 fluid ounce = 29.6 ml
1 pint = 473 ml
1 quart = 946 ml
1 gallon (128 fl. oz.) = 3.785 liters

liters x .2642 = gallons
liters x 2.11 = pints
liters x 33.8 = fluid ounces
gallons x 3.785 = liters
gallons x .1337 = cubic feet
cubic feet x 7.481 = gallons
cubic feet x 28.32 = liters

Weight

0.035 ounces = 1 gram
1 ounce = 28.35 grams
1 pound = 453.6 grams

grams x .0353 = ounces
grams x .0022 = pounds
ounces x 28.35 = grams
pounds x 453.6 = grams
tons (short) x 907.2 = kilograms
tons (metric) x 2205 = pounds
kilograms x .0011 = tons (short)
pounds x .00045 = tons (metric)

Acknowledgments

PHOTOGRAPHY

Warm thanks to photographer Evan Bracken (Light Reflections, Hendersonville, NC) for his skill with the camera, his great sense of humor, and for the support and friendship he extended to all involved throughout this project. All photographs not otherwise credited are by Mr. Bracken.

Special thanks to photo stylist Skip Wade for his impeccable taste, his great imagination, and his consistent hard work.

Thanks also to photographer Richard Hasselberg (Black Mountain, NC) whose photos appear on pages 26 (top), 27 (bottom), 32, 51, 66, 68, 69, 81 (top), 84 (bottom), 85 (top), 87 (bottom),102, 111, 112, 139 (bottom), 140, 147 (middle), 148, 150, 151, 152, 165 (bottom), 166, 167, 174, 204 (bottom), 206, 212, 226, 232, 233, 240, 245, 247 (bottom), 249 (bottom), and 278.

We are deeply grateful to the following for their generous photographic contributions: T. A. Allen (Out 'n' About Treesort, 300 Page Creek Rd., Cave Junction, OR 97523), page 115; Mary Brittain (The Cottage Gardener Heirloom Plant Nursery, Ontario, Canada), pages 132 and 133; Gary Chandler (McKenzie, TN), pages 105 (top), 120, 121 (top), 122, and 123 (top); Christine Dombrowski (Dallas Horticultural Center, Dallas, TX), pages 136 (top) and 137; Robin Dreyer (Celo, NC), pages 9 (top), 24 (top), 29 (top), 41, 81 (bottom), 83 (top), 85 (bottom); Clyde S. Gorsuch (Dept. of Entomology, Clemson University, Clemson, SC), page 27 (top); Robert Gusick © (New York, NY), page 114; Monrovia (Azusa, CA, 1-888-PLANT IT), pages 48 (bottom) and 121 (bottom); Jane Portalupi (McLeod and Portalupi, Woodinville, WA), page 13; Steven J. Prchal (Sonoran Anthropod Studies Institute, Tucson, AZ), page 103 (bottom); Hunter Stubbs (horticulturalist and photographer, Richmond Hill lnn, Asheville, NC), pages 30 (right), 36, and 58.

LOCATIONS

Very special thanks to Dr. Peter and Jasmine Gentling for sharing their extensive horticultural knowledge and for allowing us to photograph their exquisite gardens.

Many thanks to the following North Carolina residents for permission to take photographs of their gardens. Their generosity, patience, and encouragement made this book possible: Jan and Simon Braun (Asheville); Wade Bryant (Asheville); Cindy Causby and Dave Campbell (Asheville); Diane Rodgers Claybrook (Asheville); John Cram (Kenilworth Gardens, Asheville); Ian and Jo Lydia Craven (Burnsville); Eve Davis (Hawk and Ivy Bed & Breakfast, Barnardsville); Bill and Donna Jean Dreyer (Burnsville); Susan Fennelly and Ken Minnich (Asheville); Hedy Fischer and Randy Shull (Asheville); Rick and Gwenn Ford (Asheville); Robert and Jacqueline Glasgow (Beaufort House Victorian Bed & Breakfast, Asheville); Grove Park Inn (Asheville); Stephanie Harris (Asheville); Carol Hire (Asheville); Steven and Martha Howard (Asheville); Randall and Mary Johnson (Asheville); Chris and Melonie Knorr (Asheville); Karl and Beth Lail (Asheville); Peter Loewer (Asheville); Marla Murphy (Gourmet Gardens Herb Farm, Weaverville); Penland School of Craft (Penland); Richmond Hill Inn (Asheville); Bonnie Sheldon (Asheville); Colleen Sikes (Asheville); C.B. Squires (Herb Mountain L.P., Weaverville); Kay Stafford (Asheville); Taylor and Webb (Asheville); Linda Tuuri (Asheville); Dr. Peter and Cathy Wallenborn (Asheville); Kenneth and Claudia Wienke (Asheville); Patricia and Gary Wiles (Cumberland Falls Bed & Breakfast, Asheville); Dr. John Wilson (Black Mountain); Lassie York Woody (Asheville); University of North Carolina at Asheville Botanical Gardens (Asheville); Lisa and Rice Yordy (The Lion & the Rose Bed & Breakfast, Asheville).

PROJECT DESIGNS

Our thanks to the following designers:

Kevin Barnes (Asheville, NC): rustic bench, page 78

Robin Clark (Asheville, NC): tool shelf, page 14; potting bench, page 20; trellis planter, page 60; bluebird house, page 128

Amy Cook (Asheville, NC) garden journal, page 116

Eve Davis (Barnardsville, NC) moss-lined hanging baskets, pages 44 and 45

Nora Mosrie (Black Mountain, NC): painted glass lanterns, page 260

Sam Smith (Sam Smith Woodworking, Asheville, NC): portable utensil rack, page 196

Mark Strom (Lotherien Studio, Asheville, NC): screened box to protect food, page 178; sun shade, page 206; game table, page 278

Catharine Sutherland (Asheville, NC): Humpty-Dumpty piñata, page 252

Skip Wade (Asheville, NC): take-it-home station, page 222

GARDEN ART DESIGNERS

We are grateful to the following crafts-people for allowing us to photograph their garden art:

Holly Olinger (Hurricane Art Metal, Charlottesville, VA): suncatcher spires, page 84

Gwendolyn Ottinger (Black Mountain, NC): Brown and white scraffito pot, page 40

Tzadi Turrou (Celo, NC): mosaic stepping stones, page 81.

RESEARCH AND WRITING

For their research and writing skills, we are indebted to the following people: Julie Abbott (Asheville, NC); Trent Bouts (Asheville, NC); Susan Carol (Asheville, NC); Amy Cook (Asheville, NC); Holly Clark (Leicester, NC); Katie DuMont (Gerton, NC); Naomi Friedman (Asheville, NC); Ben Gilbert (Asheville, NC); Clare Hanrahan (Asheville, NC); Christy Hicks (Asheville, NC); Megan Kirby (Asheville, NC); Christopher Mitchell (Asheville, NC); Chris Rich (Asheville, NC); Paul Schattel (Arden, NC); Clarke Snell (Marshall, NC).

Thanks also to our superb indexer, Jackie Flenner (Asheville, NC)

RECIPES

We thank writer and chef Diana C. Stoll (Asheville, NC) for contributing the menus and recipes on pages 184, 227–229, and 243–245.

Thanks also to Chris Bryant (Asheville, NC) for creating the menu and recipes on pages 235–236.

ADVICE AND INFORMATION

For his horticultural advice, magnificent ponds and waterfalls, and help with location scouting, we thank Steve Haun (Tanbark Landscape Company, Inc., Asheville, NC).

For the information accompanying the miniature orchard plan on page 161, we thank Hunter and Donna Carleton (Bear Creek Nursery, Northport, WA, 99157).

For research assistance, thanks to Malaprops Bookstore (Asheville, NC).

PROPS

For allowing us to tap their knowledge and their stockrooms, we thank the following people and businesses: Genevieve and Larry Burda (Do It Best Hardware, Mars Hill, NC); Citizen's Ace Hardware (Asheville, NC); Complements to the Chef (Asheville, NC); Enviro Depot (Asheville, NC); April Garden (Asheville, NC); Dana Irwin (Asheville, NC); The Kansas City Barbecue Association (Kansas City, MO); Malaprops Bookstore (Asheville, NC); Marla Murphy (Gourmet Gardens Herb Farm, Weaverville, NC); T.S. Morrison & Co. (Asheville, NC); Vanessa Osborne (Grovewood Gallery, Asheville, NC); Molly Seiburg (The Gardener's Cottage, Asheville, NC); Bonnie Sheldon (Asheville, NC); Colleen Sikes (Asheville, NC); Claire Solomon (Asheville, NC); Weber-Stephen Products Co. (Palatine, IL); Hugh and Susan Wingard (Asheville, NC).

Index